Praise for the first

Lessons Learned

Practical Advice for the Teaching of Psychology

Lessons Learned

Volume 2

Practical Advice for the Teaching of Psychology

Editors:

Baron Perlman
Lee I. McCann
Susan H. McFadden

American Psychological Society

www.psychologicalscience.org

Published by
American Psychological Society
1010 Vermont Avenue, NW
Suite 1100
Washington, DC 20005-4907

Production Editors: Brian Weaver and Eric Jaffe

International Standard Book Number: 0-9626884-3-6
Library of Congress Catalog Number: 2003110545

To order copies of *Lessons Learned* Vol. 1 or Vol. 2:
Call (202) 783-2077 or go to
www.psychologicalscience.org/lessons

AMERICAN PSYCHOLOGICAL SOCIETY

www.psychologicalscience.org

Acknowledgments

The American Psychological Society's support for **Teaching Tips** as a column in the APS **Observer,** and for the publication of this book has been unwavering. We thank the APS for its continuing efforts. Specifically, we thank Alan Kraut, Brian Weaver, Eric Jaffe, and Sarah Brookhart, all at APS, for their interest in the column and the teaching of psychology.

We also acknowledge our students. They make our work on improving our teaching worthwhile. Were it not for their intellectual curiosity, wisdom, problems, energy, and presence in our classrooms, we would not be teachers.

We sincerely thank the authors of the **Tips** columns who have contributed this book's chapters. Their ideas, collegiality, and interest in sharing their insights with colleagues make this book possible. They have taught us far more than we had ever hoped to learn. Their tolerance of our editing and requests for revisions have been met with understanding and patience. We greatly appreciate their ideas and the time they spend polishing and deepening what they have to say.

Finally, we thank Doug Bernstein who, through his stewardship of the National Institute for the Teaching of Psychology, provides us new ideas and authors, and serves as a constant reminder of the importance of the teaching of psychology.

Baron Perlman
Lee I. McCann
Susan H. McFadden

Contents

PART I   Teacher Development

PART II   Course Planning

PART III   Beyond the Text or Classroom

PART IV   Pedagogical Skills

PART V   Themes Across Psychology

PART VI   Tests and Grading

Preface

One of the hardest things teachers have to learn is that the sincerity of their intentions does not guarantee the purity of their practice (Brookfield, 1995, p. 1).

Teaching Tips has been a regular column in the American Psychological Society **Observer** since 1994. Teachers of psychology in many settings ranging from high schools through doctoral institutions have told us the column gives them ideas about teaching, provides a basis for discussion with colleagues, and supports them in the hard work of continuing to teach well. Our goals for the column have remained consistent through the years: to share a wide variety of effective teaching methods; to suggest new topics that might be incorporated into psychology courses; and to enhance the quality of psychology education at all levels.

In 1999, the first six years of columns were collected in a book published by APS — **Lessons Learned: Practical Advice for the Teaching of Psychology**. It organized the columns topically, an approach that was helpful to regular readers of the APS **Observer**, some of whom may not have had the opportunity to read the original column. In addition, we soon learned that many universities adopted the book for their teaching assistant training programs. Mentors for teaching assistants have also found this collection to be valuable. We are pleased that doctoral programs are becoming more attentive to educating people in the intricacies of teaching.

After the publication of the first collection, we wondered whether we would have enough ideas for columns to gather into a second book. These concerns proved groundless, thanks to the many people who surprised and delighted us with their innovative suggestions for columns. The readers and writers of these columns have established an important community in our discipline of people who truly care about excellent teaching. One of the most gratifying parts of our editing work comes from our contacts with people with a passion for exploring the many diverse components of high quality education in psychology. Some of these individuals have been teaching for many years and some are just starting out in this profession.

There is some new organization in the current volume, reflecting the ideas of our authors and perhaps the Zeitgeist of teaching since 1999. We begin with several chapters on *Teacher Development* (Part I) and then continue with more ideas on *Course Planning* (Part II). Although there are two chapters on use of the Web, we have deleted a separate section on using technology and instead placed these chapters where they best belonged. Use of technology in teaching has become so ingrained and widespread it no longer is "special." We believe this development is positive, as the focus can once again return to quality teaching and what students learn instead of use of the technology per se. We have added a new section, *Beyond the Text or Classroom* (Part III) to reflect the amount of teaching that either brings in ideas from the world outside the classroom, or moves students into that world. Part IV contains seven chapters on the *Pedagogical Skills* all teachers need in their pedagogical repertoire. Once again we present a section (Part V) on *Themes Across Psychology,* with ideas teachers can use in a wide range of courses.

This volume contains no chapters on writing. We have included a separate section (Part VI) on *Tests and Grading.* We are especially pleased with Part VII, *Enhancing Student Learning, Performance, and Participation.* These chapters focus on providing students every opportunity to succeed and thrive. Finally, as was true in Volume 1, we end with a section (Part VIII) on *Student and Faculty Integrity,* a topic we believe in strongly.

As the editors of this column, we have experienced the excitement of applying many of these ideas to our own work with students. Thus, one result of our editing work has been the improvement of our teaching. What one might call "pedagogical epiphanies" frequently occur as we work with writers to develop and polish their columns. Each of us has taught psychology for 30 years or more and we are happy to say that we are still learning ways of doing our jobs better. We hope that some of our excitement about the quality of ideas in this book is apparent to our readers.

Baron Perlman
Lee I. McCann
Susan H. McFadden

American Psychological Society

References

Brookfield, S. D. (1995). *Becoming a critically reflective teacher.* San Francisco: Jossey-Bass.

Perlman, B., McCann, L. I., & McFadden, S. H. (Eds.). (1999). *Lessons learned: Practical advice for the teaching of psychology.* Washington, DC: American Psychological Society.

About the Editors

Baron Perlman is Editor of *Teaching Tips*., a column on the teaching of Psychology that appears in the APS *Observer*. A Professor in the Department of Psychology, Distinguished Teacher, and University and Rosebush Professor at the University of Wisconsin Oshkosh, he has taught psychology for 30 years.

Lee I. McCann is Co-Editor of *Teaching Tips*. A Professor in the Department of Psychology and a University and Rosebush Professor at UW Oshkosh, and a former Consulting Editor for *Teaching of Psychology*, he has taught psychology for 38 years.

Susan H. McFadden is Co-Editor of *Teaching Tips*. A University and University of Wisconsin System Distinguished Professor, and a Rosebush professor at UW Oshkosh in the Department of Psychology, she has taught psychology for 32 years.

American Psychological Society

Part I

Teacher Development

Managing Teaching Loads and Finding Time for Reflection and Renewal

Rosalyn M. King
Northern Virginia Community College

ONE OF THE GREATEST challenges of teaching is not to let it consume all of our time and energy. We struggle with effectively managing teaching loads and schedules to find time for the many other activities, events, and responsibilities in our lives. This includes time for other academic responsibilities, family, friends, personal endeavors, nourishing the soul, and simply time for reflection, renewal and reinvigoration.

In this chapter I explore the complexity of teaching and its effects on our time and energy. Further, I examine how we might more effectively manage our schedules and loads to have time for reflection and renewal, which is vital to being able to give more of ourselves to others as well. This exploration begins by revisiting our reasons for teaching in the first place.

Who Is the Self That Teaches?

I first saw this question raised by Parker Palmer in his book, *The Courage to Teach: Exploring the Inner Landscape of a Teacher's Life*, (1998). I believe this to be the most fundamental question that all who teach should explore. When answered it is truly at the core of why we teach. Palmer states: "The more familiar we are with our inner terrain, the more surefooted our teaching — and living — becomes." (p. 5)

Initially, many of us decided on a career in teaching because we had a passion for it. We also have a need to help people learn. Palmer's major query about teaching is why so many of us lose our enthusiasm as the years go by. Why do we face potential burnout? What are the hidden messages we can discover from revisiting our initial reasons for teaching? I believe there are many. For starters, our passion for something can lead to overwork if we aren't careful. This is an important realization. Many of us love teaching passionately and it may be difficult to draw the line and find true balance. Somehow, it seems we become caught up in the day-to-day rudiments and routines of teaching and lose touch with ourselves and our lives.

Teaching Can Generate Stress and Potential Burnout

Teaching is a complex profession. Depending on the type of college or university, teachers may be juggling many responsibilities such as teaching a number of course overloads at non-research two- and four-year colleges and universities, or fulfilling teaching and research requirements at research colleges and universities. Even more demanding than the complexity of teaching is the fact that teaching can also generate a high level of stress, fatigue, and lead to burnout. Contributing factors to this stress can include:

- ◆ Unclear expectations.
- ◆ Spending many hours in class.
- ◆ Classes that take more preparation time or having a high number of course preparations in a given semester.
- ◆ Handling classes with large enrollments, planning productive activities, or dealing with difficult or very needy students.
- ◆ Dealing with social and learning issues, such as AIDS, learning disabilities and attention-deficit disorder.
- ◆ Newer curricular and teaching approaches, including the use of technology.
- ◆ Time involved in student advising and conferences
- ◆ Increasing demands from administrative, clerical and committee duties.
- ◆ Increasing diversification of expertise.
- ◆ Campus politics and meeting the economic necessities of the institution.
- ◆ Changes in administrative demands or administrative leadership.
- ◆ Lack of financial and personnel support.
- ◆ Time pressures and deadlines.
- ◆ Continual overload of work.
- ◆ Dealing with inequities and inequalities.

These factors may be compounded by student attendance, attention, discipline, and lack of motivation. The latter can be especially stressful because uninterested students disrupt a classroom and the work of other students. Moreover, teaching uninterested or unmotivated students can be exhausting and damaging to a teacher's positive sense of self.

Increased Workloads, Less Student Contact

Demands on teachers are increasing — more work, more students and less time (Easthope & Easthope, 2000). The increased demands of workloads outside of the classroom, and on time and energy, result in teachers having less time for preparation, teaching, and interaction with students. The quality of care for students is one of the first things that overworked teachers decrease, leading to tremendous hidden and long-term impacts on the college climate in addition to effects on the attitudes, self-esteem, and motivation of both faculty and students. This can especially be the case when teachers are too pressured to carry out many of the caring activities they perceive as part of their professional identity.

How do teachers cope? Not always well. Some teachers adapt to the changes imposed upon them; many accept what they consider to be chronic and persistent overload as a normal part of their life; some indicate they attempt to do planning or decision-making "on the run;" some adapt to the increased workload by reducing their commitment to professional teaching through reducing their input into the teaching task; others opt to work part-time. One faculty member reported:

"I don't do as good a job now as I did three years ago, four years ago, because there is just not the time. If you have a 25 percent increase in workload something has got to give and basically it's preparation and it's marking. There will be less of that time for everything." (Easthope & Easthope, 2000, p.16.)

A no-win situation develops when teachers strive to satisfy all the needs of students and requirements of the administration. The resulting reduction in service to students generates the most stress and guilt.

Teachers see this as a grave loss, both to themselves and to their students. In brief, teachers sacrifice activities important to them (Milem, Berger & Dey, 2000) such as time spent advising and counseling students.

Increasing Isolation and Emotional Sterility

According to Robert Kraft (2000), there is an isolation or aloneness and emotional sterility in faculty life that seems dangerous and perhaps toxic — a paradox since teaching is supposed to be a most rewarding enterprise. Kraft reports on a tenure-track professor who quit her job because she found it to be so dreadfully lonely.

Technology Produces Stress

Many faculty reported keeping up with technology as stressful (67 percent), almost equally for men and women teachers (Higher Education Research Institute, 2000). Nonetheless, all faculty believed that technology was educationally beneficial. We are all familiar with the challenges of having to learn new technology in addition to planning our teaching, not to mention the time involved both in mastering it and learning how to incorporate it into our instructional programs in the classroom.

Effective Ways to Manage Teaching Loads and Avoid Stress

On top of all of these teaching-related stressors faculty face increased pressures in their personal lives. Whether this be financial, child-related, caring for aging parents, or a host of other issues, work can spill over into one's personal life; and the personal can negatively affect teaching and other academic work.

It is essential that those of us who teach, learn to manage our personal and professional lives or we may experience chronic stress and eventually physical and mental burnout. The suggestions which follow come from the literature as well as from a survey I administered to senior faculty and administrators from two and four-year colleges and universities.

Find Balance

"Take time for self, be responsible for the decisions you make (those big papers to grade, essay exams, etc.), block out time for yourself each week, walk around campus and spend time with colleagues. If you view teaching as a life long task, you are not upset if you are a bit slow, or a bit tired. The goal is to reach students and have something to give each day." (Baron Perlman, Professor of Psychology, University of Wisconsin Oshkosh, personal communication)

This colleague also recommended that if at all possible, leave your teaching on campus and take time to relax at home. Even better, try to find a bit of relaxation at your college or university each day. If you work at home, take time for things you cherish and enjoy. At work, block out free time in your appointment book and keep it sacred. Go for a walk on campus; visit with a colleague for a few minutes.

Reward Yourself

Know what you find rewarding about teaching and try to do a bit of this each day. Recognize when your teaching is going well and feel good about this. Do not move immediately from one task to another, reward yourself with things you consider as incentives.

Establish Meaning and Relevance

"We need to do a better job at connecting our subject matter to some larger purpose and to our student's daily lives. My field (history) is too often presented as a collection of random events and facts to memorize. We shouldn't hesitate to search for meaning or a moral, even though our conclusions must remain tentative." (Patrick Reed, Professor of History, Northern Virginia Community College, Loudoun Campus, personal communication)

Develop Short- and Long-Term Goals

"Ask the question: Where do I want to be in five years and what must I do to get there? The most important thing is an assessment of balance. This should be evaluated every couple of years to make sure the short-term (five year) and long-term (20 year) goals will be met or changed as required. Write these goals out and examine how they may shift and change over the next 20 years (Joan Roy, Head, Department of Psychology, University of Regina, personal communication).

Connect With Colleagues

Talk about how things are going for you with peers and colleagues. Establish a support system. This can be done face-to-face or via e-mail with colleagues at your institution, and others who work at other institutions across the country. Talking with others helps us clarify and maintain perspective and feel "grounded." Making these connections with colleagues also is an excellent way to relieve or minimize stress.

Manage Time

Do not attempt to accomplish too many tasks in a day. Prioritize and leave a bit of time for yourself. There is always tomorrow, although it may not feel like this is true sometimes. Several colleagues had suggestions for managing time better:

"Try new scheduling methods, use a palm pilot. I've learned to say 'no' to students and administrators when I know what they're asking me to do will reduce my ability to accomplish my goals. Surprise! People actually understand that you're busy and will not mind being put off for a little while. When I first started teaching, I felt a need to be available all the time, but now I realize it is better for students to understand my time is limited so they should plan ahead and use our time together more effectively. This often leaves more time for informal conversation." (Laurence Nolan, Assistant Professor of Psychology, Wagner College, personal communication)

"Don't procrastinate and don't let tasks pile up to an overwhelming burden. Keep to your schedule." (Arnold Bradford, Professor of English, Northern Virginia Community College, Loudoun Campus, personal communication)

"Have lecture notes, assignments, projects, etc., already planned, organized and completed before the course begins." (Christopher Blake, Assistant Professor of Spanish, Northern Virginia Community College, Loudoun Campus, personal communication)

Try to Pay Attention to Detail

Although sometimes difficult because of lack of time, try to pay attention to detail. For example, try to proofread exams to catch typographical errors, or ask a colleague to proof when it becomes difficult to see the errors. Have an extra dry marker for the board or pen for the overhead projector, an extra battery for the microphone or extra bulb for the overhead projector. Also remember to review your course syllabi and class schedule of activities on what you will be covering in the week ahead and modify as necessary.

Negotiate a Realistic Teaching Schedule

Try to negotiate a "sane" teaching load and schedule. For a morning person to teach all late afternoon or evening classes is insane. Different sections of the same course are often easier than teaching a different course each hour.

Maintain a Positive Attitude

Teaching is a wonderful way to make a living. Immovable bureaucracies or difficult students are part of work. Do not let them consume you. Try to develop a tolerance for unavoidable stress and cognitively restructure such situations, minimizing your sense of frustration, and looking for potential positive outcomes. Keeping what it is we do in perspective helps maintain a realistic appraisal of how things are going. Try to develop a realistic expectation for the amount and quality of your teaching. Tell yourself "job well done" when you deserve it.

Appreciate the Joy of Teaching and Learning

"Teaching is a constant learning process. Those of us most invested in this adventure would correlate 'the joy of sex' with 'the joy of teaching and learning' — it's always pleasurable, it's always a high (when it works for teachers and learners), and it's always different; and, in another realm of analogy, it truly is a 'religious experience.' We owe it to ourselves and our students to feel the weight, trepidation, and responsibility that young Martin Luther felt before conducting his first mass. Besides making our craft a passionate and holy quest, we must 'count our coups constantly ... i.e., never let too much time go by without reflecting on all the good we do and the recognition of it by our students and peers." (Beverly Blois, Division Chair, Communications and Humanities Division, Northern Virginia Community College, Loudoun Campus, personal communication)

Summary

I end this article where I began — with the inner self. Yes, teaching can be stressful. While mastering stress is a lifelong task, it can badly interfere with both the intellectual and emotional attractions of teaching. The important virtue to remember about teaching and managing stress and loads is that we must not get carried away with our passion, seek balance in our lives, and remember to reserve a part of the love we extend to others for ourselves. Find comfort in the awesome role you are playing in many people's lives. The world is a much better place because of the works and gifts of teachers. Without dedicated teachers, there would be no civilized world. Most of us love what we do. Celebrate the high points. If you can't seem to find any high points, then it is probably time to reassess where you need to be.

Remember to stay in touch with your inner self. Be forever mindful of who you are and the reasons you hold teaching in high esteem. Manage the pedagogical stressors positively and keep in the forefront of your thinking those things that are true, beautiful and good about teaching.

References and Recommended Readings

Brookfield, S. D. (1995). *Becoming a critically reflective teacher.* San Francisco: Jossey-Bass.

Danielson, C. (1996). *Enhancing professional practice: A framework for teaching.* [Online]. Available: www.ascd.org/readingroom/books/danielson96book.html.

Easthope, C., & Easthope, G. (2000). Intensification, extension and complexity of teachers' workload. *British Journal of Sociology of Education, 21*(1), 43-58.

Gmelch, W. H., Wilke, P. K., & Lovrich, N. (1983, April). *Sources of stress in academe: A national perspective.* Paper presented at the annual meeting of the American Educational Research Association, Montreal, Canada.

Higher Education Research Institute. (2000). *Executive summary: The American college teacher: 1989-1999 HERI Faculty Survey Report.* [Online]. Available: www.gseis.ucla.edu/heri/heri.html

Kraft, R. G. (2000). Teaching excellence and the inner life of faculty. *Change 32* (3), 48.

Milem, J. F., Berger, J. B., & Dey, E. L. (2000). Faculty time allocation. *Journal of Higher Education 71*, 454.

Palmer, P. J. (1998). *The courage to teach: Exploring the inner landscape of a teacher's life.* San Francisco: Jossey-Bass.

Trower, C. A. (1999). Alleviating the torture of the tenure track: All it takes is a little show and tell. *The Department Chair: A Newsletter for Academic Administrators 9*(4). [Online]. Available: http://gseweb.harvard.edu/~hpfa/torture.htm.

Simple and Effective Methods for Talking About Teaching

STEFFEN POPE WILSON
Eastern Kentucky University

KATHERINE KIPP
University of Georgia

TRADITIONALLY, COLLEGE teaching has been an individual endeavor. An instructor prepares her course without the assistance of colleagues, delivers course material without feedback from peers, assigns grades without the guidance of others, and handles problems as they arise on her own. There is something secure and sacred about this privatization of teaching, and we often are uncomfortable opening up this area of our professional lives to others. The opposite is true for our scholarship; we feel uncomfortable moving forward on a research project without long discussions with our colleagues, seeking their input and opinions on the numerous aspects of research.

Recently, there has been considerable interest in making teaching more public by engaging in more discussion about it. There are a number of reasons why we should be motivated to engage in such dialog.

Teaching Improvement

Conversations between individuals about their teaching improves their pedagogy. By discussing our teaching philosophies, problems, and methods with our colleagues, we refine our approach to teaching, learn new methodologies and solutions, grow in maturity and depth, and move the field of teaching forward. Talking about teaching challenges us to become aware of the assumptions that drive our approach to teaching. By making these assumptions known, we can better understand how our teaching methods reflect these assumptions and we may be challenged to change our assumptions, and consequently, change and improve our teaching methods.

Teaching Becomes an Intellectual Activity

Through discussions, we begin to challenge ourselves to consider teaching on an intellectual level. By doing so, we will begin to question the logic of our choices, consider the methods of instruction and solutions that others have chosen, and create a scholarship of teaching to empirically investigate and validate the effects of our teaching practices on learning.

Teaching Becomes Public

Talking about teaching makes it a public enterprise, helping others both within and outside of the Academy to understand its complexities, and factors that both facilitate and hinder it. Once teaching is made public it becomes more valued. If we value teaching, we will be more motivated to continually improve the quality of our pedagogy.

Teacher development. Early in one's career, a teacher often sees himself as imparting knowledge to the student, and the student passively absorbing this knowledge. As the teacher matures, he begins to see students as active participants in their education, and teaching becomes collaboration between student and instructor. Perceiving students as active participants in their education is considered superior to simply imparting knowledge. Discussing teaching can facilitate the movement through these stages and help faculty more quickly achieve teaching excellence.

Collegial connection and support. Through discussions we will learn that our colleagues also value teaching, discover those with whom we have similar teaching interests and approaches, we may learn of others who have experienced similar teaching struggles, and also develop a network of supportive colleagues who can help us to solve teaching dilemmas. These connections prevent an instructor from having to "reinvent the wheel" each time a new teaching issue arises. We also can "recharge our batteries" when we discuss teaching with our colleagues, and return to the classroom with renewed energy and enthusiasm. All it takes is one good idea to energize a faculty member for the upcoming semester. Discussions of teaching can also help us develop interpersonally satisfying relationships with our colleagues that extend beyond the classroom.

Methods for Talking About Teaching Effectively

There are a number of methods of discussing teaching and all are beneficial. The method(s) that faculty prefer may vary across an academic career, their style of learning, anxiety level, and so forth. But the sooner in their career faculty learn the joys and fascination of "teaching talk," the more depth and breadth they can bring to their teaching philosophy and work with students.

Informal Discussions

The simplest method of discussing teaching is informally with colleagues. Stopping by a favorite colleague's office and asking for advice, or mentioning a teaching topic during informal conversations in the hallway or at lunch is an easy way to open or continue communication about teaching. A more organized, but still informal method is for a department to hold regular discussions on teaching topics of current interest. In a small department, teaching circles or brown bag lunches can include colleagues from several disciplines. Some departments and universities hold annual teaching retreats during which faculty can get away from campus and discuss teaching.

Teaching and Learning Center

Many colleges and universities have campus centers to promote teaching development and excellence. Attending seminars and workshops hosted by these centers is an excellent way to engage in dialog on teaching with colleagues from across disciplines and to get new ideas from visiting speakers. One also can promote teaching dialogs by volunteering to host such a workshop. Serving as a host challenges us to more carefully consider the topic of discussion and colleagues' ideas. Or invite someone from the teaching center to your department to facilitate your own discussions on pedagogy. It often is nice to have someone outside the department to "lead," control, and direct the discussion.

Teaching Consultants

Many colleges and universities have consultants available to work one-on-one with faculty to improve teaching by identifying problems, offering solutions, or helping them see their students, course goals or teaching philosophy in a new light. Most consultants are from outside one's department, so there is no conflict of interest and less discomfort associated with opening up your teaching to a critical observer. If such a resource does not exist on your campus, consider forming peer consultation groups. An entire department also may be interested in utilizing a consultant outside of the department or college.

Teaching Conferences

A number of national and regional conferences on teaching are held each year. Attending one of these conferences allows us to discuss teaching with colleagues from other institutions who have similar interests. Because posters and presentations may be peer reviewed, the information one receives at these conferences is often high quality and novel. In addition, most faculty who attend such conferences are genuinely excited about teaching, and participants will often find this enthusiasm contagious.

Peer Review and Portfolios

Peer review of teaching is currently being implemented across the country as a tool that can be used for personal reflection as well as tenure, promotion, and post-tenure review decisions. Peer review often entails classroom observations, and compiling a course or a teaching portfolio. Both of these portfolios contain a variety of documents related to one's teaching in general or to a specific course. The process of compiling the documents that are part of a course or teaching portfolio, along with peer observation, can highlight both the strengths and weaknesses in our teaching. If done correctly, such a process can improve our teaching by providing reinforcement for continuing the positive components of our pedagogy, offering potential solutions to resolve weaknesses, and generating ideas for new teaching strategies.

Productive Discussions

We have all experienced teaching discussions that degenerated into a disagreement with our colleagues or elicited a litany of complaints about students, colleagues, the administration, or the field of teaching as a whole, leaving us with negative attitudes. There are a number of rules to prevent such problems from occurring and to ensure that our discussions are productive and collegial.

Focus on Student Learning

Student learning and mastery of information should be the focus of all discussions of teaching, even if the discussion is on an unrelated topic. For example, in a discussion of problem students, solutions should focus not only on decreasing the behaviors that make these students problematic, but also on how we can respond in ways to improve their achievement.

Focus on Solutions

Discussions of teaching should be focused on solutions to problems, instead of on the problem itself. Initial comments may be needed to define a problem, but to be maximally beneficial discussion should emphasize solutions. At the same time, it should be recognized that every solution does not work for every person. Additionally, some of what faculty confront in their teaching are not problems, but "conditions" (e.g., class size, heterogeneity of student body) for which there may be no answers.

Remain Collegial

Faculty love to debate, argue, and disagree. The culture of academia teaches us to think about the ideas of others critically, and then to provide a quick, and occasionally negative response. Because we see our teaching as a private and sacred enterprise, this approach to interacting with colleagues will prevent discussions of teaching from being productive. We need to listen to our colleagues in discussions of teaching with non-critical ears, and be slow to pass judgments on what they say. One of the "ten commandments" of success as a faculty is to learn the value of keeping one's mouth shut and listening.

Voluntary Discussions

Forcing discussions will not achieve the desired goal of improving teaching. Leaders should model discussions to demonstrate that they can be a non-threatening way to improving teaching, and then let others join, as they feel comfortable.

Frequent Discussions

Teaching issues arise continually throughout the academic year. To address them in a timely manner, regular discussions should be held in either formal or informal settings. In addition, the availability of regular teaching discussions sends the message that improvement of teaching is something that should occur continually, not just once or twice a year.

Focus on Success

In addition to discussing our problems, we should take time to affirm what we are doing well in the classroom and with our students. This approach can help us feel that teaching is not always an uphill battle, but also a battle won.

What Can We Talk About?

What can we talk about during these discussions? Here are several suggestions to help get you started.

Probably the simplest way to begin a discussion of teaching is by asking colleagues how they handle a specific teaching issue. For example, you might ask how do you:

+ Handle make-up tests?
+ Grade group assignments?
+ Encourage class discussion?
+ Balance lecture with discussion?
+ Teach attachment theory?

Most of us like to talk about ourselves, so this is an effective method of starting a conversation.

Actual Teaching

Go watch other faculty teach, and paradoxically, preferably not in psychology. You will learn more by watching colleagues in other disciplines and it is often more fun to do so. Ask them in advance and explain that you want to visit their class in order to learn from them. Try to talk with them after class about how it went, and what they were trying to achieve. Bring back your observations and insights to your colleagues.

Teaching Cases

Another way to start discussion and discover solutions to common classroom problems is to discuss teaching cases. Teaching cases are especially useful because they are not specific to any person in the group, and therefore, they are a non-threatening way to discuss solutions to problems. You will learn as you read and discuss teaching cases that faculty are sometimes their own worst enemy and at other times, we are at the mercy of the actions of our students, colleagues, and administrators.

Ethical Dilemmas

Faculty can discuss ethical dilemmas they have faced recently or that are of frequent concern. This topic requires a willingness to open up to colleagues, but it can elicit helpful suggestions for thinking about and resolving ethical dilemmas. A discussion of common ethical dilemmas and solutions also can help new faculty learn the cultural norms and policies within the department and university. For a start, you may want to consider how you:

- ◆ Address plagiarism, and what methods do you use to prevent it?
- ◆ Achieve equity in grading group assignments?
- ◆ Respond to requests for extra credit, and how do you balance these requests with remaining fair in your grading practices?

Content

Faculty, especially those who teach different sections of the same course, should discuss how they approach content. Many topics can be discussed:

- ◆ Do you feel that breadth or depth is more important?
- ◆ Does your approach to breadth versus depth change for different courses?
- ◆ How do you use the text to supplement content presented and discussed in class?
- ◆ How prepared are your students?
- ◆ How are your students doing in courses for which the one you teach is a prerequisite?

Student Feedback

This is a good topic to consider towards the end of a class term when students are completing evaluation forms for their courses. You can ask colleagues:

- ◆ How do you feel about the feedback you receive for your courses?
- ◆ Do you add additional items to your student evaluation forms? If so, what items have you added and what have you learned from these items?
- ◆ How have changes you have made in your classes influenced student comments either positively or negatively, or had no influence at all?

Academic Issues and Beliefs

Teaching takes place within a context of individual beliefs and the demands of our college or university. To truly understand our own and colleagues' teaching it is fun and interesting to step back and look at the world of academe. Such topics might include:

- ♦ The place of teaching after one is tenured. Does teaching take a back seat to scholarship or does one's commitment to teaching increase?

- ♦ What does it mean to be a faculty member? Is being an academic truly a calling and if so, how does one balance, teaching, service, scholarship, and one's own personal life?

- ♦ What does one gain and lose by being a "local" (someone whose efforts emphasize the department and college in which one works) versus being a "cosmopolitan" (a faculty who emphasizes reputation and efforts beyond the local institution and regional, national and international forums and groups)?

Conclusion

Regular and collegial discussions of teaching, no matter what the format, can promote growth and excellence in college and university teaching. What is important is that you make discussions of teaching a regular part of your professional life. Doing so will improve the quality of your teaching, enhance your collegial relationships, and help to de-privatize teaching, making it a public and intellectual domain worthy of our respect, and the respect of those outside of academia. It will also lower your stress and bring some fun to your work. Who could ask for better than that?

References and Recommended Readings

Bernstein, D. J. (2002). Representing the intellectual work in teaching through peer-reviewed course portfolios. In S. F. Davis & W. Buskist (Eds.), *The teaching of psychology: Essays in honor of Wilbert J. McKeachie and Charles L. Brewer* (pp. 215-229). Mahwah, NJ: Lawrence Erlbaum.

Brookfield, S. D. (1995). Holding critical conversations about teaching. In S. D. Brookfield, *Becoming a critically reflective teacher* (pp. 140-159). San Francisco: Jossey-Bass.

Giordano, P. J., Awalt, H. M., Ingham, R. O., Simpler, S. H., Sims, G. E., & Kendall, E. D. (1995). Enhancing teaching by participating in an interdisciplinary faculty improvement group. *Teaching of Psychology*, 22, 123-125.

Hutchings, P. (1993). *Using cases to improve college teaching: A guide to more reflective practice*. Washington, DC: AAHE.

Johnson, D. E. (2002). Teaching, research, and scholarship. In S. F. Davis & W. Buskist. (Eds.), *The teaching of psychology: Essays in honor of Wilbert J. McKeachie and Charles L. Brewer* (pp. 153-162). Mahwah, NJ: Lawrence Erlbaum.

Kugel, P. (1993). How professors develop as teachers. *Studies in Higher Education, 18*, 315-328.

Palmer, P. J. (1998). Learning in community: The conversation of colleagues. In P. J. Palmer, *The courage to teach* (pp. 141-161). San Francisco: Jossey-Bass.

Perlman, B., & McCann, L. I. (2002). Peer review for meaningful teaching enhancement. In S. F. Davis & W. Buskist (Eds.), *The teaching of psychology: Essays in honor of Wilbert J. McKeachie and Charles L. Brewer* (pp. 189-201). Mahwah, NJ: Lawrence Erlbaum.

Seldin, P. (1997). *The teaching portfolio: A practical guide to improved performance and promotion/tenure decisions*, (3rd ed.). Bolton, MA: Anker.

Shulman, L. (1993). Teaching as community property: Putting an end to pedagogical solitude. *Change, 25*(6), 6-7.

Using a Scholarship of Teaching Model to Enhance Your Teaching

Tami J. Eggleston
McKendree College

Gabie E. Smith
Elon University

HAVE YOU EVER TRIED to improve your teaching? Our assumption is "yes," but that these attempts have not always gone well. Have you ever wanted to make a change, but didn't know exactly where or how to start? Have you ever felt slowed down by a sense of academic inertia and needed a jump-start to make a change? Did your changes actually improve your course(s) and student learning or did you simply assume you succeeded or fell flat? We have good news; there is a strategy and process that will help improve your teaching — the scholarship of teaching model. We can imagine some eyes glazing over at the mention of theory and models and you may be asking, *Can a theory or a model really help enhance courses through better teaching and learning?* In this article, through simple steps and teaching examples, we hope to help you make effective pedagogical changes to increase student learning.

A couple of years ago, we tried to incorporate more technology into our teaching and developed what we thought was a clever classroom activity that involved assigning "virtual personas" for students to use on electronic discussion boards. For example, a young white male student might be assigned the role of a 40 year old Latina woman and then have to respond to a discussion prompt such as explaining attitudes about counseling or child rearing. The first semester was a dismal failure but we were not discouraged, assuming that we were teaching an unusual group of students. The next semester, we replicated the same assignment with the same results. So, we asked a colleague in the English department to assist with fleshing out the personas and the discussion questions. Interestingly, she was so intrigued by the virtual persona activity she also tried to incorporate it into her teaching. Although three faculty members thought the activity was original and had great possibility, it was clear that the students had very different ideas. They were still not posting, and when they did their answers were unclear and they were certainly not getting what we thought they should from the assignment.

We decided to apply some of the scholarship of teaching model to discover what was wrong, and help us to modify the activity. A primary tenet in the scholarship of teaching is the importance of assessing activities and getting feedback from students, so we asked for their feedback and got some specific suggestions: write better directions, provide assistance for finding research about their new persona, provide an exemplar for a good post, and improve some technology issues. After hearing from the students, we finally (and easily) determined what needed to be changed.

This virtual persona saga demonstrates a process that involves changing our courses to enhance teaching and learning with deliberation and a specified goal. The theoretical model of the scholarship of teaching developed by a variety of scholars, and modified into a simple five-stage model in this article, can assist instructors to make effective changes in the classroom, provide opportunity for sharing this information, and even bring fun and excitement to the endeavor.

Underlying this model is the understanding that the best teachers modify their courses to improve the teaching and learning process. The seemingly simple decision to improve the processes of teaching and learning quickly generates many questions such as what classes to modify, where to make changes, what to change, why make changes, and eventually, whether the changes did indeed enhance teaching and learning.

What Is the Scholarship of Teaching?

Boyer (1990) and Shulman (1993) are leading proponents of a scholarship of teaching that views the act of teaching from the perspectives of design, enactment and critical analyses. "Pedagogical procedures must be carefully planned, continuously examined, and relate directly to the subject taught" (Boyer, 1990, p. 24). In addition to making the process of teaching more scientific, additional benefits include increased excitement in the class, decreased chance of instructor burnout or stagnation, greater chances of faculty collaboration, more systematic and reflective activities, and ultimately enhanced learning for both instructor and student. The importance of the scholarship of teaching model lies in the fact that it does not emphasize a few techniques, strategies, or teaching tips, but rather focuses on a more macro level complex, integrated, and theoretical process for looking at pedagogy (Menges & Weimer, 1996).

Taking the Scholarship of Teaching Into the Classroom

Based on the theoretical approaches to the scholarship of teaching and our experiences, we propose a five-stage model for making meaningful and manageable changes in your courses.

Stage 1: Identify the Challenge or Need

Be reflective. Reflect on your classes or topic areas within a class with an eye for what could be enhanced or needs improvement. Have an open critical mind and listen to students. We actually keep a teaching notebook to list challenges, needs, and ideas as they present themselves in the classroom. We have found that when you take time to observe your classroom, challenges and research ideas become readily, and sometimes painfully apparent.

In more traditional empirical approaches this would be considered the development of the hypotheses. This first step is paramount in deciding what, where, when, and why you will modify your courses. For example, an instructor teaching Health Psychology might want to add more substance to his or her class by additional physiology and neurology. The dilemma is that the class is sophomore level and the professor worries that adding the biopsychology may be "too much." In this case, the need and challenge are clear.

Look to colleagues in other disciplines and other colleges to develop innovative activities. One of the exciting aspects of the scholarship of teaching model is the inherent collaborative opportunity. Sharing and learning with others will be both invigorating and fun. The health psychology instructor may want to talk to other faculty at his or her institution or colleagues teaching health psychology elsewhere for advice about additional biology in the course. Do not make changes for the sake of change, or change everything in every course at once.

Ask yourself the following questions:

- ♦ What course most needs change to increase teaching and learning effectiveness?

In our course using the virtual persona saga, we decided our class needed more emphasis on ethnic and cultural diversity.

- ♦ What is your primary challenge in this course?

Ours was two-fold. In addition to adding diversity issues, we wanted students to utilize more technology.

- ♦ What is/are the primary goal(s)/outcome(s) that you want to achieve?

This was a difficult question, but we decided that applying theory to real world issues, developing empathy, and using technology were important goals. Interestingly, we had few readings, discussions, speakers and films/videos designed to increase empathy and understanding.

Stage 2: Develop the Teaching Technique

Create a change (activity or technique) to address the identified need. This step begins with creative generation of ideas that become progressively more specific in focus and purpose. Rather than simply *plopping* something into your course, the addition is now clearly linked to a pedagogical need. For example, an instructor teaching child psychology may decide that there is a need for an observational learning component in the course and, therefore, must find appropriate places for the observations to occur.

Start small. Small ideas often grow into meaningful classroom learning. You probably do not need to change an entire course. For the child psychology instructor, a small change may include simply asking for a one-hour observation of children at any location (school, day care, shopping mall, etc.) and a one-page reflection paper. Over time, with some student feedback, this project could evolve into a larger project with a service learning component and a longer paper.

Remember that pedagogy and learning come first. Let your pedagogical needs and challenges guide the process of improving your courses. Keep your focus on the outcome — effective teaching and learning. Reading pedagogical books such as *Teaching to Transfer* (Hooks, 1994) may assist with articulating your primary, global pedagogical objectives.

For this stage, ask the following questions:

- ♦ What change or innovation could be made to your course to meet your challenge or goals?

In our case, we had a new technological tool and with the right assignment believed that empathy and understanding diversity issues could be enhanced. Once a goal is clearly identified, it is important to make sure that there are classroom activities that meet the goal.

♦ What could I eliminate to allow for more time on the new activity?

By adding more time for a virtual personal project, a "tired" outline summary for one of the chapters was eliminated to allow more time for student work and faculty evaluation.

Stage 3: Just Do It!

Implement the activity in one or more classes. Although some of these alterations may be time-consuming and perhaps risky, we have found that altering classes increases the energy level in the class fueled, in part, by our own enthusiasm. If the class is being altered to meet an identified need or challenge, the activity will seem worthwhile to the students if the instructor presents it in this light. For example, an experienced clinical psychologist may believe that the DSM gives students great structure for organizing and categorizing various disorders. Yet, the instructor may find that the students find the DSM confusing and they do not have enough insight and information to fully utilize the DSM classifications. What to do? The instructor can tell the students that they are going to embark on an experiment. They will receive more information about the DSM in one module of the abnormal psychology class (e.g., mood disorders) and less in another module (e.g., anxiety disorders). After the two modules, the instructor informs students that they will be asked for their feedback about what approach they believe helped increase their learning (e.g., the DSM-extra or the DSM-light). Students will appreciate knowing that you care about their learning.

Don't be afraid to fail. Even when changes are not effective, the excitement and the process create energy and enthusiasm in the classroom. The only way to truly fail is to not try to improve teaching and learning.

When implementing a change in teaching, think about the following questions:

♦ Are my instructions clear?

One of the biggest problems with our virtual persona assignment was that the instructions were vague with phrases such as "research your persona." When we revised the assignment, we gave specific Web sites for students to visit to get more information about their persona.

♦ Is the timing correct for the intervention?

In our initial attempts, the activity was placed early in the semester, but students needed more course content and familiarity with the technology for the activity to be successful. Therefore, we moved the activity to later in the semester.

♦ How are you going to "sell" the activity to the students?

If you are incorporating an activity to meet a need, challenge, or primary goal, tell the students. The students are more likely to see the value of the activity when they understand the underlying rationale. For example, in our early attempts with the virtual persona activity, we did not bother to tell the students what we hoped they would learn from the activity. Needless to say, they did not figure it out on their own.

Stage 4: Did It Work?

Perform multidimensional assessments of the innovation. These assessments can be simple Likert-type items or open-ended questions measuring students' perceptions of the innovation, attitudes towards participation, and self-reports of knowledge or ability improvements. For example, many instructors use a classic film of Milgram's research in Introduction to Psychology or Social Psychology. The instructor probably believes that there is enough "set-up" with an introduction and transition including emphasizing the importance of this classic film. However, do we know if the film is viewed by the students as classic and relevant or old and outdated? After the film, an instructor could hand out a brief survey asking how the video was related to the topic, if students understood the video or had additional questions, if they thought the video helped their learning, and if they thought of replications or alterations to the study that needed to be done after seeing this video. This survey provides the instructor important feedback. It also allows the students a chance to reflect on the video, making them more attentive viewers.

Whenever possible, assessment results should be anonymous and confidentiality assured. Other assessments include performance measures (such as scores on exams, papers, or project folders) and behavioral measures, including attendance, participation, preparation for class, or retention in major. For more information on classroom assessment, see Angelo and Cross (1993) and Brookfield (1995). Interestingly, we often fail to ask students what works and what does not. Most faculty have standardized campus-wide teacher evaluations, but these often fail to provide specific and constructive feedback that would suggest effective changes.

To assess your changes, ask yourself the following questions:

♦ What questions could I ask students about specific activities that I use in class?

Finally, after the failed attempts we asked students if the instructions were clear, if they could find resources easily on the Internet, if they had any problems using the technology, and if they had suggestions for improving the activity. With this specific feedback, we were able to make the changes necessary to make the assignment a useful learning experience.

♦ What questions could I ask students about things they like in certain classes or things they would like to see altered?

In addition to asking about the persona assignment, we also asked for feedback about what students felt they learned from different assignments and general suggestions for an improved learning environment.

♦ What do students perceive as the big picture or primary goals or outcomes?

Perhaps one of the scariest questions involves what students see as the reason for different activities in the class. In our early attempts with the virtual persona, students were literally dumbfounded as to why we were doing the activity.

Stage 5: Share Your Knowledge

Disseminate the information. This can be done by talking with colleagues, making scholarly presentations, writing for publication with external peer review, participating in "teaching circles" on campus, making reciprocal classroom observations, or applying for grants. Too many times we make excellent changes but then keep them private. We both have gotten many of our best teaching tips while conversing or just hanging out in offices with our colleagues. We also have found that sharing our ideas on campus via informal teaching circles helps to create a community of teachers. If teachers want to collect more data and formally share their work, there are a variety of avenues. For example, the *Lilly Teaching Conference* and the *National Institute for the Teaching of Psychology* are invigorating opportunities.

To start the sharing and collaboration, ask yourself:

♦ How could I share information about my teaching with my colleagues on campus?

For example, we both added a cross-cultural project to our human sexuality course that involved student presentations about sexual topics (e.g., birth control, prostitution, marriage) in countries around the world. After we shared our activity with other colleagues, they easily implemented the ideas into their own psychology classes and even into other disciplines.

♦ What conferences on teaching might I consider attending?

These conferences help you identify your challenges and goals and also provide specific ideas for when, what, where, why and how to improve learning.

Conclusion

The five-stage teaching as scholarship model (or from another perspective, conducting pedagogical research) can be used to improve teaching and learning experiences. Not only does it enhance the classroom, but it can also lead to presentations and possibly publication opportunities. In addition, it is fun and invigorating to collaborate with others who are also passionate about teaching.

Of course, there are other ways to improve teaching. We have emphasized the importance of identifying specific needs, making precise changes, and then evaluating outcomes. An alternative approach is to look at the "big picture." List all of the projects and activities in one of your courses and determine what is missing, what could be deleted, and what can be improved. We believe this global course evaluation or teaching portfolio approach is beneficial and complements the teaching as scholarship model. In sum, whatever methods help make effective changes to the classroom and allow for greater knowledge of the teaching process are valuable. As Boyer (1990) noted, "Good teaching means that faculty, as scholars, are also learners (p. 24)."

References and Recommended Reading

Angelo, T. A., & Cross, K. P. (1993). *Classroom assessment techniques: A handbook for college teachers.* San Francisco: Jossey-Bass.

Boyer, E. L. (1990). *Scholarship reconsidered: Priorities of the professorate.* Princeton, NJ: Carnegie Foundation for the Advancement of Teaching.

Brookfield, S. D. (1995). *Becoming a critically reflective teacher.* San Francisco: Jossey-Bass.

Carnegie Foundation for the Advancement of Teaching Web site. www.carnegiefoundation.org.

Cross, K. P., & Steadman, M. H. (1996). *Classroom research: Implementing the scholarship of teaching.* San Francisco: Jossey-Bass.

Glassick, C. E., Huber, M. T., & Maeroff, G. I. (1997). *Scholarship assessed: Evaluation of the professoriate.* San Francisco: Jossey-Bass.

hooks, b. (1994). *Teaching to transgress: Education as the practice of freedom.* New York: Routledge.

Menges, R. J., Weimer, M., & Associates. (Eds.). (1996). *Teaching on Solid Ground.* San Francisco: Jossey-Bass.

Shulman, L. S. (1993.) Teaching as community property: Putting an end to pedagogical solitude. *Change, 25*(6), 6-7.

The Course Portfolio

WILLIAM CERBIN
University of Wisconsin LaCrosse

WHAT DO WE MEAN BY "teaching?" Too often teaching is identified only as the active interactions between teacher and students in a classroom setting (or even a tutorial session). I would argue that teaching, like other forms of scholarship, is an extended process that unfolds over time. It embodies at least five elements: vision, design, interactions, outcomes and analysis. (Shulman, 1998, p. 5)

If, as Lee Shulman contends, teaching entails an extended process of vision, design, interactions, outcomes and analysis, then where is teaching documented so that we can study it, discuss it, learn from it, understand it, replicate it, build upon and improve it? In other areas, our scholarly investigations evolve into manuscripts, articles, chapters, and monographs. What is the pedagogical equivalent of the research manuscript?

Frankly, the record of my teaching resides mainly in computer files and files of course syllabi, course assignments, lecture material, and student work. Any reader would have to infer from these artifacts, the vision, design, and interactions of the course, as well as what effect the course had on student learning and development. Only a forensic scientist or an archaeologist could construct a facsimile of my teaching from the artifacts I have accumulated. This is a common scenario. We lose good ideas about teaching because we do not preserve them. We fail to build and refine good ideas about teaching because there is so little upon which to build.

We need something equivalent to a "manuscript in progress" that explicates the vision, design, interactions, outcomes and analysis of teaching. I nominate a type of teaching portfolio — a course portfolio — as a viable candidate to fill this void. Such a portfolio is a superb mechanism for reflection on and improvement of one's teaching. It emphasizes a significant element in teaching, an individual course. Engaging in the course portfolio process necessitates a close look at:

- ♦ *Vision*: One's goals and hopes for a course
- ♦ *Design*: What and how students will engage the subject — what they will read, discuss, experience, study, and hopefully learn
- ♦ *Interaction*: The nature and quality of teaching and learning in the course
- ♦ *Outcomes*: What students actually learn changes in their knowledge, abilities, sensibilities, and attitudes
- ♦ *Analysis*: Conclusions about student learning, successes, shortcomings, surprises and changes one would make to improve the course

The Course Portfolio

Broadly defined, a teaching portfolio is "[A] factual description of a professor's strengths and accomplishments. It includes documents and materials which collectively suggest the scope and quality of a professor's teaching performance" (Seldin, 1993, p. 2). Portfolios at their best are more than collections of teaching artifacts (i.e., syllabi, assignments, evidence of student learning). They include analysis and reflection; they put forward an argument, make a case, summarize and explain an inquiry into teaching and learning.

Trying to make a coherent argument about, or sense of, all of one's teaching is an unwieldy prospect. A more manageable unit of analysis is the individual course. Our teaching lives are organized around courses. Our teaching often varies among courses; we teach a certain way in one and differently in another. A course is an identifiable entity with certain learning goals, teaching strategies, assignments intended to accomplish those goals, and outcomes (i.e., student learning). As a goal oriented endeavor, a course resembles an "experiment," as the following description suggests:

- ♦ The course begins with significant goals and intentions, which are embodied in its design and expressed in the syllabus and other documents (such as a proposal to a curriculum committee).
- ♦ Those goals and intentions are enacted or carried out in appropriate ways as the course material unfolds over the term.
- ♦ And, as a result, certain outcomes emerge: students grasp (or do not) the key ideas/methods/values of the

field that shaped the course design and enactment. (Hutchings, 1998, p. 16)

The course-as-experiment analogy suggests that a course portfolio is the write-up that documents the investigation of teaching and learning in the class. In it, the instructor explores questions about what, how and why students learned or did not learn what they were taught (or what the instructor intended them to learn). The investigation may be a broad exploratory study that examines what students actually learn in the course (i.e., to what extent they attain the stated course goals). Or, instructors might pursue specific questions inside the course, such as "Why can't students apply theoretical perspectives to behavior in real contexts?" or "Why is it so difficult for students to distinguish between causality and correlation?"

What if Instructors Developed Course Portfolios?

Imagine that you developed a course portfolio for one of the important classes each of you teach. What might be the consequences and benefits?

Deeper Understanding of Teaching and Learning

Portfolio authors report that moving from informal or episodic reflection to more sustained and systematic inquiry leads to deeper understanding of their teaching and how it affects student learning. As one biologist said about her portfolio development experience:

> Too many times, my good ideas about teaching are lost because they pass through my brain as fleeting thoughts or as unwritten resolutions to "do better." The opposite is also true. I repeat mistakes or make due with old strategies because I have not taken the time to rethink my game plan for a lesson or activity. My sense is that the very act of capturing those fleeting thoughts, of formalizing the game plan, of facing the failures, and of underlining the successes will help me to new places with my teaching. (Langsam, 1998, pp. 60-61)

An English professor suggests that portfolio development influenced his concept of teaching:

> What most surprised me was how the portfolio increased my sense of unrealized potential in the classroom. I began to see teaching and learning in a more scholarly

way — comprising a body of knowledge much in the way one's "discipline" does. ... I began to read more selectively in the research literature on teaching and learning, discovering new ideas and strategies for use in the classroom that made me more aware of the cognitive atmosphere in my classes. I saw — increasingly — many more opportunities to apply principles of good practice in my classes. (Mignon, 1998, pp. 69-70)

In my own case, I discovered fundamental discrepancies between my professed learning goals for the course and students' actual performance. The course syllabus indicated that critical thinking was an important goal of the course but, on close examination, I found I actually did little to facilitate the development of students' thinking. I certainly expected it on papers and examinations, but I was not really teaching it. Another realization came when I started to explore why students had so much difficulty applying newly learned concepts to novel situations and problems. I discovered that students were capable of paraphrasing and parroting back information but had little understanding of the material. This has led to a long-term study of students' understanding in my classes (Cerbin, 1992, 1995, 1999).

I doubt my experience is unique; there are always gaps between instructors' goals and students' performance, and gaps between instructors' goals and their own teaching practices. So, in an abnormal psychology class, an instructor who wants students to develop greater tolerance and empathy for mentally ill people finds she spends almost no time on that goal during the term. Or, an instructor who wants students to achieve a conceptual understanding of statistical inference finds that students do the computations adequately without understanding statistical principles. Or, an instructor in introductory psychology finds that students' misconceptions about human behavior remain unchanged as a result of the class.

Of course, the payoff for better understanding of teaching and learning should be better teaching and learning. The gaps between intentions, teaching practices and student learning provide the problems to be solved. Good course portfolios do not stop with analysis of problems — instructors often think through possible solutions, implement changes in their courses and assess those changes.

Changing the Discourse of Teaching and Learning

Discussions among instructors about teaching often stall or wander because participants do not share a common language, and because the topic lacks a concrete context. A course portfolio puts a problem in a specific context for all to see and examine. Imagine the difference between hallway conversations with colleagues about teaching and one that begins like this, "I've written about several new lab experiments I'm using in experimental psychology class and how students have done on them. Would you mind reading it and giving me some feedback on it?" Moreover, course portfolios may alter the discourse about teaching, as instructors shift from idiosyncratic or personal issues (i.e., my problems and successes in my class) to "problematics that are inherent in the teaching of the subject area" (Hutchings, 1998, p.88). For example, psychological research has shown that students' prior knowledge plays a key role in new learning. In our classes students' intuitive theories of behavior affect their learning of new disciplinary knowledge. But we have not addressed this general problem as a community of teachers.

Advancing the Practice of Teaching

Developing course portfolios might lead individual instructors to new discoveries and improvements in their teaching. Those ideas may have broader implications for advancing the practice of teaching. Other instructors could benefit by reading about how colleagues have grappled with the significant teaching and learning issues. Course portfolios could serve as a kind of pedagogical text with a variety of uses. Departments could use course portfolios as the basis for focused discussions about teaching and learning throughout the program. Advanced graduate students might study course portfolios as part of their preparation for teaching, and also produce a course portfolio as part of their TA experience. New faculty might benefit from being able to read portfolios of key courses in a department. Departments might ask senior faculty members to create "legacy" course portfolios to pass on their work to future generations of instructors. And so on.

Writing a Course Portfolio

Decide on a purpose. Start with a purpose for creating a portfolio. The purpose could be personal growth — to rekindle enthusiasm for teaching, to stimulate teaching improvement, or to reflect on one's development in teaching. Another purpose is to generate new pedagogical knowledge and influence teaching in the field. Still another is to demonstrate teaching performance for job application, promotion, tenure, or post tenure review. Of course, it is unlikely you would write one without a purpose, but purpose is important because it helps determine what goes in the portfolio.

Find a focus. Focus on a question, a problem, a dilemma, a predicament, a topic, or an issue of interest that helps structure and organize portfolio development. A good rule of thumb is to pursue a problem that is personally important in your teaching.

Adapt the portfolio to the audience. Who will read the portfolio and why? The audience for a personal growth portfolio might include the author and a few trusted colleagues. The audience for a portfolio in a tenure decision will be colleagues making a high stakes decision.

Anticipate the data and evidence you need. Collect the artifacts you need to make your case. Save student work, course evaluations, and copies of important materials. Videotape classes, etc.

Reflect on your practice. Portfolio development is an opportunity to examine one's basic assumptions, beliefs and teaching practices. Tell more than how you teach; explain why you teach the way you do.

Start small. Put aside analyzing the whole of the course. Build a single portfolio entry around an interesting question, experience or finding. This could be an analysis of a single class period or something you notice about students' interactions, or something about your own teaching worth exploring (e.g., trying small group activities for the first time in a large lecture class).

Seek feedback. Talk to colleagues about your work. Ask them to read it and discuss it with you. Don't pass up the opportunity to have a good discussion about teaching.

What to Include in a Course Portfolio

Purpose, focus and audience will help determine the contents of a portfolio. But, keep in mind four major categories — design, enactment, results and analysis.

Design. Discuss underlying assumptions and beliefs about teaching. How does your teaching philosophy translate into goals and practices? What are the learning goals and objectives of the course? What factors affect course design (required vs. elective, level of course, characteristics of students, etc)? Include an annotated syllabus that explains not only what the course entails, but why it is put together that way.

Enactment. What do students experience in the course?

Include copies and explanations of important assignments, projects, learning activities, and exams that address the course goals. Consider including video or audio excerpts of actual teaching-learning episodes or classroom observations by colleagues.

Results. How are students changed by the course? What did they learn? How are they different with respect to knowledge, skills, dispositions, values, beliefs? What did they not accomplish that you hoped they would? This section need not scour every aspect of student learning, but should highlight how students performed with respect to the course objectives. Try to include the students' perspective through course evaluations or other forms of student feedback.

Analysis. What are your conclusions about the course, about the issues you investigated, about your teaching and student learning? Given the results of the course, what would you change to improve it?

Summary

A course portfolio examines teaching and learning in a single course. By structuring systematic inquiry into teaching, the portfolio development process can lead instructors to important insights about their teaching and its effect on student learning. Portfolios also have the potential to influence scholarly discourse about teaching — to foster systematic, focused discussion of significant issues and problems. As a source of pedagogical knowledge, portfolios could be used as texts to learn more about teaching and learning, and to advance the practice of teaching.

References and Recommended Readings

Cerbin, W. (1992). *A learning centered course portfolio.* [Online]. Available: http://kml.carnegiefoundation.org/gallery/bcerbin/Resources/Course_Portfolio/course_portfolio.html

Cerbin, W. (1994). The course portfolio as a tool for continuous improvement of teaching and learning. *Journal of Excellence in College Teaching, 5,* 95-105.

Cerbin, W. (1995). Connecting assessment of learning to the improvement of teaching through the course portfolio. *Assessment Update, 7*(1), 4-6.

Cerbin, W., Pointer, D., Hatch, T., & Iiyoshi T. (1999). *The development of student understanding in a problem-based educational psychology course.* [Online]. Available: http://kml.carnegiefoundation.org/gallery/bcerbin

Hutchings, P. (1998). Defining features and significant functions of the course portfolio. In P. Hutchings, (Ed.), *The course portfolio: How faculty can examine their teaching to advance practice and student learning,* (pp.13-18). Washington, DC: American Association for Higher Education.

Hutchings, P. (1998). A course portfolio for a creative writing course. In P. Hutchings, (Ed.), *The course portfolio: How faculty can examine their teaching to advance practice and student learning,* (pp.85-90). Washington, DC: American Association for Higher Education.

Langsam, D. (1998). A course portfolio for midcareer reflection. In P. Hutchings, (Ed.), *The course portfolio: How faculty can examine their teaching to advance practice and student learning.* (pp.57-63), Washington, DC: American Association for Higher Education.

Mignon, C. (1998). Post-tenure review: A case study of a course portfolio within a personnel file. In P. Hutchings, (Ed.), *The course portfolio: How faculty can examine their teaching to advance practice and student learning,* (pp. 69-70). Washington, DC: American Association for Higher Education.

Samford University Problem-Based Learning Project. [Online]. Available: www.samford.edu/pbl. (Samford is involved in a university-wide effort to incorporate problem-based learning throughout the curriculum. Faculty who redesign PBL courses develop course portfolios to document their work. The portfolios undergo external peer review and are then published by the institution.)

Seldin, P. (1993). *Successful use of teaching portfolios.* Bolton, MA: Anker.

Shulman, L. (1998). Course anatomy: The dissection and analysis of knowledge through teaching. In P. Hutchings, (Ed.), *The course portfolio: How faculty can examine their teaching to advance practice and student learning,* (pp.5-12). Washington, DC: American Association for Higher Education.

Teaching a Course You Feel Unprepared to Teach

Todd Zakrajsek
Central Michigan University

LIFE IN HIGHER EDUCATION is full of surprises. Like everyone else, sooner or later you will probably agree to teach a course you do not feel well prepared to teach. This might be a course in an area in which you have no formal training, or that is "just" outside your disciplinary training, a topic area you never really mastered in graduate school, or a course very different in format from how you have taught before. There are a number of factors that result in a course needing to be covered by someone other than the regularly scheduled faculty member. In such situations, the department chair has the difficult task of finding someone to cover the course. This article is presented to give guidance to those who accept such an assignment.

Where to Begin

You have been asked to teach this course and although it makes you a bit nervous, the chair has assured you that you will do a great job. Your first decision is whether to accept the assignment. There are many issues related to this decision. Most colleagues will appreciate your being a "team player" and putting the good of students and the department ahead of your own interests. Balance their good will against your upcoming workload and your ability to adapt to new stressors in your life. Although accepting such an assignment will test your nerves, it also allows you to learn an area of psychology new to you. It will be very time consuming, so if you have an overload at present, are working on a major grant proposal, or are already teaching a course you have not taught before, it would be wise to pass on this opportunity.

Find out why you are being asked to teach this course. If it is a new curricular need, determine to what extent this will become "your" course. If it has been taught before, why is the instructor no longer teaching it? If the past instructor obtained permission to give up teaching the course because of a grant or other opportunity, talk to that instructor and find out why this particular course was released. It may well be that it is a scheduling issue, but it could also be a course that burns people out. Do not accept the assignment if the course has moved from person to person in the department and each vows never to teach it again. There are good reasons instructors are passing on this course. Also keep in mind that the moment before you say "yes" or "no" is your best time for bargaining. Consider asking for a graduate student to help you with searching the literature, grading, or even helping with some class sessions as a TA. You may even be able to negotiate extra secretarial support or undergraduate student help for that semester. Overall, I would suggest always taking a day or two to think about whether or not to accept this assignment. It is a big commitment, and taking a bit of time to make this decision is reasonable.

Let us assume your situation allows you to accept this new assignment. Let us also assume the best-case scenario that you have a few months before your class is scheduled to begin, and the freedom to construct or design the course as you see fit. Three major areas will serve as good places to start: gather as much information as you can about how the course has been taught in the past; make decisions upon which you will build your course; and monitor your class closely once it begins. If you have only days to prepare, and/or the components of the course are already selected (syllabus, text, course schedule), skip the first two sections and proceed (quickly) to the last section on monitoring your class and being ready to adapt.

Gathering Information

Find General Course Information

Check out the college catalog and find out as much about this course as you are able. Read the course description and any objectives that are listed. Is it a required course, and if so, must students take that course or is it an option in a list of courses from which students must select? Find out if prerequisites are listed for the course. I once accepted an assignment to teach a research methods course and was told statistics was required. When I looked, the college catalog did not state what I had been told. I went back to the chair and he said statistics was strongly encouraged, which students often interpret as very different from required.

Talk With Colleagues

Your best resources are instructors who have taught this course at your institution in the past and those who teach the same topic at other institutions. If you find information on the Web, e-mail instructors with questions. New collegial friendships will emerge. Also consider contacting instructors from the university where you completed your graduate and undergraduate work.

Faculty are typically *very* receptive to speaking with colleagues regarding a number of course topics and resources: syllabi; past textbooks, tasks, and assignments; motivational level and preparedness of the students; examples of good and inadequate papers; course traps (e.g., modules that have too many core concepts and materials; particularly difficult material); and types of exams.

Obtain Course Syllabi and Materials

Course syllabi allow you to see how the course was structured, assignments and exams used and the weighting given to them in establishing final grades, types of extra-credit assignments (if used), relevant films and videos, original sources for reading, ideas for guest speakers, relevant Web sites, the pacing of the course, and course objectives. Textbooks assist in identification of whether the course was taught from a theoretical or applied orientation, the number of core concepts per chapter and module, applications to students' lives (the one-page "boxes" many texts use), and the reading/comprehension level of students.

Determine what tasks and assignments you can require such as service learning, group projects, computer assignments, poster sessions, or homework assignments.

Learn About Typical Students Taking the Course

Talk with colleagues regarding students' motivation and ability level. Is the course typically a popular one? What kinds of students typically enroll? Do many students find the course content boring? Does the course have the reputation of being easy or difficult? For example, merely because a course is required, do not assume that students are enrolling because they must take the course. Required courses are the backbone of any program and motivated students may understand well that the material is vital to an understanding of the discipline. Ask prior instructors of the course how students feel about the course and whether students have the prerequisite knowledge they are supposed to possess.

Exams and Grading

Copies of old exams may be helpful. These exams will indicate the level of difficultly, degree of discrimination of concepts expected of the students, and coverage of material. Regardless of the information requested, delicately inquire as to what worked well, and what did not. Be respectful of the person who has agreed to help you. You may be amazed (both positively and negatively) at what you hear and see. If you do not agree with something done when someone else taught the course you are preparing, thank the faculty member for the input and keep those opinions to yourself as you design your version of the course.

Examples of good and inadequate work in papers and essay exam responses exams are helpful, if available. This information will not only help you to assess the ability level of the students, but also the commonly accepted grading practice for the course. It may prevent an awkward situation of you agreeing to teach what is viewed as a challenging course and end up assigning a great number of *A* grades. Likewise, you do not want to fail or give many *D* grades in a course in which students typically do well.

Foundational Decisions

Once you have basic information regarding the course, you need to make decisions regarding what your course goals are (aside from your own survival). Design the course with a minimum number of specific course content areas you will cover and then teach them very well.

As mentioned in the previous section, it is helpful in determining content coverage to review copies of syllabi and texts previously used. Stick closely to what has worked before. This is not the time to design the "perfect" course. If you feel the need to personalize a syllabus, but are not sure where to find resources, check Internet sites. For example, Society for the Teaching of Psychology has a program called "Project Syllabi." You can easily obtain a number of syllabi for about any undergraduate course. Thirty course categories are listed, and they currently have 22 syllabi available for "Introduction to Psychology." (see www.lemoyne.edu/OTRP/projectsyllabus.html)

Too Much Content Is the Antithesis of Good Teaching

When making decisions about content, resist the urge to add more to what has been done by other instructors. It will always seem like a good idea, before the course starts, to cover chapters that others deleted and/or to assign two term papers instead of the one that is typically assigned for the course. Your goal is to teach the course as well as possible, and to do this you will need more time to prepare for each class session. Extra material and assignments will make your job much more difficult. If you teach the course well, there is a high probability that you will have the opportunity to teach the course again and at that time you can add and delete topics and assignments.

Share Your Course Planning With Others

Once your syllabus and descriptions of course assignments are drafted, you should show them to others who have taught this course; also talk with your chair. They will appreciate the collegiality of your seeking their wisdom regarding this course and may offer valuable feedback.

The Text

Once you decide on the major content of your course, you need to select a text. If the text is already selected, plan your content around it. You may certainly have to adjust the course content based on the text, but it is preferable to design your course and then select the text, as opposed to allowing the text to drive the content. That said, do be sure to adapt to the text to some extent. It is *rarely* a good idea to assign two or more textbooks to a single undergraduate course whereas multiple short books of specific topics are fine. If the course text is already selected for you, or if you select a different text than has been used previously, do *not* complain about the selected or previously used text to people in the department. After all, you have never taught the course.

If you can select your own text, it is a good idea to use the same one that has been used previously. This continuity allows you to ask those who have taught the course specific questions as the semester proceeds, and may even allow an opportunity for that faculty member to cover a course session for you (helpful if you are particularly uncomfortable with a particular content area). Of course, it is best to have a text with which you are comfortable and one that fits your style. If the one used in the past does not fit you, select one of your own. One source to evaluate texts is www.facultyonline.com. This site lists many options by subject areas. In addition to linking you to Web sites of publishers (allowing you to order desk copies online), it also lists top selling textbooks and the faculty who use them. This is helpful in determining the level at which the book is written. If you teach at an institution with open enrollment, avoid texts regularly used at highly selective institutions.

Request desk copies of several competing texts for the course. The books will help you understand the material, give you ideas for discussion topics, and you may well end up teaching the course again and desire to switch books. Look for textbooks with lots of practical examples, great short summaries of pertinent research, and descriptions of applications. You may want to select a theory-oriented book for your students to read and then have at hand several application-oriented books to help with lecture ideas, or vice versa. If you have five to seven good texts to draw information from, rotate when you use them and explain to the students where you found the material. A statement such as, "Phil Zimbardo explains the topic this way," followed the next class period by a similar statement about another textbook author gives credit to the author and shows the wide variety of places from which you draw your course knowledge.

It also is a good idea to locate a handbook in the area in which you are teaching. The handbook will summarize key research studies and offer insight into important areas of the field. This is much less time intensive than digging through original research and comprehensive textbooks in the area of study.

Ancillary Materials

Pay close attention to the ancillary materials for the text you are going to use. Good ancillary materials include classroom discussion ideas, tips for covering certain topics, and even collaborative learning ideas. Ask the textbook representative if additional resources are available: videos, Web resources, transparencies and other support.

Do Not Shy Away From Using Guest Speakers

Using guest speakers can be critical in enriching students' experiences in a course where the instructor is trying to accurately present the basics in an interesting manner. Be certain these speakers have the correct areas of expertise and ask others in the department for suggestions. For example, if you are teaching developmental psychology, a college daycare worker might come to your class to talk about early child social development. If done well, your students will learn a lot, you will learn a lot, and you will save hours of additional preparation time. Another excellent choice for a guest speaker may be the person who regularly teaches the course.

Invite speakers as early as possible, as the probability of the person agreeing is directly related to the amount of time before the event. It is important to invite only a few such guests. Students do not respond well to guest speakers for every class period, as they will conclude that you are having others teach the course for you.

Class Presentations

Even if you do not normally use student presentations in class, consider their use. Meaningful class presentations are not to be done as filler, but to give the students a chance to prepare some material on the topic to be covered and to give you a bit of a break. Consider having these presentations midway through the course, not at the end, allowing you to bring closure to the class and to cover critical components missed during the student presentations.

At this point you have a syllabus, goals, a text, resource material, and potential resource people lined up to help you in creating a positive learning environment for your students. Now it is time for the class to start.

The Course Begins

Monitor the Class and Be Ready to Adapt

Start the class the way you would any other. Classroom civility is important in any class, but vital in a course that you teach for the first time, as there is a greater possibility of tension at some point in this course. One important consideration is whether to tell your students the course is not in your major area of study. To do so is to be completely honest with the students and will be beneficial if you struggle with some content areas. However, this information also invites students to question your ability to teach the course well. Even the minor things that tend to go awry in any course might be perceived by the students as an inability on your part, due to a lack of training in the specific course being taught. I would suggest you decide based on your personality. If you have great rapport with students and tend to see class as a learning environment for everyone it would be beneficial to tell them of your situation and build a "we're all in this together" feeling. If your classes are typically designed such that you are the expert in the course and students are to see you as a resource, then it might be wise to not go into detail about the fact this course is outside your traditional area of expertise.

Get Feedback From Students

Once the class is underway, get information frequently from the students about how the course is progressing. Classroom assessment techniques (CATs) allow you to assess what the students know, think, and feel at any point in the semester (Angelo & Cross, 1993). The one-minute paper is vital. This assignment, typically done at the end of a class session, asks students to write for exactly one minute about what is working well in class and what is not. It will take you about five minutes to go through 40–50 responses to such a prompt. Be certain to address the main points in the next class session or students will stop writing. Although I recommend CATs for every course, it is much more important when you are teaching something for the first time. This information will allow you to adapt as the course proceeds.

Consider asking students for their peeves about the course one-third and two-thirds of the way through. If you use student evaluation and opinion forms, use them at the halfway point instead of the end of the course so you can make meaningful changes for the rest of the semester. Some faculty even request a few student volunteers to meet periodically and every week or two provide feedback on what is working well in the course and what might be hindering learning.

Keep It Basic

A common mistake of instructors teaching a content area for the first time is to prepare too much information. Over-preparation will cause you to rush through the class, lecture too much, and be more concerned about teaching than learning. It is a natural consequence. Whatever amount of time you spend preparing, you will want the students to hear that material. Prepare a solid amount of material and then stop. If you incorporate class activities with students working in groups, you will not get though as much material as you expect. Also, if you are teaching in a 75-minute block and run out of material at 65 minutes, spend time talking to the students about the material in an informal dialog for 10 minutes. Or talk a bit about how the class is going and what can be done to better facilitate their learning. That is time well spent.

The Web

There is a lot of information on the Web. Although use of the Web could have obviously been listed in the previous section on preparing for the course, it is highly likely this source will be used for last-minute information and classroom demonstrations. Take a bit of time and search the Web before class sessions. You can sometimes find entire presentations, placed on the Web by other instructors who teach the same topic. The American Psychological Association's Society for the Teaching of Psychology, maintains another wonderful source of material. This site has a variety of teaching tips and resources pulled together for easy use: http://teachpsych.lemoyne.edu.

Summary

Keep the course in all its facets simple. Your goal is to survive. After all, you have never taught this course before and are not well prepared in training to do so. Obviously, many aspects of teaching a course you are not prepared to teach are the same as the courses you have taught many times. But no one expects everything to work perfectly, and you will have to adapt. If something goes badly, tell the students you are disappointed that it went badly and what you expect to do to prevent that from happening again. They know when things do not go well and appreciate your honesty. That said, consider that some things will not be as bad as *you* fear. Do not over apologize.

There will be times you will regret having agreed to teach a course you may not feel prepared to teach, but keep in mind the beneficial aspects of doing so. You will be introduced to a new area of psychology, and as we all know, you learn best when you teach something. In addition, you will be learning it for the first time, and that can be an exciting time for you. If you are not overly nervous about perfection, that excitement of learning will be transmitted to the students, and they also will be excited about the material. Having your students and yourself excited about learning something new together may be the most positive aspect of teaching a course you are not prepared to teach.

References and Recommended Readings

Angelo, T. A., & Cross, K. P. (1993). *Classroom assessment techniques: A handbook* (2nd ed.). San Francisco: Jossey-Bass.

Benjamin, L. T., Nodine, B. F., Ernst, R. M., & Broeker C. B. (1999). *Activities handbook for the teaching of psychology* (Vol. 4). Washington, DC: American Psychological Association.

Dewey, R. A. (1999). Finding the right introductory psychology textbook. In B. Perlman, L. I. McCann, & S. H. McFadden (Eds.), *Lessons learned: Practical advice for the teaching of psychology* (pp. 25-28). Washington, DC: American Psychological Society.

Henry, K. B., & Deka, T. S. (2004). A new edition of your text. In B. Perlman, L. I. McCann, & S. H. McFadden (Eds.), *Lessons learned: Practical advice for the teaching of psychology* (Vol. 2) (pp. 51-59). Washington, DC: American Psychological Society.

Mullins, P. A. (2004). Using outside speakers in the classroom. In B. Perlman, L. I. McCann, & S. H. McFadden (Eds.), *Lessons learned: Practical advice for the teaching of psychology* (Vol. 2) (pp. 119-126). Washington, DC: American Psychological Society.

Nilson, L. B. (2003). *Teaching at its best: A research-based resource for college instructors* (2nd ed.). Bolton, MA: Anker.

Perlman, B., McCann, L. I., & McFadden, S. H. (Eds.). (1999). *Lessons learned: Practical advice for the teaching of psychology.* Washington, DC: American Psychological Society.

Part II

Course
Planning

A New Edition of Your Text

KELLY BOUAS HENRY
TEDDI S. DEKA
Missouri Western State College

IT'S BOUND TO HAPPEN almost every three years — the text that you worked so hard to select and then worked even harder to incorporate into your course comes out in a new edition. For many faculty, this can be a vexing addition to an already heavy workload. They may feel like the course is finally "working" and now they have to revise and start again. Other faculty staunchly refuse to alter their course in the face of changing editions, assuming the substantive change is less than minimal and motivated solely by the publisher's desire to "beat" the used book market. While shrieking in frustration may have some therapeutic value, there are ways to make the new edition work to *your* advantage: All it takes is a little advance planning.

New Editions: Why Do They Do This to Us?

New editions are often unwelcome to faculty, and viewed as offering no real benefit except profit for the publishers. While publishers are certainly interested in profits, that is not the only reason to revise a text. New editions often incorporate changes suggested by students and faculty using the text, and colleagues of the authors, and they nearly always include new information. These changes often result in some degree of re-organization, or perhaps a different slant, to make the material more accessible.

New Editions Create Opportunities

From a faculty member's viewpoint, there are still good reasons to take advantage of the opportunities new editions provide.

Re-vamp course content. Many of us teach the same course year after year and the content can become stale after a while. New editions offer the impetus for a careful evaluation of what we teach in a course, and how the current text complements our goals and presents course content. Changes in text content can serve as motivation to think about the course we are teaching, what changes we might make in it, and whether we might be better off with a completely different text.

Re-assess students' needs. If you read the course goals listed in your syllabus, and the introduction to the text you use, you will have a good sense of what you are trying to accomplish with your students. But to decide how the new edition fits your course structure and goals you need to think about your students. What do students need to learn? What do students want to learn? What would be most useful for your students given their typical background? Where does the course fit in the curriculum?

Bypass professional ennui. Doing the above need not be terribly time consuming. In essence it is a mini course portfolio, where you use the publication of a new text edition to think about what you want students to learn, what they need to learn, the pacing of the course, and so forth. Engaging in this process can help you minimize how stale you become, especially if this is a course you teach regularly.

Catch up on new research and theories. Most faculty teach, in part, because of the intellectual nature of the undertaking. A new text edition allows teachers to keep current on new research and theory, and at times to discard dearly held but outdated ideas. But there can be excitement in seeing an area of psychology evolve.

Adopting the Latest Edition or Changing to a Different Text

Once you have decided how you want the course to progress, and what student and department needs must be met, you can better assess if the new edition can do the job for you, or if you need to switch books altogether. You need not do this work by yourself; colleagues and students can be quite helpful. Understanding the types of changes new editions usually entail — changes in the style, in the order of presentation, and in content — can help with this decision.

Style Changes

Authorship changes can create style changes in the text. Often, these changes occur because the publisher received feedback from people who have used the text and improvements were needed. Although some professors may feel it is important to read the entire text when this type of change occurs, we submit that reading one to two chapters (in very different content areas) will give you a sense of any style changes that have occurred. At that point, you can decide if you still like the text enough to continue with the new edition. If it seems like something you cannot live with, then it is time to start shopping for a new text altogether.

The Order of Presentation

Changing the order of presentation for material is another change that occurs frequently in edition changes. These changes are fairly easily identified by turning to the table of contents, and do not necessarily require a great deal of alteration in lecture. If you have worked hard to develop a "flow" of connections between topics that you want to retain in the classroom and if the order change is minimal, assigning chapters out of order is probably the best solution. Most textbook chapters are self-contained, and assigning them in non-sequential order will not cause difficulties for the student.

A Change in Content

The most time-consuming aspect of dealing with a new text edition occurs when the content is altered. The publisher's transition guide (see below) is an important and efficient way to identify content changes. If the text has changed too much for your liking, it is time to consider a different text.

Talk With Your Colleagues and Students

Your colleagues may be using the text you use, or different ones, for reasons you have never thought of. They may help you define your criteria for selecting a text by clarifying your own reasons for the texts you have used. It is also good practice to talk with students about why you have asked them to purchase the text you did. If done early in the semester, this invites them into the course and the learning process. And their feedback can be invaluable as you evaluate a new edition's offerings.

Look at the New Edition Yourself

This will take a bit of time. Read the preface and introduction to see what the author(s) says about the new edition. As noted, if there are new co-authors see if the writing quality and style is similar to the present text.

The most efficient way to determine what has changed from the old to the new edition is to get your hands on the transition guide provided by the publisher. Most publishers are happy to provide them because they make good business sense: They increase the chances that you will not seek a different book because they have made it easy for you to identify new or improved areas in the new edition, and the text authors get a chance to show you that they continue to update their text. The transition guide is exactly what you need to determine quickly and accurately what has changed, and therefore what changes may be required in your course. Most publishers have these guides available on their Web sites.

Look at the Ancillary Materials

As you determine whether to stay with the same publisher or not, you might find it useful to examine the ancillary package the publisher is marketing with the new edition (and compare it to other text ancillaries). The quality of the ancillary package can have a big impact on how much time the instructor spends generating in-class or online activities, PowerPoint slides and images for lecture materials, review guides, and grading exams. If the publisher is adding a lot of ancillary support to the text, it tells you something about the publisher's investment. Students can help you with part of this evaluation process. If the publisher is spending a lot on resources to help students be more autonomous in the learning process, and the students perceive the resources as valuable, then you can have some assurance that staying with the new edition and its supporting cast of ancillaries will be worthwhile.

Have Your Students Help

Many of our colleagues have enlisted the assistance of their students in the text selection process with great success. If you are waffling on whether to stay with the new edition of your old text or go to a new one, student input can help you decide. For example, consider creating an extra credit assignment for students in a course in which you anticipate a new edition. Students could read and compare chapters across two different texts and provide the instructor with a written, critical review.

Students feel empowered when asked to participate in this part of the education process and typically take the assignment seriously. Their feedback can help you determine whether it is time to switch to a new text altogether, or to transition to the new edition of the present text.

Be careful and specific in what you want to know. For example, students may like a new edition because it has more displays (pictures and one page topics), more headings, more summaries, and the like. In brief, there is less text for students to read. These may not be your criteria, however.

Making Compromises

Sometimes there are good reasons to stick with a new edition, even if you think a change to another text is justifiable. You may be teaching a distance education course and have had to put a lot of time into agreements with the publisher that allow their images and exercises to be used over the television or Internet. Changing to a new text creates the need for a completely new set of agreements, as well as the need to change the images and exercises you use. These types of changes can be hugely time consuming, and instructors need to evaluate if changing to a new, "better" text is worth this time investment, especially if the new edition is adequate.

The timing of the change to a new text, in general, is also worth considering. If you are considering changing from the new edition to another text altogether, it is worth looking ahead in your schedule to determine if you will be able to accomplish the changes in the time you have available. For many of us, summers provide the best opportunity to do so. If you've found an alternative to the new edition of your old text, but won't have blocks of time (like summer) to re-vamp the course for the new text, you may compromise and use the old or new edition until you can adequately incorporate a completely new text.

Sometimes our compromises for staying with a new edition rather than switching to a preferred alternative have little to do with our own schedules and preferences, however. Many of us have evaluated textbooks that are excellent, but do not suit the needs of our students. Perhaps the most important student need to consider when evaluating a text is its readability. An alternative text may be outstanding, but if your students aren't up to its reading level, then you are better off sticking with the new edition. Departmental needs also are part of this decision. Some departments allow each instructor to choose his or her own text when teaching the same course (e.g., Introductory Psychology), while others require instructors to use the same text. Using the same text across instructors can yield a variety of benefits: it makes coordination between instructors easier and it helps to develop a relationship with the publisher's representative that can result in a better total "package" for both you and your students. If a new edition is coming out, but instructors can't agree on an alternative text to switch to, it may well be worth the compromise to stay with the new edition until an agreement can be reached.

If you are unconcerned about the timing of changing texts or the impact of a change on students or colleagues, then you can comparison shop — evaluating the new edition against its competitors. If the new edition is not going to meet your needs, you will need to find a different text. Reviewing other textbooks for potential adoption is a task that consumes a considerable amount of time. If a different text improves student learning and your course, it is time well spent.

If You Choose the New Edition

Timeline

One of your first concerns may be whether the new edition will be available in time for you to organize your course and prepare your lectures, other in-class activities, and class assignments. Unfortunately, book representatives often provide optimistic availability dates that do not account for production difficulties, so it is a good idea to call the production editor to verify when the new edition will actually be available. If there is a concern that the book will not be ready after speaking with the production editor (this will depend on your risk tolerance), you can always continue to use the previous edition for the upcoming term, and then transition to the new edition the following term. There are usually enough "used" copies floating around for one more semester.

New or Substantive Change in Content

The first thing to look for as you examine the transition guide and the text itself is the nature of the change. Some content changes are simply updates of references to current events so that the examples referred to will remain topical to the students. The narrative of the text needs to be tied to daily life to keep students interested. Imagine an introductory text coming out next year that makes no mention of how research on social psychology relates to managing the escalating conflicts between the United States and Iraq, or how health, stress and coping relates to the terrorist attacks of September 11, 2001. These types of changes are probably the kinds of things you are naturally doing as your course evolves over time anyway. A quick skim of each chapter as you prepare your lectures will help you identify these changes and make lectures, discussion, and in-class work more contemporary.

Other content changes can be more vexing to a time-pressed faculty member. Just as changes to make the narrative topical are necessary, changes in substantive content are, too. Consider what students would be reading about if they were still using an introductory text that is a mere four or five years old. The research is constantly changing, and students need to be equipped with current perspectives.

Determine if Content Changes Are Something You Cover in Class, and What to Do Next

There are a couple of strategies for dealing with substantive content changes in ways that do not necessarily mean writing entirely new lectures or class activities.

New material that you will not cover. Most instructors don't cover the entire content of the text in class but rather a smaller portion of the material. The substantive changes that have occurred in a new text edition may not necessarily have occurred within the areas you choose to cover. In this case, you need not change your presentation plan much at all; simply update the exam where needed.

Material covered in class. If the change did occur in material that is covered in class, you may find that the text has finally "caught up" to your teaching. Some specialty areas are constantly being updated (e.g., adulthood and aging) and faculty who teach these courses must stay abreast of new research. In this case, further support from a new-edition is welcome and the changes cause few waves. Faculty who teach broader introductory courses are more likely to find some of the changes are outside or on the fringe of their areas of expertise. These changes should be looked at as an opportunity to update yourself without having to hit the journals and sift through this information on your own. If you are entirely too pressed for time to deal with a major change in a lecture or two, though, you can always present the older material as a historical backdrop of where the research began. Then point out how the research of the past (which you shared in class) links to the current work (in their text), but leave the details of the current work to their reading.

What About Exams?

Substantive changes in content will require some adjustment to your exams. We look at new text editions — and the new test banks that accompany them — as opportunities to write new exams, or at least revise old ones. Using the same exam over and over can be a bad idea for lots of reasons, not the least of which is the high probability that they will become fixtures in student-created test banks. Usually new editions emerge every three to four years, which is probably longer than you should use the same exam. While you might be able to use an old exam with a text that has changed fairly minimally in content, probably a few items will need to be altered. This is a good time to item analyze old tests and revise or replace "bad" questions or questions that do not distinguish "good" from "poor" students very well. If you have "modulized" your exams (see below) the task of revising exams congruent with course goals is that much easier.

Make It Easier Next Time

It makes little sense to have your lectures, exams, and other course materials so dependent on the text that if the text changes, you find your course in upheaval. There are steps you can take to protect the work you have.

Modulize Your Lectures

As you build lectures/classroom experiences, try to make them self-contained presentations or activities so that you can easily shift the order in which they occur. Doing so allows you to be responsive to changes in your text with minimal effort on your part (*after* you've done the work of creating the modules, that is). Although this takes a little time in the development phase of the course, doing so can substantially minimize stress associated with moving from one edition to the next, or even when adopting a different textbook.

Some faculty build on previous content, or have examples and content that refer to specific themes (e.g., nature and nurture in General Psychology) throughout the course. Changing the order of some material, if the new edition changes its order of presentation, does not affect a course's core themes. But you may have to carefully read your lecture notes and inspect assignments to make sure you are not referring to material that now comes later in the text and semester, not earlier as it used to.

Modulize Your Exams

This work (in the same way as you modulize your lectures) is a real time-saver. Organize your exams into small chunks, perhaps even labeling what each section tests over (e.g., information processing, forgetting, etc.). If you have modulized your lectures and exams in a consistent manner, it is fairly easy to update your exam at the same time that you are updating your lectures and class activities. In this case, you may not find it necessary to re-write the entire exam but rather just a few items that apply to content changes in the new edition.

Conclusion

A new text edition does not mean you have to spend your time starting from scratch. Planning your course so it is adaptable to changes in content may take time up front but will be worth it when your text goes into a new edition. Edition changes are always going to happen. Using these tips, hopefully the transition to a new edition will actually benefit you, your students and your course without great time expenditure.

References and Recommended Readings

Davis, B. G. (1993). *Tools for teaching.* San Francisco: Jossey-Bass.

Dewey, R. A. (1999). Finding the right Introductory Psychology textbook. In B. Perlman, L. I. McCann, & S. H. McFadden (Eds.), *Lessons learned: Practical advice for the teaching of psychology* (pp. 25-28). Washington, DC: American Psychological Society.

Hutchings, P. (Ed.). (1998). *The course portfolio: How faculty can examine their teaching to advance practice and improve student learning.* Washington, DC: American Association for Higher Education.

McKeachie, W. J. (2002). *McKeachie's teaching tips* (11th ed.). Boston: Houghton Mifflin.

The First Day of Class

Baron Perlman
Lee I. McCann
University of Wisconsin Oshkosh

EVERY TIME WE THINK we are on top of our teaching, even briefly, a host of pedagogical issues nibble at our consciousness — course content, method of presentation, critical thinking, writing across the curriculum and others. Only the first day of class seems comparatively luxurious. Show up — distribute course materials — answer questions — and leave early. At least this is one class meeting we don't have to worry about or spend a lot of time on. Wrong!

The first class meeting is critically important to the entire course to follow (does the primacy effect ring a bell?), deserves careful consideration, and is full of pitfalls. During your first class meeting you want to be interesting, organized and well prepared, clear, enthusiastic, and create a favorable climate for positive interpersonal relations. You want to structure the first class meeting to your students' benefit and to your own.

In this chapter, we review a variety of issues and ideas for you to consider as you prepare for your next first class periods. Do not use them all, but pick and choose those that will serve your students well.

Questions to Consider

In your first class meeting you are communicating a great deal of critical information about yourself and the course in what you cover and how you behave. It is not unusual for teachers, especially new teachers, to be nervous and exited on the first day, just like the students are. Our advice is to plan the first class meeting carefully and then *teach deliberately*. Put your feet up for a few minutes and consider the following questions.

- What are your goals during a first class meeting and have you budgeted sufficient time to achieve them?
- What tone do you want to set — laid back and informal organized and content oriented, or some of both?
- Assuming some of the first day is devoted to "housekeeping" tasks, what do you cover and what do you save for a later class?
- What can you do to draw students into the intellectual realm of the course?
- What should you tell students about yourself, your teaching style, and why you teach that way?
- What can you tell students about how to do well in your class?
- What do you tell students about cheating and academic honesty?
- What can you do to ease students' concerns?
- What do you do so that students with several first classes beginning on the same day will retain the important material about your course?
- How can you have students participate and what level of participation should you expect?

Objectives/Purposes of the First Class Meeting

A first class meeting has multiple objectives. Do you see the first class meeting as mostly "housekeeping," drawing students into the intellectual realm of the course, emphasizing the affective, beginning your coverage of course material, or all of these? Your goals should fit not only who you are and what you value as a faculty member, but also should fit the level and size of the course. You will be explicit and belabor the obvious in an introductory course with primarily first-year students more than in a senior course for majors. For example, not all first year students may understand what a syllabus is and they can benefit from an explanation of how it functions as an informal "contract." Regardless of your specific objectives for the first class meeting consider the following suggestions.

Create rapport. Be patient. Beginnings of semesters can be difficult for students. Be calm. Be respectful of your students! Tell students about your teaching career, your academic interests, why the present course is important to you and why you like it. Many students never really get to know their teachers. View the first day as a chance to begin a relationship with your students. Depending on class size, call each student by name from a class list, and get to know students by asking for a show of hands for majors, minors, and so forth. You also have an opportunity to gather information about them that will help build this relationship. It does not take long to read 50 index cards with students' year in school, number of psychology credits, major, reasons for taking the class, hobbies, and the like. Such information will help you get to know them.

Communicate the nature and content of your course. In doing this you have an opportunity to explain why students should take your course and how they will profit from it.

Emphasize important aspects of the course. If something is important, overtly cover the details. Be sure to stress elements that may be idiosyncratic or differ somewhat from more "boilerplate" courses.

Use what you know about psychology. Present critical information first or last in the class meeting. Assume that students will not retain all of the details presented during the first class meeting, and repeat crucial information later. This is especially important for first year students.

Prepare for the First Day

There is much that you cannot control during first class meetings, but prepare as best you can. In addition to decisions on tone (see below) and time spent on first day tasks, other preparation should include the following:

- ♦ Visit the classroom if you have not taught there before to learn how to use the lights, sound system, computer equipment, etc. Do you need chalk, or a marker for a whiteboard?
- ♦ Decide on seating arrangements and lighting, music or silence before you begin.
- ♦ Write and update handouts and the syllabus, and have sufficient copies printed. Bring these materials to subsequent class meetings for students who miss the first day. Make sure you also bring copies of all required texts and materials.
- ♦ Check with the bookstore to make sure the required texts have arrived and that there are a sufficient number of copies.

The First Day

Once again, implementing all of the following suggestions would take more time than is available in most first class meetings. Consider what you are doing now, and make changes based on those ideas that seem most helpful.

Arrive at the Classroom Early and Dress Professionally

Arriving early allows you to make sure the class door is unlocked, the room is laid out the way you want, and to kibitz with students as they arrive. Dress professionally. Many sources recommend this, and you can always dress down later. Be prepared to stay late to answer even more questions.

Start Slowly and Cover the Basics

The biggest mistake most faculty make on the first day is to cover too many topics. Students often have several *first* classes in one day and are absorbing a great deal of information all at once. Take care of basics. Make sure all students belong in the course. Ask if anyone wants to *add* the class, and before doing anything else either sign them in, start a waiting list, or tell them you are sorry, but they cannot be added to the class. Identify the course number, title, number of credits, when and where the course meets, where exams are held, course prerequisites, and so forth (if included in syllabus, review it). Obtain student e-mail addresses if you will be contacting them via e-mail or will have an electronic course bulletin board. Some faculty identify important drop dates. Introduce your TAs if you are using them, and explain their role.

You have another important decision. You need to help students settle down and focus. Whether you do this by simply introducing yourself and telling students what the first day will entail after everyone is quiet, or by doing something "dramatic" to get their attention, is up to you.

Introduce Yourself

Spend a few minutes talking about yourself. Tell students your name and title, office hours, e-mail address, phone, and Web page address. Tell students your office location and provide them a map if it is difficult to locate. Describe your policy on phone calls to your home. Tell students how you wish to be addressed (e.g., Dr. Smith, Professor Smith, Ms. Smith, the Grand Guru Smith, the Great and Powerful Oz, or just plain Joe). Talk about your educational background and professional experience and interests, particularly as they relate to this course, and include whatever personal information you want students to know. Students, and especially juniors and seniors, really are interested in who you are, how you got into the profession, how you came to be teaching at your college or university, and for how long.

Texts and Other Materials

Students need to know the text title, edition, author, and date. State which texts are *required* or *recommended* and why. Tell students why you chose this text (e.g., author's credentials, readability). Tell students to buy the book and ask if they are available in the bookstore. Provide the location(s) of other assigned materials (e.g., reserved reading desk at library Web) and whether they can be purchased or are on reserve. If you are using electronic materials be clear how and when you will assist students in accessing them. If there are other required materials such as calculators, identify them.

Course Description and Requirements

Students need basic information regarding what the course is about. Do not assume they have opened the text; most have not. Inform students what the course's place is in the curriculum, why they should take this course (general education, major requirement), and whether the course is primarily lecture, discussion, small group work or some combination of all. Briefly review course objectives. Such objectives are becoming more important with increased emphasis on assessment. Identify your course's extra costs such as lab fees or required or elective out-of-class opportunities such as field trips.

Distribute and review your syllabus. Briefly! We know at least one faculty member who gives a quiz on his syllabus the second week of the course. He wants students to read it! Emphasize the following course requirements:

- Exactly what a student is expected to do
- Important dates in the syllabus (e.g., assignments, reviews for exams, tests, guest speakers)
- Required reading not included in lectures
- The student work load (how much time and preparation the course will require)
- Reading assignments (where listed, how much, and so forth)
- Attendance policy
- Number and type of tests or laboratory exercises
- Study aids (practice exam questions or outlines)

- How changes will be communicated for dates of exams and other required in-class assignments
- If films and videos are used, are students tested on their content? Repeat this information when they are shown.
- Number and type of papers, expected content. Hand out a model paper, or place copies on reserve or on the Web. Delay the detailed information on what contributes to a paper's grade (e.g., intellectual level, quality of writing, level of referenced material read) to a later class meeting. If you use a *scoring grid* for papers, distribute it when you discuss the papers in depth.
- Class participation (e.g., in-class, e-mail bulletin board), oral presentations, or group work
- Grading

Grading Procedures

Decide what to emphasize, such as how you grade (curve, absolute standard), policy on incomplete grades, penalties for late work, and extra credit opportunities, and consider presenting grade distributions from previous classes. If attendance is required, what is its percentage of the final grade? What is the percent each exam, quiz, paper, and assignment counts toward the final grade? Do you give multiple choice, short answer, matching, or essay exams?

Sometime in the next week or two present detailed information on your grading system (e.g., letter grades, total points across the semester, or some other approach), urge students to highlight this information on the syllabus, and if relevant, briefly describe how you grade group work. Explain your policy on exams or assignments missed because of weather, athletics, ill children, etc. What is your makeup policy and what happens if an exam is not made up? Do students fail the course, or pass the course but receive an F on that assignment? Directly before your first exam discuss whether students can drop an item or contest items, and rules for exams (e.g., picture ID, sit every other seat). Be prepared to explain grading again and again throughout the course.

Academic Honesty Policy and Cheating

Review the academic dishonesty policy statement in your syllabus. Define how cheating is defined in the course including crib notes, plagiarism on papers, turning in someone else's work as your own, and purchasing term papers; and talk about your efforts to minimize cheating and why doing so is important. Many faculty stress their responsibility to general society to emphasize moral behavior. Tell students you reserve the right to meet with them about their assignments/exams and behavior, and will do so in private.

Course Rules

Often course rules can wait for the next class meeting. Can students tape record lectures or bring food to class? What class decorum issues need discussing, especially in a large class? Do you assign seating? If you have a small class meeting in a larger classroom do you want students to sit near the front of the class? If you are teaching a laboratory course, review safety rules for students, explain use of equipment and other rules, and give a tour if needed.

How to Do Well

- ◆ Spend a few minutes offering advice on how to do well in your course.
- ◆ Distribute or read letters in which students from the same course in past semesters offer advice on how to do well.
- ◆ Emphasize that most learning occurs out of class.
- ◆ Give advice on how many times students should read each chapter, how they can best prepare for each class, and use of a study guide, if available.
- ◆ Emphasize the importance of coming to class, reviewing lecture notes, and asking questions.
- ◆ If you value discussion and questions, show students you mean this by entertaining questions and listening carefully the first day.
- ◆ Talk about how students might obtain a tutor. You will cover this material individually with some students later in the semester, but most students make the mistake of waiting too long to obtain a tutor.
- ◆ Encourage students to form study groups, and to study with academically strong peers. Give them your estimate for expected time devoted to your class (rule of thumb is two or three hours out of class for each class hour).
- ◆ Invite students with special needs such as older students returning to school, foreign students, and transfer students to meet with you early in the semester.

- Provide a printed list of important and relevant campus resources (e.g., counseling center [test anxiety]), reading/study center, writing center).
- Ask students to obtain names, telephone numbers and e-mail addresses of two or three classmates to be used for obtaining lecture notes, or anything missed when absent.

Setting the Tone

By now you have already done a great deal to set the tone for the course in your patience, clarity, and organized style, or in your impatience, distance, and preoccupation with your needs and not theirs. But there is more you can do. If you want to stress course content, begin lecturing or conduct a class discussion. You can make an assignment for the next class, but ensure that it is relevant and important. If you want to emphasize the relevancy of the course to students' lives or general society, develop a relevancy exercise. If you want to learn what your students know, give a pre-test of some kind.

Ask students what they have heard about the class and dispel myths about the course. This may be an opportunity to lighten the tone a bit and to ease student anxiety. Use humor (e.g., "Instructor receives 10 percent of all chocolate brought to class," or "I received my PhD from Michigan State University, bonus points for wearing MSU apparel."). Ask what their first day rituals are or what they are feeling the first day of class, and then share what you are feeling. If you emphasize writing, have students write something.

Save Time for Questions

Students often are extremely quiet during the first day of class. This reluctance may be due to not knowing the instructor. Some students want the class to be dismissed as soon as possible and asking questions keeps them in class longer. To increase participation try to ask questions that students can/will answer. If questions are not forthcoming provide important information on questions you know students need answers to: How difficult is the course (*Can I do the work?*)? Is the course fair? Will you help students?

Conclusion

Thought and attention to the first class meeting benefits your students greatly. You want to demonstrate concern for what they need to know, and for the anxieties most students have as they begin a course. The tone you set is one you can build on throughout the entire semester. By carefully structuring the first day, you will have grown as a teacher, given some thought to the art and craft of what we do, and shown students that starting a course well is critically important to what follows. We wish you a *good first day!*

References and Recommended Readings

Davis, B. G. (1993). *Tools for teaching.* San Francisco: Jossey-Bass.

Diamond, R. M. (1998). Developing a learning-centered syllabus. In R. M. Diamond (Ed.), *Designing and assessing courses and curricula: A practical guide* (pp. 191-202). San Francisco: Jossey-Bass.

Johnson, G. R. (1995). *First steps to excellence in college teaching* (3rd ed.). Madison, WI: Magna.

McKeachie, W. J. (2002). *McKeachie's teaching tips: Strategies, research, and theory for college and university teachers.* (11th ed.). Lexington, MA: D.C. Heath.

Nilson, L. B. (2003). *Teaching at its best: A research-based resource for college instructors.* (2nd ed.). Bolton, MA: Anker.

Perlman, B., & McCann, L. I. (1998). Students' pet peeves about teaching. *Teaching of Psychology, 28,* 201-203.

Perlman, B., & McCann, L. I. (1999). Student perspectives on the first day of class. *Teaching of Psychology, 26,* 277-279.

Wolcowitz, J. (1984). The first day of class. In M. M. Gullette (Ed.), *The art and craft of teaching* (pp. 10-24). Cambridge, MA: Harvard.

Parting Ways: Ending Your Course

TAMI J. EGGLESTON
McKendree College

GABIE E. SMITH
Elon University

MUCH EMPHASIS HAS been placed on the use of activities at the beginning of a course to provide opportunities for introductions, begin to create a comfortable classroom atmosphere to encourage discussion and learning, or develop a sense of community and group identity. In many teaching books (e.g., McKeachie, 2002; Perlman & McCann, 2004) there is an entire chapter devoted to getting started and what to do on the first day of a course such as breaking the ice, introducing the teacher and textbook, and allowing time for questions. Much less attention has been given to the equally important task of providing closure at the end of a course or seminar. After a great deal of time developing a sense of comfort and community in the classroom, ignoring class endings seems awkward and abrupt to both students and faculty. Use of "parting-ways" techniques:

- Provides emotional and psychological closure to the classroom thereby reducing awkwardness.
- Acts as an opportune time to summarize central ideas and review content.
- Wraps up the class in ways that add to students' entire semester-long experience and sense of accomplishment.
- Stimulates interest in the topic area and possibly the major.
- Increases the connection between faculty and students by recognizing the importance of taking time to say good-bye.

Many faculty members do not typically use parting-ways (Eggleston & Smith, 2001). Our recent survey of college faculty from a variety of disciplines at two different institutions demonstrated that faculty members typically end their courses with final projects, papers, and review sessions. Some faculty did more: approximately 42 percent reported that they took the time to say good-bye to their students, and 30 percent responded that they tried to leave their students with some final "words of wisdom". We also surveyed students at the same institutions: 90 percent reported that they would appreciate more closure on their courses.

The lack of class-ending activities is due to a number of factors including time constraints, attempts to complete as much course material as possible (Pescosolido & Aminzade, 1999), being unaware of useful techniques, or feeling uncomfortable saying good-bye (Wagenheim, 1994). But faculty can overcome these obstacles, and we hope to provide a least one way to end the class that is useful for each reader.

It Is Important to Provide Closure Academically and Emotionally

Parting-ways can serve many purposes depending on the specific dynamics of the course, the goals of the instructor, and time available. End of the class activities may:

- ♦ Summarize the course material or act as a review of the course goals and objectives and what students have learned, or the course's most important ideas. Most textbook chapters provide a summary at the end of each chapter, instructors should think of a way to provide a summary to the class.
- ♦ Give students some memento from the course experience. Just as with a memorable trip, people enjoy having something to remember important events in their life.
- ♦ Provide an opportunity for faculty and students to say good-bye. After all, you have spent a lot of time together. If a classroom community has been established, then time needs to be dedicated to end the class.
- ♦ Contribute to a sense of accomplishment. In one sense an activity can put closure on the class from an academic or learning based perspective. Completing your class should be seen as something worthwhile and important.
- ♦ Create the feeling that the class has come to a culmination and it is time to move on.

Clinical practitioners, i.e., counselors and therapists, understand the importance of closure from an emotional and psychological standpoint. Before students truly feel ready to leave the class and move on to other classes or graduation, they should feel like the course has been completed.

When we presented this topic at the 2001 National Institute on the Teaching of Psychology (NITOP), many professors indicated they thought that these were wonderful ideas, but they were not using them. Most often it was faculty teaching group dynamics or group psychology who used closure techniques. However, all classes are a special form of a group, and emphasizing, even if for a few minutes, the task of adjourning needs attention.

Academic Parting Ways

Most faculty who use a parting-way report that the few minutes of new course content they "lose" is more than made up for by the summary over the lifespan of the course or by the good feelings engendered by thanking the class for their hard work and in some way winding down a semester long experience. Here are some ideas:

Projects, Letters, Brochures

These techniques allow you to focus on what was learned throughout the course. In addition to a final paper or presentation and comprehensive exam items, students can:

- Write a letter detailing their own development in the course and what they have learned.
- Write "letters to successors" to students enrolled in the course in the future, detailing what can be gained from the course as well as broader advice on being a successful student.
- Review the course concepts through completion of a project, such as developing an informational brochure for incoming students. This activity has been used effectively in several Psychology courses, including Health Psychology and Drugs and Behavior.

Pre/Post Tests and Video Summaries

Knowledge pre-tests and post-tests also can be used as a review for students and emphasize accomplishments at the end of the semester.

We administer "intuition" tests at the beginning of the semester that consist of true-false items to assess students' initial ideas, myths, and common sense beliefs about psychology.

Saul Kassin delivered the opening session at the 2001 NITOP and discussed having students make predictions about the results of famous psychological studies before providing them with the "answers." Kassin believes this activity will help to dispel the "I knew it all along belief" or the "hindsight bias." Not only does a pre-test of intuitions or predictions illustrate incorrect ideas, but also using it as the course ends provides some closure. Have your students complete the same set of questions during the first and last weeks of a course. Students receive their pre-tests back and can be asked to write a reflection paper on how their perceptions of the topic area have changed over the semester. Students often make such comments as "Wow, I didn't realize how much I learned this semester," "I can't believe that I thought that."

E. R. Klein, a philosophy professor, (Pescolido & Aminzade, 1999) suggests an end of the year activity asking one question, "What is philosophy?" It would be fascinating to see the answers to the question, "What is Psychology? " It would further be interesting to compare these answers depending on the specific course being taught (e.g., physiological, abnormal, development.)

Distribute a two-to-five page essay at the beginning of class discussing a variety of psychological topics (e.g., classical conditioning). Tell the students to highlight in yellow everything that they do not fully understand. Chances are most of the page will be highlighted. At the end of the semester, redistribute the essay and ask them to highlight all that they do not fully understand with a different colored highlighter. Students will be impressed with this visual demonstration of how much they have learned.

Show one of the videos in Zimbardo's (1989) "Discovering Psychology" series on the future of psychology or applications of psychology as a way to review and wrap up the class.

Lists, Games, and Objectives

Changing the tone of the course and introducing something that can be fun and different sustains students, and can help them remain focused on the course. This can be a favorite for faculty members and students alike at the end of a tiring semester.

Lists of names and research studies. In many courses professors provide students with numerous names and/or research studies throughout the semester. A fun and educational way to review these lists is to have students, meeting in small groups, compile their own "Top 10" lists of the most important or significant studies or theories discussed. Allow the students to share their lists and argue with other groups about the rankings. It is interesting to hear students debate the merits of Milgram and Festinger in a Social Psychology Class.

Review session as a game. Review sessions for the final exam are a common activity during the last week of classes. James Wangberg developed a way to bring academic closure and also have a sense of celebration by having the review session in the form of a game of charades (Pescosolido & Aminzade, 1999). Other game style activities such as "Jeopardy" or "Who Wants to be a Millionaire" also could be adapted as a fun way to review for the final exam.

Revisit course goals and objectives. Many professors start a course introducing students to the course's objectives and goals. Fewer professors revisit them at the end of the semester. Specifically, a professor could show how each objective was met using the assigned readings and specific activities. This may allow students to reflect on what and how much they have learned. Students may provide other examples of which the teacher was unaware.

Meaningful Projects

Many professors have a final paper or project that they think of as integrating the course, and very important and meaningful to what the students learn. Students often view these traditional papers or projects as simply more work. Certainly, some courses seem linked to the traditional paper, but some minor changes to the assignment can make it more meaningful for the students.

Invite an outside group for comprehensive project presentations. Final group presentations to the class and to relevant others in the university community communicate to students that their work is real and interesting to others. For example, invite residence life groups to presentations on such topics as STD's, drugs, health, or study skills.

Integrate service learning and helping into course endings. Group service learning projects can be a meaningful activity for classes. For example, a faculty who teaches adult development may consider holding the last class at a local group home or facility, leading bingo or another activity. This allows students to have fun, say good-bye to each other, and do something worthwhile in the community at the same time.

Emotional Parting Ways

Parting-ways can be elaborate but the simple can have great power. Taking the time to say "good bye" and "thank you" to students can be very effective. One professor discussed standing at the front of the room and after thanking students for their contributions and hard work, applauding, literally, the students for their participation in the class. Kevin Shannon suggested taking time to shake hands with each student as he or she leaves the final day as an effective way to formally say good-bye (Pescosolido & Aminzade, 1999).

Something to Take With Them:
Reflections, Certificates, Quotes, & Fortunes

When a person goes on an important trip or vacation, most of us bring home some memento of the experience to help us remember this important time in our life (e.g., a seashell, a postcard). A course could be considered such an important trip.

Wagenheim (1994) suggests having students complete sentence stems such as, "Something I have learned about myself _____," or "Something I have learned about groups _____." These sentence stems could then be shared with other students and kept as a written reflection of the course.

The faculty may want to consider raffling off flowers, t-shirts, or other items. The t-shirts could be creative with examples of related topics such as "I passed Human Sexuality class," "Ask me about my ID", or other course topics.

Use of certificates of achievement or completion as mementos is often times very appropriate. Certificates can include a quote for each student or recognition of a personal achievement ("To Bob Smith for completing SPSS and finally learning what a negative correlation means"). In addition, certificates can provide a humorous ending to the class. Other students can take part in making class certificates by having each student write a positive comment on each other's certificates.

Particularly meaningful quotes can be distributed to students, or put on an overhead at the end of the last day of the course or during the final as a way of ending the class. For example, one of the authors has placed the following quote from the movie

Awakenings, which the class watched on an overhead at the conclusion of a course, "The human spirit is more powerful than any drug. It needs to be nourished with work, play, friendship, love. The simplest things. The things we have forgotten." H. Goldstein (personal communication, May, 1999) has posted several suggestions for closing words of wisdom on the electronic discussion group in Teaching in Psychological Sciences (www.frostburg.edu/dept/psyc/southerly/tips).

In larger classes, fortunes can be distributed to students, rather than individual certificates. The fortunes are slips of paper containing either a brief summary of an important lesson from the course or a quote selected by the faculty member that reflects something about the course content or the class dynamics. Students are given the opportunity at the end of the last class or the final exam to draw a fortune from a container. To personalize the fortunes, faculty members can print them on mailing labels and then attach labels on the back of their business cards, and distribute them to students. Students often appreciate receiving the business card of a faculty member, even without the fortune. Quotes related to specific topics can easily be obtained via a variety of quote web sites such as www.quoteland.com.

Paul Berghoof reported reading a story or a parable as a way to end the course (Pescosolido & Aminzade, 1999). Because of student stress during finals week, this parable may have a greater impact if it is relatively short and read the week before finals.

Keep in Mind the Following

This chapter had as one of its goals to inspire teachers to consider how they and the students part ways as a course ends. The following considerations are important to keep in mind when making decisions about ending the class.

Relevance to the course. The activity will be viewed as more meaningful if it linked and related to your course content. Service learning at a nursing home, for example, seems much more appropriate for an Adult Development or Gerontology course than for a Tests and Measurement class.

Your own style. Certain activities are not for all instructors. Just as we all have our preferences for lecture styles, group discussions, and other pedagogical activities, find activities that fit your unique teaching style.

Type of closure (academic or psychological and emotional). At the end of the semester, many instructors are busy and may not take the time to explore how they would like to end their classes. Faculty members will need to decide if they are more interested in an academic review of the material and course objectives or psychological and emotional parting-ways. Some may desire both types of closures and need to do two activities.

Existence or lack of community. In some classes due to time constraints, meeting times, the course content or class size, students may not have a developed a sense of community. In that case there is less need for psychological or emotional closure. An academic activity will probably be the most applicable. Distance learning and virtual computer classes may require less closure and a different type of activity would be appropriate (for example, an electronic thank you card sent to students in a virtual class would seem very appropriate).

Time investment. Some activities take more time to develop and carry out in class. Some will need to be included in your syllabus to allow for students to complete them and understand how they contribute to a final grade. It may be beneficial to start with the small, easy, and time efficient techniques before moving to more elaborate activities.

Small versus large classes. It is important to modify your ending activity based on the size of your class. Individual certificates and top 10 lists may work better in a smaller class whereas fortunes seem suitable for larger classes.

Course and campus climate. Courses that are personal in nature and where a great deal of sharing has taken place (for example, many clinical and counseling or human sexuality classes) may need a more complex activity than less personal classes that tend to have less sharing (for example, a physiological psychology class). In addition, some college campuses portray themselves as "caring" and "student centered" and parting-ways activities seem especially useful on such campuses or for such faculty.

Good luck as you integrate parting-ways into your classroom. Here is a quote for you, our reader:

> Education is what survives when what has been learned has been forgotten. (B. F. Skinner)

References and Recommended Readings

Eggleston, T. J., & Smith, G. E. (2001, January). *Creating community in the class: The use of ice breakers and parting-ways.* Poster session presented at the National Institute on the Teaching of Psychology, St. Petersburg Beach, FL.

Maier, M. H., & Panitz, T. (1996). End on a high note. *College Teaching, 44,* 145-149.

McKeachie, W. J. (2002). *McKeachie's teaching tips: Strategies, research and theory for college and university professors* (11th ed.). Lexington, MA: D C Heath.

Perlman, B., & McCann, L. I. (2004). The first day of class. In B. Perlman, L. I. McCann, & S. H. McFadden (Eds.), *Lessons learned: Practical advice for the teaching of psychology* (Vol. 2) (pp. 61-69). Washington, DC: American Psychological Society.

Pescosolido, B. A., & Aminzade, R. (1999). How to end courses with a bang. In B. A. Pescosolido & R. Aminzade (Eds.), *Fieldguide for teaching in a new century* (pp. 287-289). Thousand Oaks, CA: Pine Forge.

Wagenheim, G. (1994). Feedback exchange: Managing group closure. *Journal of Management Education, 18,* 265-270.

Zimbardo, P. (1989). New directions. *Discovering psychology* [video series]. Boston: The Annenberg/CPB Collection.

Getting Started on the Web: Enhancing Instruction in Psychology

PAMELA I. ANSBURG
Metropolitan State College of Denver

MICHAEL CARUSO
University of Toledo

SALLY KUHLENSCHMIDT
Western Kentucky University

THERE ARE FOUR GENERAL attitudes among teachers about integrating technology and instruction: excitement about new technology, thoughtful consideration of technology as a tool for societal change, interest to the extent it serves students, and rejection or avoidance of technology (Clemmons, personal communication, February 13, 1999; Rogers, 1995; Rocklin, personal communication, March 8, 1999). Your personal response may be included in some combination of these types and you may have additional concerns, such as lack of time or limited resources. However, the use of Web pages and the Internet has changed and will continue to change how we instruct students. Can you be a master teacher without its use? Certainly. But using the Internet will give you new options for instruction. This column provides a starting point for those interested in supplementing traditional instructional techniques with Internet resources.

The Internet Helps Instructors of Psychology Meet Their Pedagogical Goals

The Internet can convey information about the course. It is a tremendous tool for broadcasting messages to students 24/7. The message may be as simple as a course syllabus or it may provide supplemental information on topics for which there is never enough class time.

The use of graphics and other media on course Web sites makes information more exciting. Web sites are motivating for some students. Graham (2001) noted that her Web site provided Child Development students greater opportunities to become engaged with the course material. Further, most students appreciate the ease of information access and the opportunity to repeat information at a pace appropriate to their skill. Hurlburt (2001) provided brief streamed audio content that allowed students to pause and review material; the students reported that this capability was valuable.

Given that many students turn first to the Internet for resources, we need to teach them how to evaluate these sources of information, just as we were taught to distinguish among various journals and other print media. There are many Web sites devoted to helping instructors foster critical thinking about Web site content (see www.lib.vt.edu/research/evaluate/evalbiblio.html for a relevant bibliography). The University of California at Berkeley's library provides an excellent rubric students can follow when evaluating electronic information (www.lib.berkeley.edu/TeachingLib/Guides/Internet/Evaluate.html).

Some Words of Encouragement and Advice

You do not have to be able to write computer code to develop a Web site. There are many ways to generate Web pages, some of which are geared specifically for those of us who know close to nothing about computer programming (see section below for more on this topic). Of course, the more technical skills you have, the more flexibility and control you will have. But even with little or no skill, you can still produce effective Web pages.

If you do plan to integrate Web pages into your classes, start slowly. Create a home page first and then begin to work on a specific course Web site.

Initially, designing Web pages will be time-consuming; avoid working on more than one course a semester. Further, because there are many areas to specialize within Web design, seek advice on which areas will be most helpful to you and then specialize, just as you do within psychology. You don't try to understand every aspect of psychology. You don't need to understand every element of technology:

Everyone faces a learning curve; some are just better than others at hiding it. To maintain a sense of accomplishment, set up small goals that are easy to reach. Don't work to the point of frustration. If you find yourself becoming annoyed, take a break and return to the problem later. Incidentally, physical discomfort will increase your frustration level. Check your position. Arms and wrists should be hanging from your shoulders and slanting downward, not stretched upward or sideways at any point. Take frequent breaks to stretch and relax.

When orienting to a new software package, first learn to execute critical commands. For example, knowing how to save your work, how to retrieve a saved file, how to undo a previous command, and how to exit the program will save you much anguish. You can do it.

Just as it is easier to revise a lecture than it is to generate one, to maintain Web pages takes much less time than developing them. Once you have created a Web page, the time involved in making slight modifications, such as adding a link or uploading an announcement is negligible. You decide how much or how little you want to modify your pages; the less editing you do, the less time it will take.

Get advice from someone more experienced who can help you break the task into manageable, easy steps. Seek feedback from students, other faculty who have well-designed pages, and your instructional technology staff. Use their suggestions to revise your existing pages and to help in the development of new ones. Although this process is continuous, it is not necessarily a time-consuming one.

What Can I Post on the Internet to Enhance My Courses?

A Reasonable Starting Point

Create a single home page (shared by all of your classes) that lists your phone number, fax, e-mail address, office location, and class schedule. Some faculty members add their research and teaching interests, as well as some personal information (e.g., favorite hobbies). Then add course specific pages as links off your home page.

Basic Items to Include on Your Web Pages

A course syllabus and other information. The most basic form of a course specific page is one that hosts a course syllabus.

You also can post class announcements, such as changes to the schedule, as well as assignments and handouts. To minimize maintenance, post a sample syllabus with a header indicating the official syllabus is available in class.

Lecture outlines. Students appreciate the posting of lecture outlines so that, in class, they can spend more time actively involved with the material rather than on writing notes that simply parrot the lecture. According to Doctorow, Wittrock, and Marks (1978) when students reorganize information they are more likely to remember it. If students are free from worrying about verbatim note taking, they can be encouraged to use more effective active note-taking and listening strategies. It is up to you to decide just how much lecture material you want to post. You will need to balance the benefits cited above against the potential pitfalls (e.g., Will student attendance decrease? Are you providing too much help to students?); your decision may vary depending on the course and the students.

Links to other sites. Doing this allows students to explore a topic in greater detail or to experience psychological phenomena that otherwise might involve too much class time or expensive equipment. For example, students can test their recognition memory at a site maintained by NASA (http://olias.arc.nasa.gov/cognition/tutorials/index.html) and can witness the dissection of a sheep's brain at a site maintained by San Francisco's Exploratorium (www.exploratorium.edu/memory/braindissection/1.html). The Public Broadcasting Service Web site presents animations on how drugs influence neurotransmitter activity (www.pbs.org/wnet/closetohome/science/html/animations.html). Integrating some of these links with the course requirements is a terrific way to help psychology come alive. Many textbooks have accompanying Web pages intended to help you reach this goal, but you'll need to check each one carefully because their quality and accessibility vary tremendously.

How Do I Get Started?

To create a basic Web page, you need to create text, integrate graphics into your page, and test and then upload the page onto a Web site.

Creating Text

For those who have no computer programming knowledge: Hypertext Markup Language (HTML) is the code that underlies Web pages. You do not need to know how to program in HTML to produce HTML pages, especially if you do not mind some slight variations in appearance across platforms. Investigate whether your school provides Course Management Software (CMS) like Blackboard or WebCT, or you could ask your textbook publishers if they offer some type of CMS (most do and are happy to provide support). Because these options provide templates into which you simply type content, this route is the quickest and easiest way to develop a site. A note of warning: if you are using a Web site managed by an organization other than your institution, keep confidential student information off the site or you will violate educational privacy laws. Word processing programs are an alternative to CMS, as most current word processing programs will allow you to convert your documents to HTML with a couple of mouse clicks (typically you look under "File" and "Save As"). Powerpoint presentations also can be saved as Web pages (but they can take up a lot of memory).

For those who have no computer programming knowledge and want to learn a bit about HTML: If you want maximum control over the appearance of your Web site, then you will need to learn HTML. Basic HTML is easy and there are good tutorials available on the Web (e.g., www.pagetutor.com/). We especially recommend learning about creating tables if you want the layout of your pages to be more than just a column of text. There are software packages, HTML editors, specifically designed to create and manage Web pages. There are high-end editors, like Dreamweaver, Pagemill, or Frontpage, and free shareware editors that are available via download (e.g., http://downloads-zdnet.com.com/3150-2048-0.html?tag=dir). The interface for some of these look like that of a word processor (i.e., you do not see the HTML code), whereas others require that you actually write a program in HTML.

For the more technologically sophisticated Web page designer: Explore Web coding other than HTML. These (e.g., javascripting, java coding, CSS, DHTML, and XML) are more complicated, but allow you to add dynamic and interactive elements to your pages. There are javascript and java programs that you can cut-and-paste into your Web pages that can help with creating dynamic images and interactive elements and that are available for download on various Web sites (e.g., www.javapowered.com/werks.html).

Integrating Graphics

The basics on graphics. Adding graphics into your page can be as simple as searching a canned collection of clip art (standard in most word processing and HTML editor programs) and clicking a mouse to insert the selected image.

Want more control over your images? If you spend a few hours, you can learn to create and edit graphics with an image editor that can save graphics as .gif or .jpg files. These programs can range from very powerful programs like Adobe Photoshop to more basic programs, like Adobe Photo Elements. The Paint program on recent versions of Windows may suffice. If you scan images, or use images available on CD-ROM or from other Web sites, please be aware of possible copyright infringement issues. Also, whenever you include images in your Web pages, be sure to describe the graphic with text so that programs that do not display graphics will have a text description of the image. (This practice satisfies one of the Americans with Disability Act requirements).

Going beyond basic text and graphics. There are programs and Web sites available for creating online quizzes, discussion boards, e-mail forms, hit-counters, search engines, and other niceties. Links to programs and tutorials to help you create pages for your Web site are available at *Developing Web Pages for Psychology Instruction* at http://homepages.utoledo.edu/mcaruso/webpaper.html.

Final Steps

Test your work. Because a page can look different when viewed in Internet Explorer versus when it is viewed in Netscape, preview the page in both browsers. Also, check to make sure your page looks right on both PC and Macintosh computers.

Post it on the Web. Your final step is to post your newly developed pages and graphics to the Web. If you are using Web-based CMS, like Blackboard, then all you need to do is save the pages at the Web site. Otherwise, you will need to arrange for server space at your institution and get a File Transfer Program (FTP) to upload your pages. You can take a class from your instructional technology office or ask an experienced faculty member to help you with this process.

Some Additional Advice

On Page Design

Keep it simple. Be sure to take into account that not everyone has sophisticated hardware and software. The fancier your pages are in terms of multimedia or non-HTML codes, the more likely it is that some students will not be able to see your pages as intended. It may be worthwhile to keep pages simple or to provide plain-text alternate pages to increase access to your pages.

Check your pages' compliance with basic standards for disability accessibility. Once you move into using images, tables or frames, you will need to learn about basic standards for disability accessibility to meet legal expectations for educational institutions. It is easy to check your Web page's compliance by submitting it to http://bobby.watchfire.com/bobby/html/en/index.jsp for a free evaluation. More information can be found at http://easi.cc/. Simpler design is more likely to meet disability criteria so beginner Web pages are often more accessible than those of long time developers. You should also check with your institution to see if there are local accessibility standards you need to meet.

Use a password. Remember that anyone in the world with Internet access can view public pages. Take appropriate steps to protect your intellectual property and your students' intellectual property, as well (e.g., only post student work with permission). CMS's provide password protection. You can also create passwords to sites and portions of sites you develop. Educational institutions have a legal obligation to protect some student information and that means passwords for certain materials — check with your registrar for details.

On Employing Web Pages

Responding to students' requests. Be prepared for an increase in communication with students via e-mail. Tell students your typical response time, lest they expect an immediate reply. You will need to be careful about deleting e-mails based on the familiarity of the sender's name. That e-mail from lovegod@isp.com might not be junk mail but a message from that shy, bespectacled student in your class. Tell students to give you the course and section they are in and their real name in the subject line of their e-mail. Also, make clear to students whether you are willing to accept assignments via e-mail. If you do decide to accept assignments saved as attachments to e-mail messages, be sure to have a *very* current virus checking software system. If you have large classes, you might also want to have a filtering mechanism to keep student assignments together.

Reinforcing use of Web pages in class. Be sure to reinforce the use of your Web pages during class discussions. You must alert students in-class when you post new information to the course Web site (unless you have set up an expectation that they need to check the site at some regular interval).

Attending to the "non-techie student." Do not assume that all of your students are computer literate or that they own a computer. Just as you teach writing skills you can encourage some computer literacy. When you introduce the Web component of your course, offer to help students learn to navigate the Web and to locate computer labs on campus. Just as you orient students to the course syllabus, show students how to use the course Web site. If your classrooms are set up to display the Internet, show them the Web pages. If you do not have classroom access, you can print key Web pages and show them as transparencies. You may want to provide students with an annotated hard copy of the transparencies that describes how to get to your Web site and what they'll find when they follow links. Having a student from Psi Chi or the Psychology Club hold sessions for the non-techie student also is effective. In our experience, each year fewer students need additional help.

Conclusion

Internet resources can provide a way to engage students in more active learning. Integrating these resources with more traditional pedagogical techniques will have the benefit of preparing your students for their technology rich future and give your students 24/7 access to course materials and experiences. The Internet has tremendous potential for enhancing educational experiences; it is time to start exploring how it can best serve you and your students. Technology skills are as fundamental today as are reading, writing and arithmetic. If we fail to model use of basic tools, we fail to educate our students.

References and Recommended Readings

Aberson, C., Berger, D., Healy, M., Kyle, D., & Romero, V. (2000). Evaluation of an interactive tutorial for teaching the Central Limit Theorem. *Teaching of Psychology, 24,* 289-291.

Alexander, J., & Tate, M. (1998). *Evaluating web resources.* [Online]. Available: www2.widener.edu/Wolfgram-Memorial-Library/webevaluation/webeval.htm

Brinson, J. D., & Radcliffe, M. F. (1996). *An intellectual property law primer for multimedia and web developers.* [Online]. Available: www.eff.org/pub/CAF/law/multimedia-handbook

Doctorow, M., Wittrock, M. C., & Marks, C. (1978). Generative processes in reading comprehension. *Journal of Educational Psychology, 70,* 109-118.

Eggleton, F. (1999). *FERPA: Family educational rights and privacy act.* [Online]. Available: www.wku.edu/Dept/Support/AcadAffairs/ CTL/ferpa.htm

Graham, T. (2001). Teaching child development via the Internet: Opportunities and pitfalls. *Teaching of Psychology, 28,* 67-71.

Hafner, K., & Lyon, M. (1996). *Where wizards stay up late: The origins of the Internet.* New York: Touchstone.

Horton, S. (2000). *Web teaching guide.* New Haven, CT: Yale University.

Hurlburt, R. (2001). "Lectlets" deliver content at a distance: Introductory statistics as a case study. *Teaching of Psychology, 28,* 15-20.

Lynch, P. J., & Horton, S. (2002). *Web style guide* (2nd ed.). New Haven, CT: Yale University. (Also available online at www.webstyleguide.com.)

Nielsen, J. (1996). *The top ten mistakes of web design.* [Online]. Available: www.useit.com/alertbox/9605.html

Rogers, E. (1995). *Diffusion of innovations.* New York: Free Press.

Authors' Note: This Chapter is based on an invited address given by the authors at the 13th Annual Convention of the American Psychological Society. Toronto, Ontario, Canada, June, 2001.

Course Interrupted:
Coping With Instructor Absence

RETTA E. POE
Western Kentucky University

A ROUTINE TRIP TO SEE
a doctor reveals the need to have surgery the next day. A letter
in the mail includes a summons to a month of jury duty. A
paper acceptance for an international conference means a two-
week absence. A family member is hospitalized with a serious
illness.

These normal events of daily life happen even to college professors, but higher education institutions generally make no
provisions for replacements for those on sick or personal leave,
nor are there "substitute teachers" who can be called in. When
college instructors must be absent for some period of time, they
or their department chairs are faced with arranging class coverage, but there are limited options for successfully accomplishing this task. Because the choice of options depends in large
part on situational factors, a review of those will be followed by
some suggestions for dealing with the various issues that arise
due to instructor absence.

Reasons for Instructor Absence

Instructors can be unable to teach their classes for a variety
of reasons, some planned and some — perhaps most — unplanned. Planned reasons include travel, usually for professional
reasons but sometimes for significant personal events (e.g., the
birth of a grandchild), and surgery or maternity leave. However,
most instructor absences are probably unplanned: illness, injury, surgery, family illness or injury, death in the family, jury
duty, job interviewing, instructor arrest (and possibly resigna-
tion), and instructor death. Sometimes the absence is only a

few days, but more serious problems arise when the absence is expected to be a long one, or is permanent.

Some of the issues that affect decisions about class coverage include:

- ♦ How long will the instructor be gone? Will the absence be through the end of the semester or permanent?
- ♦ At what point in the term has the absence occurred?
- ♦ Is the assigned instructor available to consult with and/or write exams and grade papers?
- ♦ Are the assigned instructor's syllabus, and records on assignments and grades available?
- ♦ What is the reason for the instructor's absence? Will there be a need to deal with students' emotional reactions to the instructor's being gone?

Advice for the Department Chair

The most important advice for the forward-thinking department chair is to arrange a system to deal with instructor absences in advance of need and thus avoid a crisis when an unplanned absence occurs. As part of this effort you should encourage the development of a departmental norm that canceling classes be avoided if at all possible and emphasize the faculty's ethical obligation to deliver the courses that have been promised. When an instructor is unable to teach his or her classes, it is the department faculty's shared responsibility to pitch in and cover classes for one another, not only out of ethical obligation to the students but also because "what goes around, comes around."

Substitutes

In planning for instructor absences, identify and explore the resources available for arranging class coverage, especially for an extended absence. When the assigned instructor's absence is expected to be lengthy or permanent, options may include hiring adjuncts or graduate students, assigning graduate teaching assistants, and paying overloads to other faculty. If the department does not have the resources to pay for substitutes, then imposing on existing faculty members may be the only option. However, you may be able to negotiate a reduction in the other duties of those assigned to fill in. Sometimes it is preferable to have a team of faculty members take turns teaching various topics in the instructor-less course; when this arrangement is utilized, it is probably best to identify one person to be the coordinator. Also, students will need to know whom to contact with questions and concerns, and whose office hours schedule to request.

Grades

Having substitutes covering classes may lead to other complications. One of the most significant concerns the grade records of the absent instructor. If these are available, problems are minimal; ideally all instructors would keep organized records in an accessible place. As part of departmental "norm-setting" you can impress on the faculty the value of keeping grade records current and accessible. However, you should probably anticipate that some faculty may object to having their grades records be available, especially if they perceive the request to be a means of monitoring their activities. To counter this, point out the need to be prepared for contingencies, including unexpected absences, and involve the faculty in identifying other potential solutions. Each faculty member could provide information about where and how to locate grade records (e.g., where the grade book is usually kept, or the file name and location of records stored on one's computer, or the name of a colleague or other person who knows where records are kept), with the understanding that this information would only be accessed under certain circumstances.

If grades are not available, then you may have to help the substitute work out a plan. One possibility would be to develop a formula for combining students' estimates of their grades at the point of instructor-change with the grades they earn after the substitute takes over (J. O'Connor, personal communication, February 5, 2001). For instance, the new instructor could ask students to estimate their grades on already-completed assignments and exams and then assign weights, both to those estimates as well as to grades earned on the remaining part of the course (depending on how much of the course has been completed, perhaps 25 percent and 75 percent, respectively). In following such a procedure the substitute may want to qualify the arrangement by stipulating that no student's final grade can be higher than the highest grade earned in the second part of the course, or higher than the grade earned on the final exam, or some other contingency. The purposes for such a caveat would be to minimize the impact if students were to inflate their estimates of grades already earned, and to insure that students continue to have an incentive to learn. One might also tell students that grades have not yet been found but may eventually be located, thus encouraging more "accurate" estimates. In developing the grading plan, it would be important to enlist students' support for working out a fair and responsible solution in a difficult situation, and the chair's role in seeking consensus between students and the substitute would be essential.

Another potentially problematic situation concerns administration of student course evaluations. If these are required at your institution, be prepared to make special arrangements in cases where significant teaching was provided by more than one instructor. For example, if the course were begun by one person and finished by another, perhaps it would be possible to arrange to have students complete an evaluation form for each instructor. If not, students will need very clear instructions about whom to evaluate as they complete the forms.

Advice for the Original Instructor

Deciding When to Be Gone

If you have any control over the timing of an absence (such as elective surgery or consulting), think carefully about the best time to be gone. As a rule, in most courses the beginning and the end of a term are the worst times to be absent. The best time to be gone is when you can plan course topics for which you have colleagues already prepared and willing to fill in. Asking colleagues to teach material that is similar to what they teach in their own courses requires them to spend less time preparing for your course and thereby reduces the size of the favor you are asking.

Syllabus Planning

Not knowing what may happen during any semester, all instructors should consider taking some steps that would make dealing with unplanned absences easier. Because syllabi are regarded as contracts between students and the institution (Keith-Spiegel, Wittig, Perkins, Balogh, & Whitley, 1993, p. 23), it is wise to leave open the option of making adjustments, should they be necessary to deal with instructor absence. Altman (1989, p. 2) recommends that instructors add to the end of their syllabi a caveat such as, "The above schedule and procedures in this course are subject to change in the event of extenuating circumstances." Also, if you know before the term begins that you will be absent for a significant period, you should take that possibility into consideration when deciding on course requirements. If possible, avoid requirements, such as required class participation, that would be difficult for someone else to implement in your absence.

Record-Keeping

Keep good records and organized files so someone else can locate your materials if needed. Make sure your grade book is accessible, or make a secretary, graduate assistant, or colleague aware of how to find a grade file on your computer (name of the file and where it is located, password for accessing it, etc.). The location of your lecture notes also would be helpful.

Planned Absences

If you know ahead of time that you will be absent, some of the options for class coverage include:

- ♦ Selecting films or videos relevant to course topics.
- ♦ Arranging for colleague guest lecturers, perhaps in a "trade-off" arrangement with you.
- ♦ Developing a class activity project that can be directed with minimal preparation by a graduate student or colleague.
- ♦ Preparing lecture(s) for a graduate student or colleague to deliver for you.

Of course, it may be necessary to rearrange course topics from your original schedule if the selected method of coverage works better for some topics than for others.

Hiring a Substitute

From an ethical standpoint, arranging class coverage so that you can do consulting work may obligate you to pay your substitute. Suppose that you make plans to do some consulting during a summer term when you are being paid an extra teaching stipend, and you ask a graduate student or colleague to teach your course for a week. In this case, paying the substitute a pro-rated amount of your stipend seems only fair. Or perhaps during the regular academic year you persuade a graduate student to cover some classes outside of his or her duties as part of a graduate assistantship. In such a situation it is important to be sensitive to the power inequities between professors and graduate students and to avoid taking advantage of a graduate student. One way to calculate a fair rate of compensation might be to find out how much adjunct faculty members at your institution earn per course and then pay the student a pro-rated amount, based on how many classes the student teaches (J.

O'Connor, personal communication, February 5, 2001). Of course, it is important to clear all the details of such an arrangement with appropriate administrators.

Sharing the Load With a Substitute

If you can do some of the instructional work from home during your absence (such as during maternity leave or recovery from surgery), you will need a good system of communication. For example, if several colleagues are covering different topics for your course, it would be good to have one person designated to coordinate the whole set-up and facilitate communication among you, the various substitutes, your students, and your secretary. Determine how much of the instruction you can manage from home using technological resources such as e-mail and posting materials on your Web site. Decide whether you can do some or all of the exam writing and grading of exams and papers, and if you cannot, designate someone to be responsible for this and for keeping you informed.

Returning to Class

If you will be returning to the class after your absence, be prepared to be flexible in dealing with students and in evaluating their work, especially if they have had to cope with taking exams written by, and having their work graded by, different people. This is clearly a situation in which giving students "the benefit of the doubt" seems appropriate. Expect some students to be angry with you for having been gone, and upon returning, express your appreciation and gratitude to the students for their patience and tolerance in a difficult situation, and to your colleagues for their help.

Advice for the Substitute Instructor

The major situational variable is whether this assignment is temporary or permanent. Are you teaching a class or two for someone who is out of town, covering a class for six-to-eight weeks while a colleague recovers from surgery, or permanently taking responsibility for a course already in progress? Regardless of the situation, there are a few basic guidelines to keep in mind.

You will need to find out from the department chair or original instructor exactly what is expected of you. Are you just to give a couple of lectures, or will you write exams, read students' papers, evaluate class presentations, assign grades, etc.? Be sure to let the students know your plans, too. Keep good notes about what material you cover — especially if you will be taking responsibility for more than one class — and be prepared to develop exam questions on the material you present.

To reduce students' anxiety, communicate as much and as clearly as you can about the nature and duration of the instructor's absence, the changes in the course (if any) that may result, what impact there may be on their grades, etc. Begin the first class by introducing yourself and telling the students what to expect. If you will be on the scene for a few weeks, don't forget to let the students know your office hours and office location, just as you would your own students. At least for a while, these are your own students.

Especially if the class you enter is small, it is a good idea to be sensitive to the "cultural milieu" of the class. There may be a well-developed sense of community, such that you become a major source of disruption. If so, acknowledge your awareness of the situation, and, if appropriate, facilitate a discussion of their reactions to the absence of the original instructor and your presence.

In general, although having a substitute instructor requires some adjustment on the part of students, you should expect to do most of the adjusting. Strive as much as possible to accommodate to the class you are visiting or have inherited, rather than expect the students to adjust to you. If the assigned instructor will return, try in advance to get an agreement with that person as to your role in assigning grades, and also how much freedom you have to indulge your personal teaching style and decide about how to cover course material.

If "filling in" will require a substantial commitment of time and effort (e.g., if you will be teaching virtually the whole course, or if the course is a new preparation for you), negotiate up front with the department chair about issues like compensation for teaching an overload, reductions in other responsibilities, and special consideration of your efforts on evaluation occasions (salary adjustments, tenure and promotion decisions).

When you are taking over a course permanently, ethically (and perhaps legally) you should consider yourself bound to follow the syllabus developed by the original instructor. As noted above, Altman (1989) and others have suggested that the syllabus is generally regarded as a contract between the institution and the students, so this means that you should not expect students to buy a different textbook, and you should make an effort to abide by the course expectations and requirements already in place. If alterations are unavoidable, explain why and apologize. Next, try to arrange with the chair and/or other administrators for students to withdraw from the course without penalty if substantial modifications of the course are necessary and are perceived to be unacceptable to some class members.

Some difficult decisions may be required if you should inherit a class for which there is no syllabus and the previous instructor is not available for consultation. You might begin by asking students to write summaries of what they understood the course requirements and expectations to be; then use the areas of agreement in their accounts as a starting point for developing a working syllabus of your own. Without a syllabus you may also have little idea as to what has been covered in the course so far; again, your only recourse is to survey the students.

Special Situations

Instructor Death

A substitute who must fill in for someone who dies suddenly has to deal with all the problems mentioned above as well as emotional issues. Students may need help in coping with their grief; the best advice is to seek the assistance of your institution's counseling center. Counseling center personnel are trained to serve as consultants to faculty in helping students, and in some cases a counselor may be available to conduct a group grief counseling session.

Jury Duty

The requirements of jury duty vary widely; in most cases, however, what makes jury duty so difficult for an instructor to manage is that jurors may not know even one day in advance whether they will be selected for a particular case. Thus, during the time of jury service faculty members often have to develop elaborate contingency plans for covering their classes. In some jurisdictions faculty may be able to arrange with court officials to postpone jury duty to a time when they are not teaching. If not, the court administrator may be able to identify days when the court will not be in session, and sometimes members of the jury pool can indicate certain dates on which they cannot be available to serve. Thus, with planning, it may be possible to reduce the uncertainty of one's schedule. To cover classes during the term of jury service options include arranging for a colleague to be on "stand-by" to teach a class if necessary, supplementing regular instruction with web-based instruction, and developing homework assignments and projects for students. Scheduling make-up classes may be a workable idea at institutions that are largely residential; however, if the student body includes a large number of commuter students (traditional or non-traditional), make-up classes should be optional.

Absence of Graduate Teaching Assistant (GTA)

GTAs occasionally have to miss classes, usually for the same reasons as other instructors. The usual practice for dealing with short-term absences is for other GTAs to fill in. Buskist notes that getting GTAs to volunteer to pitch in is seldom a problem because "they want all the (teaching) experience they can get!" (B. Buskist, personal communication, February 6, 2001). When the absence is permanent or long-term, however, a better practice is to recruit a new GTA, perhaps from the pool of applicants for assistantships. Problems with excessive or inappropriate GTA absences can usually be prevented; as Davis notes, "the best measure to prevent such absences is to give the GTAs thorough and continuous training that emphasizes professionalism" (S. Davis, personal communication, February 7, 2001).

Conclusion

The focus on prevention is probably the best overall advice for dealing with instructor absence. Although some amount of hassle is probably unavoidable in working out a remedy for the instructor-less course, instructors and department chairs can reduce the frustration of all concerned with some advance preparation.

References and Recommended Readings

Altman, H. B. (1989). Syllabus shares 'what the teacher wants.' *The Teaching Professor, 3*(5), 1-2.

Keith-Spiegel, P., Wittig, A. F., Perkins, D. V., Balogh, D. W., & Whitley, B. E., Jr. (1993). *The ethics of teaching: A casebook.* Muncie, IN: Ball State University.

Part III

Beyond the Text or Classroom

Teaching Psychology Through Film and Video

RAYMOND J. GREEN
Texas A&M University-Commerce

YOU'VE BEEN WORKING your fingers to the bone all semester and it is time for a break. So, you come up with the great idea to show a film. One of your colleagues has recommended one highly. You plan to dim the lights, hit the play button, and quietly sit in the back of the classroom wishing for some popcorn. Sounds great — what could go wrong? The film starts and before you know it you find yourself wondering — how does this fit with the material I've been presenting? This question is reinforced when one of your better (and braver!) students asks the same question as the lights go up. The next question brings up a point in the film that you had no idea would be addressed and thus you do not have an answer. This lack of knowledge helps bring questions and discussions to a halt. As you stand sweating in front of the class wondering how to tie the material in the film back to the class objectives you think — shucks, it would have been easier to lecture!

This nightmare scenario does not need to happen. Movies can be a wonderful tool for teaching psychology. However, for this to happen you need to do your homework. In this article I will discuss some of the reasons for using film in our courses as well as important rules, hints, and suggestions for doing so. I will conclude with a method for using film to teach psychology outside of the classroom.

Why Use Films?

Complement Other Course Content

There are many excellent reasons for using films to teach psychology. The most basic is that theatrical movies or educational videos can complement the text, lectures, and discussions. One of the basic rules of communication is redundancy, that is, communicating the same point in a number of different ways. Movies provide a concrete way to present important information (Anderson, 1992), sometimes in a way that grabs the class by their collective lapels and gives them a good shaking! For instance, teachers can talk about the power of Milgram's Obedience to Authority experiments until they are blue in the face and most students will just nod their heads. However, show them the film *Obedience* and many of them will squirm and giggle uncomfortably, just like Milgram's participants.

Improve Students' Discerning Eye

Filmmakers love to use psychology as a topic, perhaps because we are all amateur psychologists at heart. Thus, there is no shortage of psychology-oriented material. However, this leads to another reason to use film: to debunk inaccurate portrayals of psychology in popular film and to help students become critical consumers of popular information (Hollander, 2000). Many people have a distorted view of what psychology is and how psychologists work due to popular movies. We can use these films as a reminder that not everything presented on the silver screen is accurate and thus students should view portrayals of psychology with a discerning eye. For example, in *Analyze This*, starring Robert DeNiro and Billy Crystal, the absolute disregard for client confidentiality is appalling. Thus, I show this film clip to illustrate how psychologists "don't work."

Increase Relevancy

Finally, using fairly recent popular films allows you to "talk" in a language that students understand and frequently use. Another way to think about it is that the student tends to think of newer movies as more relevant to them and their world. For instance, you may want to use *Sybil* as a jumping off point for discussing Dissociative Identity Disorder but you may find that the students are not enthused about it and consider it dated. I guarantee, however, that you will not receive this reaction if you choose to use more recent films like *Primal Fear* or *Fight Club* (if you have not seen this movie I just ruined the ending for you — sorry!).

Using Films in the Classroom

Follow Three Critical Rules

There are a number of steps that can be taken to reduce any potential problems associated with using a movie and to make it a beneficial experience for you and your students. It is important to note that I believe that the same teaching tips apply to the use of theatrical films and educational videos, although there are generally fewer time concerns with educational videos. In my opinion there are three crucial rules for insuring successful use of videos in the classroom.

View the film before the class sees it. Previewing allows you to answer a number of crucial questions. Does the content merit the use of class time? Are there portions of the movie that can/ should be skipped? Is there any particularly objectionable material? If so, does the importance of the material outweigh the possibility of offending a student?

Always watch the movie with the class (Gross Davis, 1993). In the mind of some students, and some colleagues, a film means, "No learning today" or "The teacher is feeling lazy." If you use the film as a substitute for yourself or if you leave the room and come back when the film is over you are reinforcing these beliefs.

Be aware of copyright laws. In general, legally obtained copies of materials can be used in face-to-face classrooms for educational purposes without violating copyright laws. However, the issue quickly becomes murkier if you want to tape something off television to show in your class. At this point the Fair Use exemption to United States copyright law probably comes into effect. The Fair Use exemption allows for educational use of copyrighted material without permission of the author (amongst other uses). However, Fair Use comprises a short excerpt that is attributed to the original source. Further, the use of the material should not harm the commercial value of the material. If you plan on using a longer piece of material I suggest that you contact your University counsel to determine your University's policy concerning copyrighted material.

How Does One Find a Good Film or Video?

There is no shortage of films that contain psychological content. In fact, you stand to be overwhelmed by the possibilities if you are not selective in your approach to finding a good film! The two places that I always begin are Instructor's Manuals for the class and my colleagues. Use of the Instructor's Manual insures that the films are relevant to the course and content being covered. However, remember that this does not guarantee that the film is of high quality or useful for your particular classroom. No matter how highly recommended a film is — make sure that you preview it first. If you have more time I suggest that you use the Internet to find additional films, particularly theatrical releases that might be helpful. The best site that I have found for this purpose is www.psychmovies.com.

Know Your Classroom and Equipment

You can spend quite a while previewing films, preparing summaries, and designing exams only to have all of your efforts undermined if some basic preparation is ignored. Remember to practice operating the machinery that you will use in the classroom that you will use to show the film or video. This will help you to determine if you have the proper materials (e.g., adequate sized television, extension cords) and to check to see if there might be barriers to visibility (e.g., glare from late afternoon sun).

Time Is of the Essence in the Classroom

Most teachers feel that there is never enough time to cover what they want. So how does a professor take advantage of the benefits of movies without sacrificing other important material?

Do not feel obligated to watch a whole video from beginning to end. Feel free to use brief clips and/or sections of both scholarly and popular videos. This approach has become even easier with the advent of DVD technology that allows you to choose scenes with the push of a button.

One warning with this approach — make sure that you provide your students with the appropriate context to understand the video clip. For example, give your students any important vocabulary or proper names that they might need to know before they see the film (Gross Davis, 1993). Also, provide them with a question or set of questions that they should be able to answer/discuss after viewing the film.

Use of movies. Feel free to fast-forward through the "fluff" when using longer portions of movies. This will allow more time for discussion and tends to keep the students interested in the movie. The student feedback that I have received is that they resent "wasting time" watching material that is not relevant or appropriate. When using this approach let the students know ahead of time that you will be skipping parts of the film and take care to not undermine the continuity of the film.

When the Film or Video Takes up the Entire Class Period

Another time issue occurs when the film takes up the whole class. Often the transition to the next class is awkward and scholarly momentum is lost. One method for dealing with this problem is to provide a small assignment to be completed for the next class. This can be as simple as "Generate one thought/reaction/question related to the content of the film." These thoughts and questions can be used as the jumping off point for discussion in the next class. An alternate and frequently enjoyable assignment is to ask your students to act like movie critics and rate the film or video. Ask your students to evaluate both the overall presentation and psychological content separately. Then the next class can begin by asking how many thumbs up the film received on each factor. This assignment regenerates enthusiasm and is a much more useful prompt than "Any thoughts about the film?"

Solving Ethical Issues in the Use of Film and Video

Some ethical dilemmas arise when using movies to help teach psychology. Many times the most visually arresting images will be the most powerful for getting your point across (Anderson, 1992). At the same time these images are often controversial and may be offensive to some students. This leads to two questions:

1. Should you use the film?
2. If you do, how do you address the fact that you are presenting potentially objectionable material?

I approach this first question in much the same way that an Institutional Review Board approaches proposed research. I attempt to balance the potential benefits versus the potential costs and work to find the film that maximizes this ratio. Then, if I am going to use a potentially controversial film I warn the students about how it might be offensive (e.g., harsh language, violence, sexuality). Further, I allow students to leave if they choose to, and, when possible, I provide them with an alternative assignment that helps to cover the material (Anderson, 1992). Afterwards, I work with them to insure that they understand the important concepts covered in the film.

Test on Film and Video Material

Another potentially sticky issue is whether to test students on film content and, if so, how to test them. I agree with Gross Davis' (1993) assertion that if film material is important enough to show in class then it should also appear on a test. However, there are bounds to this logic. If you are merely showing a brief clip to highlight a concept or to spur on conversation then a test question is probably not merited. For instance, I use a humorous scene from *Monty Python's Search for the Holy Grail* where the medieval townsfolk are trying to decide whether a woman is a witch, as a way to indicate the strides that have been made in the assessment of abnormality. Using this scene gets my point across nicely but I would never test students on it.

If you are going to test students on the material you need to tell them before the movie or video. I suggest that you tell them not to take notes and that instead you will provide them with notes or a summary after the film. My rationale for this is simple. If students are taking notes they are not watching the movie. Further, for optimal viewing you want the lights turned down which makes note taking difficult. Finally, the issue arises: How should I test my students on the film content? Many films (moreso than educational videos) present potential problems in that they are more open to differences in interpretation than are lectures or textbooks. Questions pertaining to movies posed in an open-ended manner (e.g., essays) so that students have room to explain the rationale behind their answers work well. Other faculty ask two or three simple factual multiple-choice questions on exams, rewarding students, in essence, for attendance and paying attention.

Using Films Outside the Classroom

One of the most important lessons that I learned as a college student was that I could learn as much, if not more, outside the classroom as I did inside of it. For this reason I borrowed an idea from *The History Channel* and created a Psychology Film and Discussion series. The format involves inviting the university community to four different Hollywood movies throughout the semester. At the end of each a panel of "experts" leads a discussion concerning the psychological aspects of the movie. Each panel member presents a brief reaction to the film and highlights a facet that caught their interest. Then the floor is opened for questions and discussion. The panel usually consists of faculty but also includes knowledgeable and relevant community members. For instance, a lawyer would be helpful when discussing a movie that focuses on legal issues related to psychology. The film series is not used as a class requirement for any psychology course, but many professors at our university offer extra credit for attendance.

The benefits of this format are numerous. For example, time constraints are no longer a concern. Discussions can go in many different, even tangential, directions without worrying about the clock or curriculum issues. Further, this format shows students that psychology can be discussed intelligently outside the classroom. Also, the film series provides students with an opportunity to meet faculty with whom they have not previously interacted. One fringe benefit is that our department has found the film series to be a wonderful recruiting device for attracting psychology majors. Finally it is one more way your college or university can offer educational and intellectual opportunities to its general community.

Once again, an area to be careful with is copyright law. In order to avoid copyright infringement our film series follows three policies. First, the movie has to have been purchased by the university. Movies cannot be rented from the local video store. Second, the movie must be shown for educational purposes. Third, students cannot be charged admission to view the movie, so don't try to use a film series as a fundraiser!

Top Psychology Movies

To give you a head start in finding movies I have included a table (see Figure 1 on Page 110) that contains thirteen movies that are excellent vehicles for presenting psychology to your students. I have used many of these films in class and others have been used for the Psychology Film Series. Obedience is the only film in the list that is not a feature length presentation.

Conclusion

Movies can be a wonderful tool for teaching psychology. There is a lot of truth to the cliché that a picture tells a thousand words. What we must remember, however, is that movies do not provide an easy way out or a day's vacation. Successful use of a film involves as much, if not more, preparation than a traditional lecture.

Now, turn down the lights and pass the popcorn.

TOP PSYCHOLOGY MOVIES

Movie Title	Appropriate Course(s)	Teaching Topics
One Flew Over the Cuckoo's Nest (1975)	Abnormal, History	Institutionalization, What is abnormal?
Obedience (1962)	Social	Obedience to authority
Awakenings (1990)	Physiological	Oliver Sacks, L-dopa, Levels of awareness
American Beauty (1999)	Abnormal	Dysfunctional families, Projection
7 Percent Solution (1976)	Personality, History	Freud psychoanalyzes Sherlock Holmes
12 Angry Men (1957)	Social, Group Dynamics	Minority influence, Conformity, Prejudice
A Clockwork Orange (1971)	Learning, Developmental	Behaviorism, Free Will
The Madness of King George (1994)	Abnormal	Porphyria, What is abnormal?
Memento (2000)	Learning, Cognition	Memory formation
A Beautiful Mind (2001)	Abnormal	Schizophrenia
Manchurian Candidate (1962)	Cognition	Hypnosis, Brainwashing
Primal Fear (1996)	Abnormal	Dissociative identity disorder, Insanity plea
Sling Blade (1996)	Abnormal	Exceptional populations

Fig 1   Thirteen movies and the different psychological discipline they help examine.

References and Recommended Readings

Anderson, D. D. (1992). Using feature films as tools for analysis in a psychology and law course. *Teaching of Psychology, 19*, 155-157.

Bolt, M. (1976). Using films based on literature in teaching psychology. *Teaching of Psychology, 3*, 189-190.

Boyatzis, C. J. (1994). Using feature films to teach social development. *Teaching of Psychology, 21*, 99-101.

Conner, D. B. (1996). From Monty Python to *Total Recall*: A feature film activity for the cognitive psychology course. *Teaching of Psychology, 23*, 33-35.

Dorris, W., & Ducey, R. (1978). Social psychology and sex roles in films. *Teaching of Psychology,* 5, 168-169.

Fleming, M. Z., Piedmont, R. L., & Hiam, C.M. (1990). Images of madness: Feature films in teaching Psychology. *Teaching of Psychology, 17,* 185-187.

Gross Davis, B. (1993). *Tools for teaching.* San Francisco: Jossey-Bass.

Hollander, S. A. (2004). Hot off the press. Using popular media in instruction. In B. Perlman, L. I. McCann, & S. H. McFadden (Eds.), *Lessons learned: Practical advice for the teaching of psychology* (Vol. 2) (pp. 111-118). Washington, DC: American Psychological Society.

Hot Off the Press: Using Popular Media in Instruction

SHARON A. HOLLANDER
Georgian Court College

I READ ABOUT IT IN *Glamour*. Can I use information from a Web site? There was something on that in the newspaper last week. Who hasn't heard comments and questions like these in class? The popular media, by definition, is everywhere, and psychology classes are magnets for material from newspapers, magazines, the Internet, and more.

After a semester or two of smiling politely at the mention of *USA Today* or Yahoo.com, I realized that the popular media could be a valuable resource for my students. The information is often current, interesting, and accessible. Instead of trying to redirect class discussion, I decided to integrate these information sources into my courses and wanted to do so in a thoughtful manner. The results were so positive that I now encourage other instructors to use the popular media in their teaching.

Why Should I?

There are many reasons why a daily newspaper or visit to cyberspace should play a role in your course.

Reading

There is a nearly universal faculty complaint that students simply don't read enough. On-campus reading of quality materials is at an all time low. Teaching with the media encourages reading in general and more specifically, reading in psychology. Material from carefully chosen newspapers, magazines, and Web sites can be used to complement, enrich, and promote conventional academic reading.

Furthermore, these sources are read long after students complete their formal education. Be honest — how many of us reach for *An Outline of Psycho-Analysis* with our morning coffee? Pedagogical use of the media allows faculty to help shape students' life-long reading habits, both on- and off-line.

Critical Consumption of Information

Including the media in psychology lessons can help students become critical consumers of information. With the advent of the Internet and desktop publishing, everything looks credible and professional. Think about the different levels of quality among magazines alone. How does *Psychology Today* compare to *US News and World Report* or *Good Housekeeping*? With faculty guidance, students can learn to differentiate between peer-reviewed and non-peer-reviewed material, between professional and general interest articles, and between meaningful graphs and cool graphics.

Popular Media as Sources for Academic Work

Information gathering is easier than ever and once identified, quality articles in the popular media can be valuable sources for research papers and may lead the way to more scholarly inquiry.

Reduces Plagiarism

It is well known that long papers, repeat assignments, and broad topics tend to invite plagiarism. Assignments based on the popular media can be brief and are usually specific and timely, naturally counteracting these problems. Assignments and activities can be easily rotated from semester to semester making copying from sources, purchasing papers, or recycling papers from class to class extremely difficult to accomplish. It has been my experience that short papers and discussion of current articles outmaneuver even dedicated shirkers, copiers, and procrastinators.

Strengthens Students' Skills

The popular media can be used to stimulate student writing and discussion, nurture their curiosity, and deepen their knowledge. Ultimately, these assignments can strengthen students' language, computer, and critical thinking skills.

Real and Interesting

Lastly and most importantly, the discussion and writing that stem from the media can be fascinating. The choice of timely topics, the examples used, the relatively short length of most popular media articles, and the students' familiarity with the topics and people discussed make for interesting reading. These works show the application of psychology to real life. Psychologists often contribute to sources like abcnews.com and *The New York Times* and students should be encouraged to utilize them.

Copyright Is on Your Side

Most of the teaching tips which follow involve an instructor copying articles from newspapers, magazines or the Internet and distributing them to students to read. Generally speaking, copy away! There are no copyright problems. While most materials are copyrighted even if the copyright notice is not present, and copyright infringement is a crime, faculty can legally photocopy limited portions of written works for classroom use. This is considered "fair use" because your purposes are educational, not commercial, not for profit, and you are not in competition with the source or author.

Using Popular Media

Classroom Discussion

There are many ways to integrate popular media and instruction, starting as early as the first class of the semester. As an icebreaker, faculty can bring in short articles related to the course and lead small group or whole class discussions on them. Students can easily talk about these articles because they are non-threatening and in a familiar format. This technique works especially well at the beginning or end of any class session. When on track, students genuinely exchange ideas and assist each other in understanding the issues. See Kramer and Korn (1999) for tips on facilitating these discussions. They emphasize establishing ground rules, clarifying the instructor's role for the class, and providing students with training in active participation in a discussion.

Writing

Writing is not just for English classes any more, and the popular media can be used to incorporate writing into psychology classes. Both strong and weak writers can benefit from practice. Written responses, summaries, and critiques of articles are only a few examples of media-based assignments. I have students explore and review Web sites related to the courses I teach. These short papers focus on the purpose of the site, its strengths and weaknesses, and the potential benefits for specific users (e.g. psychologists, students, educators, clients, caregivers). Students can assess not just the content but the visual or numerical aspects of articles and sites, as well. Evaluation of material from the popular media can help prepare them to evaluate more complex material, such as articles from professional journals, writings on psychological theory, and grant proposals.

Speaking Across the Curriculum

Articles are great as the focus for individual or group presentations or debates. Students can do oral presentations from their critiques, prove or disprove points from an article, or debate ethical dilemmas. Phelps (1998) encourages students in her Child Psychology course to take a position on a controversial topic related to class and to defend their stance through discussion, debate, and written assignments. She recommends sources such as *Time*, *Parenting,* and *Atlantic Monthly* to garner information on topics including child welfare, day care, television viewing, and spanking. Other issues that lend themselves to this type of pedagogy and have recently received considerable media attention are teen violence, overuse of psychotropic medication, euthanasia, and culturally-sensitive books and curricula.

Critical Thinking

The media are a valuable source of information for thought-provoking long-term assignments, such as term papers or annotated bibliographies. Students can also create clipping files, portfolios, and reaction logs in following an issue of interest over an entire semester. They can look at events as they develop, examine how the issue is covered, contrast coverage in different sources, and compare points of view. It is especially eye-opening when students compare a popular article with the original research upon which it is based.

Cultural and political messages, such as stereotypes rooted in ageism, racism, and gender and disability bias, can be examined through the media. Carroll, Skinner, and Hedgepath (1998) use a heretofore unstudied form of popular media — greeting cards — to identify how women are portrayed and to sensitize students to the importance of messages from everyday items. In their Psychology of Women/Gender and Women's Studies classes, students assess both pictorial and written messages from the cards and may write personal responses to these messages. In fact, no aspect of the popular media need be overlooked in teaching critical thinking. Instructors report using everything from birth and marriage announcements to calls for human eggs and adoptable children, as well as personal ads, to encourage reflection on a variety of issues.

Net Worth

Although computer skills are extremely important, any instructor who uses technology runs the risk of being overshadowed by it. Having students use information from the Web creates its own challenges and many faculty have noticed an increase in time demands when using the Net. Although many students are quite savvy, others have little or no knowledge about how to use a computer or to locate sources of interest and will require instruction and encouragement. Will emphasis on Internet usage be at the expense of the actual content of the sites or lesson? Think about how much time, in and out of class, you would like to devote to this. Balance Net usage with other information sources, such as books, journals, interviews, and videos.

Finding Good Material

Faculty

Finding a relevant and appropriate article can be very challenging for both students and faculty. A good article should meet the same criteria as a good example in a lecture (Galliano, 1999). Scanning publications at home or in the library can be quite productive. Web-based search engines are incredibly helpful and can locate a wealth of articles relevant to any psychology course. In addition, most libraries have Infotrac, EBSCO Host, or a similar database of articles from the popular media. It is also important to note that old news may still be good news. For example, my students continue to appreciate articles on Ryan White in conjunction with lectures on HIV/AIDS. These pieces are still relevant to the issue despite being published in 1990.

Day in and day out popular media present excellent applications of psychology. Depending on the courses you teach and your subdisciplinary interests you should develop your own list of popular media sources that you read or skim regularly. To augment your list, ask your colleagues which popular media publications they find most helpful.

Students

When students select their own sites and articles, they can pursue topics that may not be covered in the curriculum or are not of general interest. However, the breadth of information of varying quality in the public domain is remarkable. Will students be able to separate trash from treasure? Recently, I required students to choose and evaluate a Web site relevant to early childhood and to e-mail me the address and a brief description which would become part of a list to be distributed to the whole class. More than one student e-mailed me what were essentially advertisements. Remember these critical points when asking students to find their own articles:

- ◆ Students may try to find appropriate articles but the instructor should provide a double check. "Advertorial" (advertising deliberately designed to resemble editorial) can be very convincing.
- ◆ Remind students to consider their source or author; look for specifics (such as facts, figures, and quotes), be wary of vague information and generalizations, and verify their information by checking or clarifying it through other sites or sources. A site on Obsessive-Compulsive Disorder set up by a pharmaceutical company will probably have different information than a site established by an advocacy or support group, though both may be factual and informative. Instructors may also want to distribute a list of preferred or exemplary sources.
- ◆ Students often do not know how to cite information from more modern sources, such as Web sites, listservs, or e-mail. Direct instruction and examples may be necessary.
- ◆ Consider availability when asking students to locate articles. Some topics are easy to find over the course of a few weeks but there may be students who need assistance.
- ◆ Inform students of which sources will be accepted and which will not.

Requirements and Grading

Articles and Web sites may be familiar but this does not mean that writing about them is, and many students report having little or no experience with this type of source in their college writing. Like any assignment, the requirements and grading criteria should be clearly articulated. Criteria for grading a media-based assignment, such as an article review, may include:

- ◆ Relevance of article to course or assigned topic.
- ◆ Level of sophistication and/or originality of the article. I sometimes tell students that academic work has a lot in common with professional diving. If you choose a very easy dive, like a brief article in *Woman's Day* you'd better do a really good job on it and it still may not stand out. On the other hand, if you select something more challenging off the high board, like a lengthy piece from *Utne Reader*, the judge (me) will take that into consideration and scores are usually higher.
- ◆ Clarity of written work, both mechanically and ideationally.
- ◆ Basic understanding of the article, usually indicated by a succinct summary.
- ◆ Depth and breadth of the evaluation. I look for three well-articulated and distinctly different points about the article in the course of a short essay.

Enriching the Class

At any point, the popular media can be used to illuminate course material, enliven lectures, add drama and humor to class, and put a face on psychological concepts and issues. For example, the media can illustrate the role of psychological science in the legal system. Miller (1997) included recent newspaper and magazine articles detailing repressed memory and eyewitness testimony cases in her course anthology for an undergraduate psychology class that examines human memory and legal issues. Students were also directed to monitor relevant Web sites.

Medical and developmental issues are often well-represented in the media. I teach in New Jersey and have been diligently clipping articles on an autism cluster in a nearby neighborhood. Published reports from parents and other articles on the cluster have been fact-filled and very meaningful to students, portraying autism in ways that far surpass a textbook. Students often contribute articles and Web addresses to my collection.

My college is also located in proximity to the McGuire Air Force Base and the influx of refugees from Kosovo has received a great deal of media coverage. Several instructors I know have incorporated articles on this crisis into their courses. Clearly, articles on both local issues and global matters have a place in the classroom.

Conclusion

Higher education and the popular media are a natural match. With newspapers, magazines, and Web sites, faculty can provide opportunities for reading and writing, curb plagiarism, help students evaluate information, and encourage critical thinking and discussion. It is important to remind students that useful information and ideas are accessible and may, in fact, be on their doorstep.

References and Recommended Readings

Carroll, K. A., Skinner, L. J., & Hedgepath, S. (1998, May). *Cultural and political messages about women: Portrayal of women in greeting cards.* Poster session presented at the Fifth Annual APS Institute on the Teaching of Psychology, Washington, DC.

Galliano, G. (1999). Enhancing student learning through exemplary examples. In B. Perlman, L. I. McCann, & S. H. McFadden (Eds.), *Lessons learned: Practical advice for the teaching of psychology* (pp. 87-92). Washington, DC: American Psychological Society.

Keating, A. B., & Hargitai, J. (1999). *The wired professor: A guide to incorporating the world wide web in college instruction.* New York: New York University Press.

Knowlton, S. R., & Barefoot, B. O. (Eds.). (1999). *Using national newspapers in the college classroom* (Monograph No. 28). Columbia, SC: University of South Carolina and The New York Times.

Kramer, T. J., & Korn, J. H. (1999). Class discussions: Promoting participation and preventing problems. In B. Perlman, L. I. McCann, & S. H. McFadden (Eds.), *Lessons learned: Practical advice for the teaching of psychology* (pp. 99-104). Washington, DC: American Psychological Society.

Miller, L. A. (1997). Teaching about repressed memories of childhood sexual abuse and eyewitness testimony. *Teaching of Psychology, 24,* 250-255.

Phelps, K. E. (1998, May). *Encouraging class debates in child psychology courses.* Poster session presented at the Fifth Annual APS Institute on the Teaching of Psychology, Washington, DC.

Using Outside Speakers in the Classroom

PATRICIA A. MULLINS
University of Wisconsin-Madison

WHEN MY COLLEAGUES hear that I often use guest speakers in my classes, I suspect they conjure up visions of me skipping out for a long weekend or, at the very least, enjoying a relaxing evening without having the next day's lecture to prepare. On the contrary, arranging to have someone speak to my class is often more work than preparing the lecture myself. Why do I do it? Not to abrogate my responsibility, but to enhance the students' learning (and mine — yes, I always sit in on the lectures). Though I may be confident in my teaching, I know that someone with expertise in a particular area will be better at communicating the subtleties of the topic from a position of authority.

A guest speaker conveys current, realistic information and a perspective on a subject that is not available from textbooks. Yet, using a guest lecturer involves more than just arranging for someone to show up at the appointed time. Over the years, I have discovered some general guidelines about using outside speakers. Whether the speaker is a colleague, a professional, or an expert nonprofessional from the community, the following information should help you decide when and how to use a guest speaker.

Why Use a Speaker?

Use the speaker to enhance the material you are covering. We have all coerced a colleague to cover a class when we are ill or are scheduled to give a paper at a conference. This is not the type of guest lecturing I am talking about. The time to use a colleague effectively in your class is when you have a topic planned in your syllabus and the country's expert on that subject is down the hall or the person doing cutting-edge research in that area is in another department on campus. You could never cover the material in the same way that they could. Even in your area of expertise, another perspective can add invaluable information. The point is to make sure that the speaker's topic fits into the syllabus on the date of the lecture. And be prepared to reciprocate.

One of my colleagues asks students at the beginning of the semester whether there are certain topics about which they would like more information. Sometimes she gives them a list of possibilities and has them indicate their top choices. Then she tries to arrange guest speakers based upon the students' interests. She finds that students appreciate the opportunity to provide input about topics they would like covered in more depth, and she tries to accommodate them, while being careful not to make any promises. This strategy works best if you know that you will have a few class sessions to spare later in the semester, because you must wait until the semester begins before you can contact speakers.

You don't necessarily have to limit yourself to arranging speakers who are experts in the class topic. Sometimes it may be more interesting to invite a guest to speak on a subject that is only tangentially related to the course. If you know of a captivating, dynamic speaker who would inspire students and make the theoretical aspects of a course more concrete, by all means, extend an invitation. This type of guest can be of great service to the students by providing an additional way to consider the primary topic and its central principles and issues. For example, having a charismatic conductor speak about conveying emotion in music would help enrich students' thinking in a class on emotions; an influential gallery curator speaking about the portrayal of depression in art could facilitate students' development beyond the boundaries of their discipline. College students often don't realize the broader applications of their knowledge, and creativity in planning this type of guest lecturer can have remarkable results.

Make Sure That the Speaker Is Credible

Books on teaching tell us how to improve our own skills but not how to insure the skills of outsiders we bring in to the classroom. There are a few points to keep in mind when considering a speaker.

Do not just settle for the person who happens to be available. The students will be most receptive to a guest speaker who communicates relevant and reliable information. It is easy to insure credibility if the person you are inviting to your class is a colleague or a professional you know or have heard speak. It is more difficult if you are doing "cold calls" to seek an expert in a certain field. If that is the case, decide on the area of expertise you are looking for, then ask your colleagues for suggestions of people or places to call — a well-respected mental health clinic, the local mental health inpatient facility, a child development center, for example — to locate a professional working in that field. Ask the receptionist who answers the phone to recommend someone on the staff who would be an interesting speaker.

Keep in mind that establishing credibility means both knowing the topic well and knowing how to communicate it to college students. I once wanted to invite a consultant in educational psychology to my class, so I called a reputable consulting company and asked the secretary who answered the phone whom she would recommend to speak to a group of college students. She considered my question carefully and gave me the name of someone on the staff who was on vacation but would be in the following week. That person turned out to be one of the best guest speakers I ever had. Not only was she knowledgeable about the topic, she was able to communicate her passion for her work in a way that excited the students.

Be on the lookout for good speakers who have specialized knowledge that would be interesting to students. Your neighbor may be an attorney who specializes in working with people with mental illness, or a judge who frequently considers insanity defenses. Your daughter's soccer coach may work for a survey research firm and would be a dynamic speaker on the use of statistics in an applied setting. A note of caution is in order, however: Be wary of individuals who solicit class time from you for the purpose of furthering a personal cause (e.g., prohibiting the use of animals in research, or promoting a product or service). None of us likes to be preached at, even if we agree with the basic premise of an argument.

Inviting Speakers

Start Slowly

Arranging outside speakers is a difficult, time-consuming process. Securing commitments from speakers requires an early start on planning your syllabus, determining the course schedule, and recruiting. You need to make calls well in advance to get on a busy person's calendar. Early planning also emphasizes to your speaker the importance of the speaking engagement. On the other hand, make sure to build some flexibility into your schedule to accommodate the speaker. For example, if you have decided that Tuesday, October 4 is the perfect day for a lecture by the local judge who hears insanity defenses, and you find out that Tuesday is her scheduled day in court, it helps to have the ability to modify your syllabus to have her speak on Thursday. If you are too rigid about days of the week or particular dates, you may have a very difficult time scheduling the desired speakers. It may be best to begin with just one outside speaker in a course and then expand that number if it seems to be appropriate. Remember that the speaker should enhance the course material, not replace it. Too many different lecturers can distract from the structure of the class.

Get the Speaker Into the Flow of the Class

Once you have the speaker scheduled at the appropriate point in the syllabus, it is important to insure that the guest lecture fits into the flow of the class.

First, send the speaker a copy of the related readings that the students will have done in preparation for the lecture. As an alternative, you can ask the speaker for a brief reading list to give the students in advance. Either way, the guest has some idea of the students' background knowledge of the topic.

Second, send the speaker an outline of the key points you would like covered, or discuss this in detail and have the speaker send you an outline, so there are no surprises. I learned this the hard way when I arranged for a health psychologist to lecture on her choice of occupation, and she shocked the class with tales of her illicit drug use and eventual conversion to a religious cult. I was expecting her to talk about health psychology as a career, and she thought I meant for her to tell her life story. Some speakers know exactly what to talk about, but others are unclear and would appreciate some ideas. A clinician who spoke to an introductory clinical class was happy to include information on salary range, time commitment, and work environment in his lecture, when asked to do so.

Third, do a brief but meaningful introduction of the speaker and the topic at the end of the class that precedes the guest lecture. This prepares the students for what to expect and enables them to begin thinking about questions to ask the guest.

If you take some time in the previous class to inform students about the upcoming lecture, they will not only be more likely to be receptive to the speaker but will look forward to hearing the lecture.

Inform the Speaker

In addition to providing guest speakers with information about the lecture topic, it is wise to discuss teaching style. Talk about the style you use in the classroom and inquire about the style the speaker finds most comfortable. It is perfectly all right if the teaching styles are different, but it does help to prepare the students for this. For example, students who are accustomed to listening to you lecture may be taken aback by a guest with a Socratic style. Their discomfort can be lessened if they know what to expect, and they can be prepared to participate.

Try to meet with the speaker before the semester begins; ask for biographical material to use in your introduction and inquire about audiovisual equipment needs. Well in advance of the presentation date, send out a packet of information, including details about the class. Time and location of the classroom are obvious needs, as is a complimentary parking sticker and/or a map of parking areas. Information about the format of the class is also useful — how much time is allotted, how much time to leave for questions, whether there will be other speakers, and how the room is arranged (moveable chairs, for example, or fixed desks). A description of the class itself is also helpful for the speaker — number of students and year in school, their knowledge of the speaker's topic, and their general interests. Some speakers ask the class members to introduce themselves and say a word about their interests, so they have more knowledge of their audience.

Make It Personal

Encourage speakers to talk from personal experience. It is an understatement to say that the best lectures are from the heart, whether guests are communicating about their passion for research or their commitment to working with mentally ill patients. A clinical nurse practitioner who specializes in working with severely emotionally disturbed children once mentioned to my class that she serves as a guardian ad litum for a severely disabled young man. Two students were so touched by her selflessness that they initiated a volunteer project at the group home where the young man is a resident.

If you have had a chance to meet with guests beforehand, you can determine their level of comfort talking about personal experiences and let them know that you may ask some provocative questions during the class. This can open up a new realm of discussion and model inquisitive learning for the students. This is also a good time to let the speaker know that you will keep track of time remaining in the class, and that you may intervene to interpret a student question. This is often comforting information for a novice or nervous guest.

Be Fair

If you are engaging outside speakers on a controversial topic, make sure they know that they are welcome to share their ideas and opinions. This gives students a point of view to consider as they form their own opinions. It is always wise, however, to insure that you have scheduled speakers who hold opposing viewpoints. It is not in the students' best interests only to hear one individual advocating a single perspective on a topic. You may not want to take up valuable class time with a heated argument (e.g., abstinence versus safe sex in a class on human sexuality), but you can schedule speakers in two consecutive classes. Or you might intentionally arrange a moderated debate — the pros and cons of psychoanalysis comes to mind as an example.

Consider the Audience

Prepare the Students

"Will we be graded on this?" If you say no, you should rethink the purpose of the speaker's visit. If the speaker is there truly to enhance the quality of the students' learning experience, then why should this information be excluded from the assessment of students? If the course does not have exams, then you need to work harder to ensure that the students show up and are respectful listeners. If you have introduced the students to the subject matter, given them some background information on the speaker, and fit the topic into the appropriate spot in the syllabus, then this task will not be difficult. Some instructors require the students to prepare questions for the speaker ahead of time; others create a respectful atmosphere by having students place name cards on their desks. A small group of students can even be selected to introduce the speaker.

Take this opportunity to teach your students the value of appropriate classroom etiquette of respect and courtesy when interacting with a guest speaker. Make sure they know that sincere applause is a sign of appreciation at the end of a talk. Encourage them to stay after class, shake hands with the speaker, and offer a personal "thank you." Let them know that a speaker is usually flattered by students' questions and requests for advice. Either the instructor or a student should escort the speaker to the door and say a final good bye. Give the speaker's name and address to the class, so that students who found the presentation particularly beneficial can write a thank-you note on their own.

Evaluate

Prepare a short evaluation form for the students to complete at the end of the guest lecture. Make sure this procedure and the content of the evaluation is known beforehand to the speaker and to the students. Ask questions that will provide useful feedback for the speaker and for you. Inquire about such issues as level of informativeness, relevance of the topic, ability to relate to students, willingness to answer questions, and enhancement of learning. Requiring completion of the evaluation form is also one way to insure class attendance.

If you form a database of speakers with contact information, speaking dates, and willingness to return, you can easily generate thank-you letters and other correspondence. If release time was required from the speaker's employer, I also send a thank you to the employer. This makes it easier to schedule future presentations. Some instructors send a copy of the thank-you letter to their dean as an acknowledgement of faculty or community members who are contributing as guest speakers.

I send a general narrative summary of information from the student evaluations along with the thank-you note. If the guest lacked experience speaking to a college class, but showed promise, I will often set up a time to meet and share some ideas for improvement. It is usually apparent when feedback and personal attention would be appreciated by a speaker.

Conclusion

Guest speakers provide an important perspective on the field of psychology and those who apply it. The variety of settings, and the diversity of activities can be described best in a personalized account. Keep in mind, too, that you are giving guest speakers the opportunity to contribute to the education of interested college students in their community. It is good public relations both for the speakers and for our students.

References and Recommended Readings

Bertelson, C. L. (1987). The three R's for guest speakers: Research, reliability, and respect. *Business Education Forum, 41,* 20-21.

Cloud, B., & Sweeney, J. (1988). Effective guest speakers require thought and care. *Journalism Educator, 42,* 30-31.

Glenwick, D. S., & Chabot, D. R. (1991). The undergraduate clinical psychology course: Bringing students to the real world and the real world to students. *Teaching of Psychology, 18,* 21-24.

Jeffrey, G. H. (1988). Seven tips for successful classroom speakers. *Instructor, 98,* 43.

Lance, L. M. (1987). Variety in teaching human sexuality: Involvement of community experts and guests. *Teaching Sociology, 15,* 312-315.

Olson, L. E. (1988). The question approach to guest speakers. *Journal of Education for Library and Information Science, 28,* 313-316.

Pestel, A. (1989). Working with speakers. *Vocational Education Journal, 64,* 34-35.

Seifert, M. H., & Smith, J. E. (1974). Improving performance of the seminar speaker. *Journal of Medical Education, 29,* 615-616.

Wortmann, G. B. (1992). An invitation to learning: Guest speakers in the classroom. *The Science Teacher, 59,* 19-22.

Faculty-Librarian Collaboration

SHARON A. HOLLANDER
BARBARA RAE HERBERT
KAREN STIEGLITZ DEPALMA
Georgian Court College

SOME FOLKS COME TO the college library fully expecting the experience be excruciatingly dull, and we are not necessarily referring to students. If truth be told, as a faculty member, I (first person throughout refers to Hollander) probably would not have partnered with a librarian or even made my way across campus for a visit. However, one of my courses, Psychological Basis of Education, mandates a library orientation session for students. Once in the session, I was impressed with the bibliographic instruction (BI). I also realized that the majority of my students did not know how to navigate the library and make the best use of its resources. The era of the library as a quiet, orderly repository for scholarly knowledge is gone. It has morphed into a more comprehensive institution, the "teaching library." I was surprised to discover that I was not capitalizing on all of the college's databases, online services, and other pedagogical supports for faculty. After the library instruction, I thought over a few questions.

What professional on campus is available to students nearly around the clock? The librarian! Library professionals serve as a support system, providing assistance, encouragement, and informal advisement to students. In addition, on many campuses, the library is the custodian of various resources that support learning, such as audiovisual labs and collections, writing and study skills centers, special collections, and coffee bars.

What do college librarians really do? Their traditional tasks include reference work such as answering students' questions and directing them to resources, and collection evaluation and development. These are important responsibilities, but the newest, and perhaps the most interesting role is that of a liaison or specialist who works with students and faculty from specific departments and schools. This includes advocacy (e.g., representing the interests of their designated school or department at library and college-wide meetings), assistance, troubleshooting, and more. In addition to traditional BI, many college librarians have become more active and involved in instruction.

Why is faculty-librarian collaboration worthwhile? Librarians and teaching faculty have many mutual goals and concerns. Both want students to develop a greater understanding of and respect for books, journals, and other intellectual property. Both want to enhance student literacy, particularly information literacy, and help students become writers, problem solvers, critical thinkers, and self-directed, lifelong learners. Lastly, both want to build the social and learning community on campus.

Librarians and faculty have a great deal to offer students and each other, especially in this "Information Age." To succeed in college, students must be able to: 1) work independently on computers, using electronic databases, online catalogues, and the Internet, as well as print resources; 2) evaluate, analyze, and synthesize information; and 3) understand issues of copyright, access, privacy, free speech, and censorship.

Obstacles to Faculty Use of the Library

Unfortunately, not everyone has embraced the idea of the teaching library and faculty-librarian partnership. Many professors underestimate librarians and view them as subordinates, sometimes as research assistants or babysitters for classes during out-of-town conferences. Some professors do not work with librarians because their students are part of a special population, such as honors or graduate students, who are mistakenly thought to be more knowledgeable and accomplished than typical undergraduates. Some faculty have simply never thought of how librarians could help them achieve course goals. Sadly, teaching itself is not valued on some campuses, so faculty may not choose to engage in cooperative instructional projects. Faculty may have encountered librarians who were unresponsive to faculty feedback and requests, had little enthusiasm for building coalitions, or may not have been interested in greater involvement in teaching or Psychology as a discipline. Social factors also affect collaboration. A fair number of professors and librarians spend most of their time working alone or with close colleagues and may have substantially different professional cultures. Finally, as with any relationship, there are a host of personality variables to consider.

Use of the College Library and Librarian in Teaching

Faculty-librarian collaboration can yield many creative projects that enhance instruction. These endeavors come in all shapes and sizes. They may be formal or informal, individual or institutional, ongoing or a "one shot" deal. Some cooperative efforts are college-wide; others involve just a few professionals.

Start With the Basics

At times, the goal is merely to get students into the library and to make contact with a helpful librarian. Incorporating a library assignment into a course syllabus is a simple but valuable type of partnership. Professors may require each student to use the reference desk to help develop a term paper. One of my colleagues asks students to come up with a set of questions relevant to their paper and to note the responses to these queries from a librarian. Sometimes a librarian must sign off on a preliminary bibliography that provides an opportunity for discussion of research strategies and the quality of references (Fister, 2002). Be sure to consult with your librarians before the assignment is defined and the course begins. They often have helpful suggestions. Also alert librarians about your assignments that send students to the library, so they can be prepared to best assist your students.

Think of Librarians as Teachers

Traditional bibliographic instruction is very broad and covers topics like library services, general information on the library's Web site and subscription databases, and the use of Internet resources. It is often offered to incoming students. Course-integrated instruction is a newer, more focused option for faculty. These are customized teaching sessions that emphasize discipline-specific information literacy. The heart of this type of library instruction is the location and evaluation of resources including specialized journals, reference materials, and databases, such as PsycInfo, ERIC, and ScienceDirect.

After instruction, a typical activity or assignment focuses on comparing popular, primary, and secondary resources. One of the more interesting versions was described by Randi Stocker, a librarian from Indiana University-Purdue University. In the lesson, students are given index cards listing various resources such as an encyclopedia entry, lecture notes, an article in *The New York Times* or a peer-reviewed study from *Psychological Science*. In small groups, students rank these from "least credible" to "most credible," Often group members tape their cards to the blackboard in rank order so they are easily visible to the faculty member and librarian who then share their views on the credibility of the items in light of different course assignments.

Librarians Are Indispensable for Independent Research Projects

After an introductory research course, the next step for my students is a two-semester research project. In fact, the independent research project is a hallmark of many undergraduate and graduate Psychology programs. This is a terrific opportunity for collaboration. Continuous faculty-librarian support is needed to help students complete high quality research projects. In a typical institutional partnership, the professor explains the specific steps in research, and the librarian demonstrates the use of relevant resources. Stein and Lamb (1998) followed this procedure, incorporating information on both the research process and research strategies into their BI sessions. In addition to group meetings, individual sessions were offered to students who needed extra help. Carrying the collaboration through to the end of the course, both the faculty member and librarian reviewed the students' research proposals, assisted with revisions, and reviewed the results.

Use Librarians to Help Students Select Research Topics

The early stages of the research process are quite important and often overlooked. Stamatopolos (2000), a librarian and instructional team member at Purdue University, assists students with research topic selection through an activity known as "The Wall," so named because a wall is used to display students' ideas. The setting for the activity is flexible. It can be staged in the classroom or in a room or area set aside for instruction in the library.

At the beginning of the lesson, students call out broad research topics related to the general theme of the class or project, and student recorders write these on paper affixed to the wall. After there are a number of these general topics on the wall, the students leave their seats and stand next to their topics of interest. Based on these common interests, groups are formed, and the members work to narrow or modify individual topics. While the faculty member can comment on the ideas from a disciplinary standpoint, the librarian can help each group identify their information needs and suggest specific reference sources. It is hoped that groups will become a natural support system for students, and if desired, group members can work together throughout the research process.

Librarians as Consultants to Students: Term Paper Clinics and More

The classroom is not the only place on campus for student learning or where faculty members can teach their students. Christensen (1994) gives one example of how to increase student success by bringing the teacher to the library. College librarians can hold term paper clinics. During these more or less structured sessions, students can get help with their research. At some colleges, faculty members also have specified office hours in the library. This on-site assistance provides a valuable and unusual opportunity for faculty and students to read and analyze sources together.

In a less formal way, the first two authors (teacher and behavioral sciences librarian) offer students, particularly those working on research projects, unstructured time in the library when we are both available. During this period, we are able to model the research process, as well as our enthusiasm for developing our ideas and tracking down information. I think the synergy is noticeable, and the queries really fly. Given many students' initial reluctance to visit the library, it is surprising and gratifying that most continue to work and ask questions well beyond the allotted time for this activity.

The value of these collaborations and work are many. Students use the library more effectively and efficiently, the quality of their work increases, and the faculty member can share responsibilities for students' development and learning with an experienced professional.

Making the Unfamiliar and Specialized Known

For upper-level students, faculty-librarian collaborative instruction may be more sophisticated and course-specific. I teach a class on assessment, and the primary assignment is a lengthy review of a standardized psychological or educational measure. Many students choose to write about one of the Wechsler scales or a popular, individually administered achievement test, such as the Woodcock-Johnson. A thorough paper on any measure requires the use of many unfamiliar and specialized resources, such as *Tests in Print,* the *Mental Measurements Yearbook, A Guide to 100 Tests for Special Education,* and various assessment-oriented journals and Web sites. Students are often surprised to learn that measures are reviewed, somewhat like movies and restaurants.

Again, the first two authors worked together to design a lesson to introduce students to these important sources of information. Every semester, we select one well-known, standardized test that would be of interest to students. Using print materials, computer demonstration, and commentary, we follow the path of this measure through many different sources. This method demystifies these references and provides a model for the research process.

Librarians Assisting With Grant Writing Assignments

I also teach a semester-long course to prepare students for a large research project in their last year of study. The class covers topics such as participant selection, research ethics, and the ever-popular APA style. Over the past year or two, I have integrated information on grant writing. Many local, state, and federal agencies, nonprofit organizations and foundations, and private corporations have money for different types of projects, and grant writing skills are valuable in any workplace. I ask students to find and describe at least three potential funders for their projects. They need not actually apply for the grant, but some do, and that's even better. Faculty writing small grants funded by their local campus also may use librarians to assist student coauthors in improving their grant writing knowledge and skills.

Technology is critical in the grant writing process. Web sites often offer the most up-to-date sources and comprehensive listings of potential funders. Tips and techniques, and many forms of proposal submission, are also online. Grant writers often use current research to support their project. Templates, spreadsheets, and word processing are also part of the relationship between grant writing and computers. To address the topic of grant writing, the Librarian and I designed a course-specific BI session that introduces students to resources like *The Chronicle of Philanthropy*, and Web sites such as the Foundation Center (www.fdncenter.org) and School Grants (www.schoolgrants.org). In addition, we guide them to the Web sites of various professional organizations such as Psi Chi (www.psichi.org), which often offer small grants specifically for students.

Librarians Can Assist With Computer-Based Projects

In addition to hands-on library instruction, professors and librarians can collaborate on computer-based projects such as designing Web pages, as well as online tutorials, courses, and course supplements. For example, through a cooperative effort, students in child and adolescent studies at CSU Fullerton learned information literacy skills through a specifically designed computer simulation that asked them to choose a daycare center by using Internet sources (Roth, 1999).

Some faculty-librarian teams have created multi-faceted, mega-Web sites for specific classes or disciplines. These sites may contain course- or program-specific data (e.g., syllabi), material on information literacy (e.g., evaluative criteria for use with print and Internet sources), and annotated references and links to selected sources (e.g., Web portals, databases, directories, other Web sites). They can also include links to multimedia resources, such as video or sound recordings. Sometimes there are complaints about technical problems or editorial choices on these sites, but most students appreciate this type of virtual collaboration.

Librarians Know Content Too: Children's Books and Beyond

With so much emphasis on scholarly material, it is easy to forget that many college librarians are quite knowledgeable about all kinds of literature. One of my colleagues, who teaches a class on reading, joined forces with the Behavioral Sciences Librarian to develop a "book talk" on popular children's literature. Both partners introduce, discuss, and display a selection of high quality books for children and adolescents. Everything from picture books to timely works for teens is included. Reference materials on children's literature also are covered.

Through this cooperative lesson, students learn about topics such as reading readiness, language development, age-appropriate themes and concerns, and children's humor. More specific issues, such as educational and therapeutic strategies with books, or literature for special populations, also can be addressed. This type of session could easily be tailored for courses on child development, educational psychology, or language and literacy. Talk with your librarians and learn if this type of instruction is available and if it could be helpful to the specific courses you teach.

College-Wide Collaborative Courses and Teaching

Although largely outside the scope of this article, it is important to note that some colleges have terrific, campus-wide collaborative teaching programs that would be of interest to many professors. Some teams are quite large and inclusive; professors, librarians, academic advisors, administrators, instructional technology professionals, and upper-level students may have a hand in planning and delivering instruction. Other groups are smaller and more specialized. For example, students on some campuses are treated to compelling, cooperatively taught courses, each developed by a faculty member, a writing lab instructor, and a librarian. If you teach general education or other Psychology courses, or if you collaborate with faculty in other fields, such as Biology or English, your librarians may be invaluable in your meeting course goals, and have creative ideas of assignments for your students.

Evaluate Your Work With Librarians Regularly: Are Your Students Learning What You Had Hoped?

Not everything works the first time, and some things never work. Therefore, faculty-librarian collaboration should be evaluated frequently and revised as needed. As with many instructional initiatives, this is not an easy process. Partners may want to examine their students and teams. Factors to investigate include students' attitudes and participation, and what they thought was useful or unhelpful, as well as their learning and achievement including appropriateness and caliber of sources used and general quality of projects and products. Some collaborators use an exam on library knowledge and a straightforward pre-test, post-test design; others distribute questionnaires on information literacy. A simple follow-up phone call or e-mail to students after a library instruction session may suit the needs of some teams. Partners may evaluate themselves in terms of the effectiveness of their interaction and instructional techniques.

Regardless of the method, any evaluation is likely to strengthen the growing belief that students can benefit greatly from the collective expertise of professors and librarians. The potential is tremendous when requests, comments, and suggestions flow freely between these professionals. There are many fine examples of collaboration in existence, and new ones are created every day. Faculty-librarian collaboration is a relatively new educational trend but, with practice and demonstrations of success, it will become tradition.

References and Recommended Readings

Buchanan, L. E., et al. (2002). Integrating information literacy into the virtual university: a course model. *Library Trends, 51*, 144-166.

Christensen, P. G. (1994). Using English department library liaisons in a term paper clinic: Reviving the scholar/librarian model. *Research Strategies, 12*, 196-208.

Ducas, A. M., et al. (2003). Toward a new enterprise: Capitalizing on the faculty/library partnership. *College & Research Libraries, 64*, 55-74.

Fister, B. (2002, June 14). Fear of reference. *The Chronicle of Higher Education,* B20.

Hardesty, L. (1995). Faculty culture and bibliographic instruction: An exploratory analysis. *Library Trends, 44*, 339-367.

McNeill, K., et al. (2003). Scholarship of teaching and librarians: building successful partnerships with faculty. *Georgian Library Quarterly, 39*(4), 4-8.

Murry, J. W., Jr., McKee, E. C., & Hammons, J. O. (1997). Faculty and librarian collaboration: The road to information literacy for graduate students. *Journal on Excellence in College Teaching, 8*, 107-121.

Rader, H. B. (2002).Teaching and assessing information skills in the twenty-first century: a global perspective. *Library Trends, 51*, 141-259.

Raspa, D., & Ward, D. (Eds.). (2000). *The collaborative imperative: Librarians and faculty working together in the information universe.* Chicago: Association of College and Research Libraries.

Roth, L. (1999). Educating the cut-and-paste generation. *Library Journal, 124*, 42-44.

Scott, W. (2000). Engelond: A model for faculty-librarian collaboration in the information age. *Information Technology and Librarians, 19*(1), 34-41.

Stamatopolos, A. (2000). An integrated approach to teaching research in a first-year seminar. *College Teaching, 48*(1), 33-35.

Stein, L. L., & Lamb, J. M. (1998). Not just another BI: Faculty-librarian collaboration to guide students through the research process. *Research Strategies, 16*, 29-39.

Stocker, R. L. *Class experience on credibility ranking of information sources.* [Online]. Available: www-lib.iupui.edu/itt/stocker.html

Thompson, G. B. (2002). Information literacy accreditation mandates: What they mean for faculty and librarians. *Library Trends, 51*, 218-241.

Integrating Service-Learning Into Psychology Courses

ELIZABETH WEISS OZORAK
Allegheny College

WHEN MY DEPARTMENTAL colleagues and I were in college, nobody talked about service-learning, although a few professors did something like it. Now, with the national emphasis on improving civic engagement among young people, service-learning has gone mainstream. A recent study of one liberal arts college found that over three quarters of the social science and humanities faculty thought that service-learning might be appropriate to a course they teach, although only about a quarter of them actually offered such a course (Rowe & Chapman, 1999). This new recognition of service-learning is supported by research demonstrating superior outcomes for students who engage in it, ranging from improved academic performance (Strage, 2000) to enhanced moral reasoning (Boss, 1994). From the Higher Education Research Institute's massive longitudinal study of over 22,000 college and university students, it is clear that although community service by itself produces some of these desirable effects, they are greater when the service takes place in the context of an academic course (Vogelgesang & Astin, 2000).

What Is Service-Learning?

A service-learning course is more than a course in which some community service occurs. Most educators agree that the term suggests course-based service that 1) addresses at least one significant learning objective for the course, 2) meets real community needs, and 3) is fully integrated into the course by means of reflective assignments, class discussion, or both. This last component seems to be especially important in realizing the academic gains that service-learning can produce.

What Are We Waiting For?

Aside from the need for more information, the most common reason faculty give for not teaching service-learning courses is that it would take too much time — their own time, and class time. As my father always says, time is the one non-renewable resource, and as a recent Teaching Tips article pointed out, most of us feel it is already too scarce (King, 2002). While it is true that setting up a service-learning course for the first time is labor-intensive, that is far less true for subsequent offerings of the same course, and even somewhat less true for other service-learning courses you may devise. Once you develop relationships with certain community partners, for example, you won't need to communicate with them as extensively or visit the site as often as you did the first time. You will know more about reflection, about how to craft assignments and integrate the students' experiences into class discussions and activities. So if you can get started and hang in there, that extra work involved in the initial set-up will pay off.

The argument about class time is more complicated. First, let's recognize that every learning activity takes time and that we are always making unconscious trade-offs, usually without data on the relative effectiveness of the activity. For example, research has offered mixed results on the efficacy of the lecture format for teaching, and yet most of us continue to lecture at least occasionally. While active learning of any kind takes more time than being told something or reading about it, students retain more of what they learn actively. Service-learning, therefore, takes its place along with lab exercises and research projects as a way for students to learn complex important lessons by doing as well as reading and thinking. I tell my students to think of the community as one of the texts for the course, a text they "read" by spending time in it and interacting with the people they encounter there.

That said, it is true that the time demands of a service project are more like those of a research project than those of a single lab exercise. There are a couple of ways to deal with this. One — the more usual — is to require the students to complete service hours outside of class, much as we would require them to collect data outside of class. In this case I find it works best to have the service sites suggest specific two- or three-hour slots and to have students sign up for a specific regular time and day of the week that fits with their schedule. The other approach is to build the service time into the class, as we build in time for a regular lab. In my department, lab courses typically meet twice a week for lecture and discussion and once or twice a week for lab, a model that works well for a service-learning course with a small number of students or where many people are needed at the same time (for example, after-school tutoring hours).

As for in-class time, service experiences make possible a number of attractive options. If a course uses discussion, it is easy to incorporate references to students' observations on site into discussion questions. Students can use their experiences as illustrations of the principles they are reading and talking about, much as we might introduce anecdotes to make a point. The advantage is that their own examples are more meaningful, and hence more memorable, for them than any we might provide. Also, students can generate descriptions of their experience that can function like case study material for analytical discussion in small groups. Upper level students might draw on their service experiences to generate research hypotheses, brainstorm data collection methods or propose interventions based on theories they've been learning.

Why Service-Learning in Psychology?

Of all the disciplines, psychology is one that lends itself most readily to service-learning, because both psychology and service are about people. It's hard to imagine a community where college students couldn't meet real needs — for tutoring, assistance with day care, preschool or after school programs, with the elderly, with at-risk youth, and so on. Likewise, it's easy to see how these experiences might help students understand human development, personality, social psychology, motivation and cognition. Indeed, psychology students have been doing this kind of service and learning for years, often under the auspices of an internship or as volunteers. What makes course-based service-learning distinctive is that important third element, opportunity for reflection, which is provided and monitored by the professor. And that's probably the element that most of us find unnerving to contemplate, since we have no experience using or evaluating that kind of teaching tool. Fortunately, there is a lot of help available, even for those who don't have staff on campus whose job it is to support service-learning (see Recommended Resources at the end of the article). Ideally, every psychology department should offer at least one service-learning course — more if size and faculty interest make it possible — and every student should be encouraged to take at least one.

Setting up a Service-Learning Course

Define Your Own Needs and Objectives First

Listing your learning goals can be helpful in developing or improving any course, but it is essential for effective service-learning. Once you have decided what you want your students to take away with them, it is easier to brainstorm possible ways to achieve these goals through work in the community. At the least, you will get a sense of the population and age group(s) that are most relevant to your course. There also may be specific skills you would like your students to acquire: observation, reporting, active listening, and so forth. If you are having trouble coming up with course objectives that are met or strengthened by sending students out into the community, then don't do it; consider putting service-learning into a different course. Since interest in the subject matter makes students especially receptive to service-learning, an upper-level course for majors with a well-matched service site can provide an ideal opportunity for students to benefit from all that service-learning has to offer. However, a general psychology class can also benefit from a service-learning component, as a recent article documents (Krechmar, 2001).

Meet Real Community Needs

It bears repeating that real service meets real needs. The community cannot be treated as just a laboratory for our students. It is no more ethical for our students to exploit community members for class learning than it is to exploit them through research. However, given the many genuine needs for volunteer help that most communities have, it is not difficult to identify a variety of genuinely useful roles that students might play. At the same time, it is important to recognize students' limitations. It is unfair to both students and community partners to put a student in a position she or he is unqualified to fill, and agencies will not always be aware of what students are qualified to do. It is up to us to be sure that the responsibilities associated with the service are ones at which our students can succeed.

Match the Site to the Needs

Now that you have identified your own needs and some likely needs in the community, you are ready to play matchmaker. At this point, if you are lucky enough to have an office of community service or support staff for service-learning, you will want to spend time with these people and pick their brains about specific sites that can meet both sets of needs and can accommodate your students without too much disruption. Clary and Snyder (1999) and their colleagues have shown that students respond best to community service when it meets their pre-existing motives. While you will not be able to gauge individual students' motives, you can make some educated guesses about students' motives as a group.

First, they will want to succeed in the course, and if what they are learning on site helps them achieve that goal, they will appreciate that the service was worthwhile, even if they didn't always enjoy it.

Second, learning more about the world through direct experience is nearly always one of the top two motives identified by those who volunteer. Sites that allow your students to learn or improve skills — as opposed to stuffing envelopes and painting fences, no matter how worthy the cause — will more clearly address both of these motives.

Check out the Site Yourself First

We would not, I hope, think of sending students into a chemistry lab without having ascertained that the experiment we were asking them to do was both safe and possible. For similar reasons, you should never send students to a site you have not visited yourself, and ideally you should spend some time talking to the supervisor, director, teacher or whoever is in charge at that site, recruiting them as your fellow educators. I go to sites equipped with a short outline of the course I hope to link with the site and a list of learning objectives. I discuss these with the supervisor and invite her or his input. I have also learned from experience that it's wise to discuss expectations of the supervisor's role in advance — for example, to find out whether students will ever work alone with agency clients. While this might not deter you from using the site, it's wise for both you and your students to know beforehand. Think about whether students need to have regular one-on-one contact with agency personnel and discuss that with the supervisor. You should also check with your administration about liability issues (in most cases, students will be covered under the same provisions already in place for internships and co-curricular community service).

More Is Better — Up to a Point

The emerging evidence suggests that up to 20-25 hours per semester produces a good service learning experience. More time in the community service may or may not produce better service-learning. A one-shot experience may be interesting and informative (or, alternatively, traumatic), but it does not offer students much chance to understand the workings of the site or to develop their own sense of efficacy. A service commitment of two to three hours a week for ten to twelve weeks is in line with the time commitment of, for example, a lab associated with a science course, and most students seem to have little difficulty working this into their schedule. However, a well-planned short involvement can certainly be worthwhile. It depends on your learning objectives. For students to develop skills or forge relationships will take longer than for them to observe social dynamics or learn what an agency does. Long-term service also requires more thought about transportation. My students have walked to their sites or have used public transportation, college-owned vehicles or carpools, and it has never been an insurmountable problem.

Orient Students Both to Service and to the Site

It seems not only fair but also wise to give students some sense of what to expect, in general and specifically from the site they will serve. I put the service component clearly in the course description and in the syllabus and discuss it in general terms on the first day of class so that those taking the course are aware that this is an important requirement. The next week or so, I have a class devoted to orienting the students to service and to the site or sites we will be using. Again, if you have support staff for service-learning, they may be able to help with this. I also find that it is extremely helpful to invite students with experience at the site(s) the class will be serving to participate in the orientation session. Their honesty and enthusiasm prepares the new recruits for what they will experience far better than my colleagues or I could do alone.

To Be There, or Not to Be There

Most professors assume that they will not accompany students to their service site, but you should think through the pros and cons of going with them at least the first time. I prefer to go with first year students, especially if the service is a one-time experience. I do not know if it diffuses their anxiety or not, but it allows me to see what goes on and sends the message that I take their service experience seriously. On the other hand, I do not go with my seniors, most of whom have spent more hours in the community than I have and are quite capable of fielding any curves they are thrown on the first, or any other, day. Think carefully about the site — since you have visited and spoken with the supervisor — and about your students in deciding whether or not to be present for any or all of their service experience. An alternative that has worked well for me and my colleagues is to use experienced upper level students as assistants who can orient inexperienced students and accompany them at least their first time or two on site.

Connect the Dots

When I began using service-learning in my classes, I assumed that the connections that were obvious to me were equally self-evident to my students. Wrong (even professors, it seems, have to outgrow some egocentrism). Especially at the beginning of the course, structure your reflection exercises and class discussion questions to guide students' attention to the kinds of connections you want them to make, without actually making the connections for them, since the joy of discovery is an important motivator for further inquiry. Questions like, "What are the requirements for a potential client to receive service from this agency?" "Where in town is the agency located? What else is in the neighborhood?" "Who talked the most in the meeting? Who talked least?" help students to be aware of key issues without giving them your interpretations. "Do you notice any patterns?" and later, "Compare this impression with your earlier ones. Do you see any differences?" draw the student from awareness into analysis.

Keep in Touch

Some students will have mundane experiences on site. Some will have very intense, even life-changing experiences, not necessarily pleasant ones. I use reflective journals as a way for to keep abreast of what students are encountering on site, and periodically I invite them to share their experiences in class. Since both of these happen only at intervals, I also have discovered that it is wise to encourage students explicitly to let me know if something significant happens — good or bad — in case the student needs some support in making sense of it. Although

I do not grade students' participation at the site, I also encourage site supervisors to let me know if students are not keeping their hours, are not doing the work they are given or are otherwise behaving in ways that are problematic for the agency. I require them to complete a certain number of hours, and if they complete less than that required number, they lose points, paralleling my approach to class attendance. Alternatively, you might make graded written assignments contingent on completion of a certain number of hours.

Checking Back With Site Personnel

Depending on the nature of the service and whether or not you were there, you may not need the site personnel's feedback in order to evaluate the students' academic work (after all, in service-learning, it's the learning that is graded, not the service). However, it's important to check back with on-site supervisors. They may have helpful comments or suggestions for future orientation or reflection. In addition, it reinforces the credibility of the partnership: you are in this together and you care what they think.

So How Do You Grade This Stuff?

Standard practice seems to be to require the service, but not to grade it, just as we might require attendance in class. I do grade the assignments that spin off their service, and after years of agonizing over how to respond to writing that feels more personal than the average psychology paper, I've evolved the following policy. Immediate reflection, whether in the form of a journal entry or a short (one or two page) response paper, is graded with a check, check-plus for outstanding work, check-minus for substandard work, and zero for late or missing work. I make comments mostly in the form of probing questions, such as: Why do you think she acted this way? What does this tell you about the challenges faced by this neighborhood? Papers and oral presentations that demand extensive incorporation of outside sources or other course material are graded on the same basis as any other such assignments, with the same standards for evidence, quality of argument, depth of interpretation and so on. Here again, I think it's helpful to think of the community experience as a text that students "read" and analyze with varying degrees of insight.

It Will Not Always Go Perfectly, and That's OK

Life is messy, and so is community service. There are a lot of variables beyond your control: people come in with attitudes and assumptions, communication sometimes breaks down, and as the saying goes, stuff happens. Not only is this inevitable, but it is usually okay. For example, one year, the teacher of an adult education program I had relied on for service opportunities in a particular course went on maternity leave at the last minute. The teacher who replaced her was manifestly incompetent, and as the semester wore on, the students became increasingly frustrated with how badly the program's clients were being served. We had some productive class discussions about what can go wrong with a basically good program administered with every good intention, and the students learned a lot. They also were profoundly impressed by the way in which the clients handled the situation, and that seemed to add something extra to the tutoring experience. In the long run, I think those students learned more than those whose site assignments went completely smoothly.

Conclusion

The most important pay-off, of course, from service learning, is what students learn. But how they learn it is also important. There is a compelling, no-holds-barred quality to community experience that makes what is learned there more memorable than anything they read or hear about second-hand. This also improves the quality of the time spent in class. Everyone, even the least confident student, has something to contribute to class discussion because everyone has had a unique experience. When students realize that the course material helps them make sense of these experiences, they also become more appreciative of what seemed purely academic before. This is the case in courses of all kinds. But perhaps psychology in particular should embrace service-learning because we have an interest in human welfare. As a discipline, we have a history of focusing on the well-being of individuals rather than of society as a whole. Following Isaac Prilleltensky's (1990) suggestion, perhaps it is time we engage students in *conscientization* — the process of becoming "[insightfully aware] of the socio-economic, political, and cultural circumstances which affect their lives as well as their potential capacity to transform that social reality" (p. 311). The students, the community — and we ourselves — stand to benefit immensely.

References and Recommended Readings

Boss, J. A. (1994). The effect of community service work on the moral development of college ethics students. *Journal of Moral Education, 23,* 183-198.

Campus Compact (2000). *Introduction to service-learning toolkit.* Providence, RI: Author.

Clary, E. G., & Snyder, M. (1999). The motivations to volunteer: Theoretical and practical considerations. *Current Directions in Psychological Science, 8,* 156-159.

Heffernan, K. (2001). *Fundamentals of service-learning course construction.* Providence, RI: Campus Compact.

Kendall, J. C., & Associates. (1990). *Combining service and learning* (Vol. 2). Raleigh, NC: National Society for Internships and Experiential Education (NSIEE).

King, R. M. (2004). Managing teaching loads and finding time for reflection and renewal. In B. Perlman, L. I. McCann, & S. H. McFadden (Eds.), *Lessons learned: Practical advice for the teaching of psychology* (Vol. 2) (pp. 3-10). Washington, DC: American Psychological Society.

Kretchmar, M. D. (2001). Service learning in a general psychology class: Description, preliminary evaluation, and recommendations. *Teaching of Psychology, 28,* 5-10.

Prilleltensky, I. (1990). Enhancing the social ethics of psychology: Towards a psychology at the service of social change. *Canadian Psychology, 31,* 310-319.

Rowe, M. M., & Chapman, J. G. (1999). Faculty and student participation and perceptions of service-learning outcomes. In J. R. Ferrari & J. G. Chapman (Eds.), *Educating students to make-a-difference* (pp. 83-96). Binghamton, NY: Haworth.

Strage, A. A. (2000). Service-learning: Enhancing student learning outcomes in a college-level lecture course. *Michigan Journal of Community Service Learning, 7,* 5-13.

Vogelgesang, L. J., & Astin, A. W. (2000). Comparing the effects of community service and service-learning. *Michigan Journal of Community Service Learning, 7,* 25-34.

Part IV

Pedagogical Skills

Rapport-Building: Creating Positive Emotional Contexts for Enhancing Teaching and Learning

WILLIAM BUSKIST
BRYAN K. SAVILLE
Auburn University

LIKE MOST OF US WHO read *Teaching Tips* columns, Sara Jamison takes her teaching seriously. She looks forward to being in the classroom, although if truth be told, some days are better than others. She prepares well-organized lectures; experiments with new in-class activities; poses challenging questions on her exams; worries about her students' intellectual growth; and reads voraciously, trying to stay atop her courses. Sara seems to go all out in her attempt to be an effective teacher.

Nonetheless, she feels uncomfortable in class. Sometimes she senses a chasm between herself and her students. Her students respect her, but they are ambivalent about whether they would take another course from her. Many don't feel comfortable expressing their ideas in class and others feel disconnected from Sara and her subject matter.

Of course, Sara Jamison is fictitious. We created her to reflect those of us who, despite our best efforts to become more effective teachers, come up short. Sara represents an amalgamation of those qualities reflective of effective teaching, but which alone don't make our teaching truly outstanding. Such qualities may be necessary for effective teaching, but not sufficient. So what is missing from Sara's teaching?

Sara's teaching seems to lack rapport, which the Random House Dictionary (1987) defines as "an especially harmonious or sympathetic connection" (p. 1601). Spanning the chasm between Sara and her students — or between any teacher and set of students — requires rapport-building: creating emotional connections between teacher and student and between student and subject matter. In this article, we reflect on the nature of rapport, offer simple suggestions for building rapport, and highlight some of the contributions that it brings to our teaching.

The Nature of Rapport and Its Influence on Effective Teaching

Rapport is tricky to understand. Perhaps that is why the voluminous literature on college and university teaching essentially ignores it. Since rapport is more of a contextual variable that sets the stage for effective teaching, it has been avoided in favor of other variables, such as methods of teaching, modes of testing, and techniques of assessing teaching effectiveness, which can be more readily conceptualized and manipulated. Nonetheless, it is prudent to consider the role of rapport in our work if for no other reason than to explore its possible contributions to effective teaching.

Rapport as an Emergent Property

Establishing "an especially harmonious or sympathetic connection" with students is not likely the result of any single act. Rather, rapport is more likely the result of many things done consistently right. In this sense, rapport may be thought of as an emergent property of teaching, or, for that matter, any kind of social relationship. In general, we must do two things for rapport to develop. First, we must extend students a warm and friendly invitation to join the "community of learning" that we attempt to establish in our classrooms on the first day of class. Second, we must adopt this demeanor every day afterwards, in or out of class, and irrespective of the myriad problems that may develop over the course of the term.

Toward this end, Joseph Lowman argued that teachers must minimize the extent to which students experience negative emotions, such as anxiety and anger, and must attempt to create positive emotions in students such as self-efficacy and positive self-worth. This approach will help students feel that their teacher cares about them, encourage them to become motivated to do their best work, and think of their teacher in highly positive ways. The positive effects of rapport do not stop with students — they affect teachers as well. As Lowman noted his 1995 book, *Mastering the Techniques of Teaching* "[M]ost college teachers enjoy classes more when they have good personal relationships with their students, and this satisfaction has a beneficial effect on the quality of their instruction" (p. 98).

Rapport as an Alliance Based on Trust

Another way of conceptualizing rapport between teachers and students is to think of it in the same way many therapists view the "therapeutic alliance" between themselves and their clients. This alliance is marked by four elements: 1) the extent to which client and therapist agree on the goals of therapy, 2) the client's ability to work toward those goals, 3) the therapist's empathy toward the client and the therapist's involvement in the therapeutic process, and 4) the emotional connection between client and therapist and the client's commitment to therapy (Gaston, 1990).

Mapping this model onto the teacher-student relationship, we might view rapport as follows: 1) the extent to which students accept or "buy into" the goals the teacher has spelled out to the class, 2) the student's ability to work toward these goals, 3) the teacher's ability to care genuinely for students and to nurture their learning, and 4) the student and teacher "connecting" emotionally and students' motivation to participate actively in their education. As such, rapport is both process and outcome. It is a process because it involves a series of steps a teacher takes that must occur for rapport to develop. It is an outcome because it emerges only when the appropriate components are present in teaching situations, leading to more effective teaching.

Central to this alliance between student and teacher is trust. Consider the point that Stephen Brookfield makes in his 1990 book, *The Skillful Teacher*:

> Trust between teachers and students is the affective glue that binds educational relationships together. Not trusting teachers has several consequences for students. They are unwilling to submit themselves to the perilous uncertainties of new learning. They avoid risk. They keep their most deeply felt concerns private. They view with cynical reserve the exhortations and instructions of teachers. (p. 162)

Clearly, trust is present in the alliance that forms between clients and effective therapists and between students and effective teachers. Whether in therapy or in teaching, such trust contributes to building rapport, enhancing motivation, and stimulating learning. If we wish students to join us as members of the community of learning, we must demonstrate to our students that we can be trusted.

Rapport as Connectedness

Akin to the notion of alliance is Parker J. Palmer's concept of "connectedness." In *The Courage to Teach* (1998), he argued that good teachers strive to forge connections between themselves and their subject matter and between themselves and their students. Such connections are the result of the individual "identity and integrity" of the teacher as it is expressed through whatever medium the teacher uses to teach. In Palmer's words (1998):

> [I]n every class I teach, my ability to connect with students, and to connect them with the subject, depends less on the methods I use than on the degree to which I know and trust my selfhood — and am willing to make it available and vulnerable in the service of learning. (p. 10)

Thus, teaching reveals our humanity, how we choose to define ourselves in our work, and the manner in which we relate to our subject matter, to our students, and to the larger world around us. If one wishes to "connect" with students — to establish rapport with them — one must expose at least part of one's self to one's students. To the extent that we are successful in this endeavor, we create an environment conducive to effective teaching, and by implication, effective learning.

Rapport Unveiled

In our view, rapport is a positive emotional connection among students, teacher, and subject matter that emerges from the manner in which the teacher constructs the learning environment. Much of the framework is provided by the teacher's disposition toward students, the subject matter, the educational process, and, in general, life. To the extent that student and teacher unite to achieve course goals, the learning environment favors increased student receptivity to the teacher and subject matter. Central to the development of such an alliance is the teacher's sense of self, as reflected in such characteristics as trust and respect, and a willingness to involve students in the learning process.

Student Perspectives on Rapport

Attempting to understand rapport by placing it within this sort of conceptual scheme is only half the story, and perhaps the less important half at that. The other half, of course, is knowing how students experience rapport.

To gain a bit of insight into this matter, we surveyed several hundred Auburn University undergraduates enrolled in an introductory level psychology course and asked them to tell us three things: 1) the extent to which they have experienced rapport in their classes; 2) the things that teachers do to develop rapport with them; and 3) how rapport affects their academic behavior.

Only slightly more than half of the students reported that they had experienced rapport with a professor. These students told us that the most common teacher behaviors contributing to the development of rapport were, in order: showing a sense of humor; availability before, after, or outside of class; encouraging class discussion; showing interest in them, knowing students' names; sharing personal insights and experiences with the class; relating course material in everyday terms and examples; and understanding that students occasionally have problems arise that inadvertently hinder their progress in their courses. Finally, the students also told us that the most common positive effects of rapport on their academic behavior were, in order: to increase their enjoyment of the teacher and subject matter; to motivate them to come to class more often, and to pay more attention in class. Thus, rapport seems to facilitate both student motivation for learning and their enjoyment of the course, and enhances student receptivity to what is being taught.

Rapport-Building

How might we build rapport with our students? Try any or all of the following suggestions for developing rapport with your students:

- ◆ Learn to call your students by name.
- ◆ Learn something about your students' interests, hobbies, and aspirations.
- ◆ Create and use personally relevant class examples.
- ◆ Arrive to class early and stay laten — and chat with your students.
- ◆ Explain your course policies and why they are what they are.
- ◆ Post and keep office hours.
- ◆ Get on line — use e-mail to increase accessibility to your students.
- ◆ Interact more, lecture less; emphasize active learning.
- ◆ Reward student comments and questions with verbal praise.
- ◆ Be enthusiastic about teaching and passionate about your subject matter.
- ◆ Lighten up; crack a joke now and then.
- ◆ Be humble and, when appropriate, self-deprecating.

- Make eye contact with each student without staring, glaring, or flaring.
- Be respectful.
- When all else fails, smile a lot, students will think you like them and your job.

Remember that any one of these actions alone is unlikely to build rapport. Instead, combinations of these behaviors implemented consistently over time produce the synergistic effects necessary for rapport to emerge in your teaching. How will you know when rapport is established? Probably the most reliable metric is the behavior of your students toward you. If they approach you with questions, comments, and personal remarks; smile or laugh during class; seek you out during your office hours, ask your advice about something; tell you that they liked a demonstration or lecture or that they are enjoying class, you can bet that you have developed some degree of rapport with your students.

Some Final Thoughts

Matters often become especially clear when we look at them from an alternative perspective. In this case, we might consider the importance of rapport-building as creating a context for enhancing teaching and learning by contrasting it with one of its antitheses, alienation. The Random House Dictionary (1987) defines "alienate" as "to make indifferent or hostile" (p. 53). Thus, sure ways to alienate your students would be to do just the opposite of the suggestions given above for building rapport: don't bother to learn your students' names; don't bother to learn anything about your students; don't bother to relate psychology to your students' lives; be late to class and rush out as soon as the period is over; don't explain your course polices; don't post your office hours, or better yet, post them, but don't keep them; make no attempt to enhance lines of communication with your students; assume your students are passive receptacles waiting to be filled with your intelligence; discourage students' questions and comments (if your students insist on speaking, ignore them, or even better, point out that their comments are lame); show students that psychology is boring and that you would rather do something other than teach; be stern, serious, and intolerant of lightheartedness; avoid eye contact, be arrogant, condescending, and narcissistic, and finally, scowl. If these don't work, then simply treat your students as if they are morons.

From this vantage, it is easy to see how rapport-building

contributes to creating a context for establishing a positive emotional classroom atmosphere and helping students learn. After all, most students view their courses as much more than mere intellectual exercises. They often develop strong feelings about their courses and their teachers, which may be positive or negative, depending on whether those teachers take steps to build rapport or to alienate them. By not actively seeking to build rapport, we may unwittingly alienate our students.

The risk of unintentionally alienating students is particularly high in large classes — say those of 50 or more students. There seem to be just too many names, faces, and lives to get to know; thus, we might assume from the outset that building rapport in a class like this is impossible. Au contraire! Most of the "do's" listed above can be implemented easily regardless of class size. After all, behaviors such as making good eye contact, telling a joke or two, or exuding passion for one's subject matter is not constrained by how many students we have before us.

Lowman's (1995) point is on target — the classroom is an emotionally charged environment. Effective teaching involves tinkering with that environment so that we maximize the chances that students will learn from our courses. Rapport-building is one way to hedge our bets that we will be successful in this endeavor. Rapport may indeed be what is missing from Sara Jamison's otherwise exemplary teaching repertoire.

References and Recommended Readings

Brookfield, S. D. (1990). *The skillful teacher*. San Francisco: Jossey-Bass.

Gaston, L. (1990) The concept of alliance and its role in psychotherapy: Theoretical and empirical considerations. *Psychotherapy, 27*, 143-153.

Lowman, J. (1995). *Mastering the techniques of teaching* (2nd Ed.). San Francisco: Jossey-Bass.

Palmer, P. J. (1998). *The courage to teach: Exploring the inner landscape of a teacher's life*. San Francisco: Jossey-Bass.

Perlman, B., McCann, L. I., & McFadden, S. H. (Eds.). (1999). *Lessons learned: Practical advice for the teaching of psychology*. Washington, DC: American Psychological Society.

The Random House Dictionary of the English Language (2nd Ed.). (1987). New York: Random House.

Safran, J. D., & Muran, J. C. (Eds.). (1998). *The therapeutic alliance in brief psychotherapy*. Washington, DC: American Psychological Association.

Acting Lessons for Teachers: Using Performance Skills in the Classroom

CATHY SARGENT MESTER
ROBERT T. TAUBER
Pennsylvania State University-Erie

WHO AMONG US HAS NOT come back from a class or two (usually around mid-semester) and sighed, "my students just didn't seem with it today?" It is very disheartening because we feel at a loss to remedy the situation. The good news is that not only is this situation not terminal, but also that you and I as teachers do have options — the class can be saved! The key to doing so often lies in the craft of the actor.

Student Motivation

We are right to be concerned about student motivation for certainly no one can learn if not motivated to attend to the subject matter. Remember, Benjamin Bloom's (1956) taxonomy puts valuing information after attending to it. The factors affecting student motivation include both elements specific to each particular student as well as elements of classroom climate. It is the latter over which the teacher has some control. We cannot change the students' family situation, personal goals, intelligence, diet or sleep habits; but we can change the atmosphere for learning that is created in our classrooms. We can accomplish that by using a tool proven successful by so many hardworking faculty members — teacher enthusiasm.

The Pedagogy of Teacher Enthusiasm

Enthusiasm as a teaching tool has often been questioned by educators who perceive enthusiasm to smack of insincerity or a lack of seriousness about one's academic endeavor. If you think of enthusiasm as disingenuous clowning then you are right to conclude it does not belong in the classroom. But that's not what we mean by enthusiasm — rather, we refer to allowing yourself to convey the true zest for learning that you feel. You are fascinated by your subject matter or you wouldn't be teaching it! To help unlock that fascination and zest, a few expressive, creative devices (learned from the world of acting) can be used and in so doing, will catch your students' attention and facilitate learning.

Vocal Animation

First among these expressive tools is vocal animation. A teacher's personal infatuation with his/her subject matter will be evident in natural variations in vocal tone: volume, pitch, rate and quality. If you have developed a habit of allowing only minimal variation in your voice, it is more difficult for the students to realize how much you value your subject matter and, therefore, less likely that they will value it. Greater overall vocal vigor then, invites students to tune in to this very exciting material to be learned.

In addition to attracting student attention, changes in your vocal tone can serve as signposts drawing the students to the most important elements in your commentary. Particular vocal devices in the "signpost" category include:

- ♦ Setting off a phrase or word with strategic pauses.
- ♦ Slowing down the articulation of the most important word or phrase.
- ♦ Speaking the most important words at a markedly lower pitch.
- ♦ Using rising inflection to signal the climactic point.
- ♦ Speaking in a noticeably quieter tone to make the students listen more closely.

A teacher can develop greater vocal vigor and come to use it naturally by the same means you would develop physical vigor — by exercise! Our voices are a resource that can be perpetually ready to serve our needs if we practice stretching our expressiveness through taped vocal exercises such as those used by professional singers. Such exercises need not consume much time since they can be done while doing something else like driving, vacuuming, watching television or playing with your dog. For instance, try reciting a memorized poem or song lyrics in a James Earl Jones or Vanessa Redgrave style or to a different beat. By regularly stretching your vocal expression, it will become more naturally varied and strong, allowing you to develop a classroom tone that can help to hold and focus your students' attention.

Physical Animation

Similarly, a physically dynamic teacher using the tools of eye contact, facial expression, gestures and postural changes commands the class' attention. With eye contact, for instance, teachers establish that they have something important to say and trust the students to attend to it. Gestures and expressions that reinforce, emphasize, encourage and clarify are tools that any teacher can benefit from using.

In this respect, our profession can learn from that of the stage actor who realizes that the playwright's written words alone convey only part of the intended message — the message is completed by gestures and facial expressions that add the all — important connotation. For instance, when asking a question of the class, you should have a look of positive expectation on your face and your gestures should be open, signaling to the students that you really want to hear their answers. The teacher whose arms are crossed while awaiting an answer is perceived by the students as intimidating, not encouraging.

The most beneficial step you can take to improve your physical animation is to videotape yourself teaching. Set the recorder up and just let it run so that you capture a full class without the intimidation of having a cameraperson following your every move. Then look at the tape and ask yourself if you could stay alert and interested during this class. If not, try one of the following:

- ◆ Stretching exercises before going to the class
- ◆ Minimizing the extent of any lecture notes to which you may refer
- ◆ Using visual aids and referencing them with appropriate gestures
- ◆ Most importantly, concentrating mentally on the intrigue of the subject matter, allowing your natural exuberance to reach out to the students

If your tape revealed yourself as a dynamic speaker, Bravo!

Using the Classroom Space

One of the easiest things we can do to revitalize our students' attention is to use the entire space of the classroom as our stage, rather than just the lectern or the front of the room. Some students like to melt anonymously into the back wall or hide behind the football lineman so that they don't have to feel involved in your communication. We can't let that happen!

Our choices are two: either move the students by rearranging their seating periodically or move ourselves. The latter is easier! Think of the whole classroom as space you can use. The instructor, for instance, who explained the concept of right-brained versus left-brained by first standing in the middle of one side of the room and then walking across to the middle of the opposite side not only reinforced the concept visually, but also held the students' attention by moving into their space.

As you respond to student comments, move toward the area of the room where the speaker is. Such movement conveys that you are mentally engaging the speaker and captures the visual attention of all the other students in that section of the room. Regular movement of this sort is particularly important in larger classes when we need to work harder to relate to all of the students, encouraging them to feel a personal involvement and responsibility in the class — a motivation to learn!

Props

For many instructors of psychology, the use of props may be second nature. It's a good thing it is because props are great attention-getters! Of course, they also clarify and make messages memorable. A colleague distributes modeling clay to her students to they can build models of the brain rather than just talk about its anatomy; another uses magazine ads to illustrate gender stereotyping in society; and yet a third involves small children in the class on developmental stages. These are all great devices and we have all experienced their positive benefits in capturing student attention and opening their minds to learning.

These are a few reminders of the do's and don'ts of using props. The criterion in every instance is to select and use props that enhance the lesson, not detract from it.

- ◆ Do select props large enough for all to see at once.
- ◆ Do keep the prop simple enough so that students clearly realize its intent.
- ◆ Do rehearse with the prop to make sure it works as intended.
- ◆ Do make sure the prop is clearly pertinent to the lesson.

- Don't use props that have to be passed among the students to be appreciated.
- Don't show the prop any earlier than or any longer than when you are talking about it.
- Don't use live animals unless absolutely necessary.
- Don't use props that require significant darkening of the room for full visibility.

That last don't is specifically applicable to overhead transparencies, slides and computer graphics. You should never transfer all of your notes to slides and just talk through them for an entire class period. In doing so, you lose that vital direct relationship with the students and create a nonresponsive environment, both of which are highly demotivating. Instead, if you want to use transparencies or PowerPoint slides, use just a few to highlight the most important points of the lesson, each with just a few words per slide to encourage the students to interact with you as you explain instead of just focusing their entire concentration on copying the notes. Again, the goal of using slides, or any prop, is to stimulate the students' attention and motivation for learning.

Humor

Another reflection of our enthusiasm for the active process of learning is the occasional use of humor. In the form of a pun, joke, anecdote or cartoon, supportive humor can enliven a lesson. One award-winning psychology professor explains that he often makes reference to his imaginary family (all of whom have funny names and even funnier occupations) as examples of particular concepts. His experience has been that the students remember the concept longer if illustrated by the antics of his imaginary cousin Orval, the tuba tuner, than the same antics of his sister Nancy, a pediatrician.

If you are not comfortable with your skill as a humorist, it's best not to go out too far on this limb. You can, however, very safely begin a file of humorous stories or cartoons you find pertinent to your field for use on transparencies or to begin a particular dayís lesson. To be effective, the humor need only be pertinent, brief, tasteful and nonhostile. My quick retelling of our dog's misadventures as a chaser of chipmunks never fails to strike a chord with the students — they can relate to the incident, find it easy to stay tuned to a funny dog story and easily internalize its point about the dangers of mistaking illusion for reality. Thus, the humor motivates their attention and stimulates their learning.

Suspense and Surprise

A surefire way to avoid student boredom is to keep them in suspense. Like the cliffhanger endings on Friday afternoon soap operas, a suspenseful or surprising classroom condition makes the students eagerly anticipate its resolution. Students wanting to hear more is motivation personified.

Suspense can be accomplished by simple things like:
♦ Keeping a particular day's activities secret.
♦ Asking students to do an assignment seemingly irrelevant to the class.
♦ Announcing a pop quiz.
♦ Masking the props set up as class begins.

Any one of these will make the class curious enough to stay tuned.

The suspense and surprise could, however, be a more elaborate concoction such as the instructor who taught almost a full class period on the topic of fear, gave the students fifteen minutes of free time and then, after only five minutes, looked up angrily and yelled "Shut up!" He then proceeded to debrief their reactions to his surprising outburst as representative of the body's natural emotional and physical fear response. This example of enthusiastic teaching was shared by a student three years after the event — its vividness in his memory is testimony to its strategic impact as a motivating device.

Role Playing

The most dramatic of the devices discovered in our research of enthusiastic teaching was that of role playing by the teacher. Involving students in role play exercises is fairly common, particularly in the social sciences; but role playing by the teacher is less frequent and quite powerful in motivating student attention.

Role playing requires fairly extensive planning potentially involving costuming, makeup, staging and scripting. The result can be quite riveting as students see a leading figure in their field of study coming alive before them, perhaps even engaging them in dialogue. Costuming can be as easy as wearing a special hat or as elaborate as coming to class in full Elizabethan or colonial dress. Psychology instructors have been known to portray Skinner, Rogers, Maslow or the characters of the famous prisoners' dilemma, all a memorable impact on students.

While this strategy may be suited especially well to a limited number of classes, there is one role we can all try to develop for the benefit of our students — the role of an enthusiastic teacher.

The Lesson of Enthusiasm

To get started on the path to achieving a more productively enthusiastic teaching persona, you need to analyze your present teaching style. This can be accomplished either by asking a trusted colleague to observe your teaching or by videotaping yourself. If the analysis suggests room for improvement, the best and easiest place to begin is with the exercises suggested earlier to enhance vocal and physical expressiveness since these tools can be used in any teaching situation. Stretch your voice! Work with Cyrano de Bergerac's soliloquy "Call that a nose," for instance. It is also appropriate to begin to incorporate movement about the room early in your efforts as that also is a tool that can be used anywhere and requires a comfortably small change in your current teaching habits. As you develop ease with these more enthusiastic strategies, work your way up to experimenting with props, surprises, humor and role playing.

Many of us, through either being so new to the profession that we lack confidence or so experienced that we lack sustained energy, can benefit from mastering the role of a motivating persona in the classroom. Today's generation of college students is not so strongly motivated by the sheer excitement of learning as previous generations — we have to "win them over." Winners of teaching awards at large and small colleges and universities have testified again and again that what works for them is accompanying their mastery of content with a set of dramatic devices that convey sufficient enthusiasm to establish themselves as credible and their subject matter as fascinating. As one award-winning instructor put it, "I use these strategies because I choose to make the learning environment come alive and make the lessons learned last beyond the next test!"

References and Recommended Readings

Bloom, B. S. (1956). *Taxonomy of educational objectives: The classification of educational goals.* New York: Longmans and Green.
Browne, M. N., & Keeley, S. M. (1985). Achieving excellence: Advice to new teachers. *College Teaching, 33,* 78-83.

Dembo, M. H. (1988). *Applying educational psychology in the classroom.* New York: Longman.

Javidi, M., Downs, V. C., & Nussbaum, J. F. (1988). A comparative analysis of teachers' use of dramatic style behaviors at higher and secondary education levels. *Communication Education, 37,* 278-288.

Lowman, J. (1995). *Mastering the techniques of teaching* (2nd ed.). San Francisco: Jossey-Bass.

Tauber, R. T., & Mester, C. S. (1994). *Acting lessons for teachers: Using performance skills in the classroom.* Westport, CT: Praeger.

Creating Cooperative Learning Environments

DIANE F. HALPERN
California State University-San Bernardino

COOPERATIVE LEARNING IS:

- A waste of time.
- A great way to avoid the hard work of lecturing.
- An ideal paradigm for lovers of social loafing.
- Another left-wing harebrained idea advocated by aging hippies.
- Some or all of the above.

If you responded like many psychology professors, you agree that there is too much material to cover in your classes to waste time on cooperative learning, and you might want to add that students paid to learn from a real professor, not another (equally ignorant) student. Lecturing works, so "if it ain't broke, don't fix it."

In fact, lecturing does work well for some educational goals. Lecturing is a *high baud rate* mode of instruction, which means that a large amount of information is transferred in a relatively short period of time.

If the instructor's goal is to convey basic information so that students can repeat or paraphrase material that the instructor spoke in class (and wrote on the chalkboard) lecturing may be a good approach.

Why You Should Consider Using Cooperative Learning (CL)

Many (maybe most) faculty believe lecturing is synonymous with teaching. After all, this is the way many of us were taught and the idea that teaching is lecturing is often supported by the culture of our departments, but the empiricists among us will be happy to learn that there is a solid body of research showing that a judicious mix of pedagogies can help students achieve a variety of educational goals.

Although lecturing appears to foster effective learning when it is assessed soon after the lecture, it is not an effective way to achieve other learning goals, such as the ability to apply knowledge in real world settings or recall information in a novel context. In other words, information learned via lectures does not transfer well — the *real* goal of learning. Lecturing is also a poor method for fostering long-term retention.

Cooperative learning offers an alternative or supplement to the one-way communication that typifies lectures and may be used occasionally or more frequently depending upon the nature of the class and the instructor's goals (see the Teaching Tips which follow).

CL is an umbrella term for a variety of educational approaches that involve joint intellectual efforts by students or students and instructors together. In CL, students are actively involved with the information being learned and interactively involved with other learners. Students work together on tasks that require them to explore, apply, question, and generate information. With CL, much of the responsibility for making learning happen shifts from the instructor to the student, where it rightfully belongs. The large literature on cooperative learning clearly shows that it is highly effective in achieving long-term learning objectives. In a meta-analytic review of 226 studies that compared cooperative and individualistic learning settings, cooperative learning produced greater *individual* achievement than competitive approaches or individualistic approaches (Johnson, Johnson, & Smith, 1998). There is ample evidence that it works in achieving many important learning goals.

Critical Features for Successful Cooperative Learning

I recall with painful clarity my early and not-too-successful attempts to use CL. I learned the hard way that CL is more than putting students into groups and telling them to work together (much like the character on *Saturday Night Live* who tells viewers to "talk amongst yourselves" while she busies herself with other things). CL activities need to be carefully planned, highly organized, and well-structured, with clearly defined subtasks that are relevant to the educational objectives. In order to be successful, cooperative learning activities must incorporate at least six critical features. (There may be others.)

To be most successful CL assignments should include the following characteristics.

Positive Interdependence

Each student depends on the other group members to successfully complete the task. This feature fosters the power of positive peer interactions — students are motivated to achieve at a high level because their classmates are depending on them. An example of positive interdependence can be found in *jigsaw* tasks, a scheme for specifying groups that gets its name from the popular puzzles that require different-shaped pieces to fit together to create the whole. With jigsaws, students are assigned to small groups, with each group specializing in one aspect of a problem or issue.

For example, in a class on theories of personality, different groups would be formed for each major theorist. Group members work cooperatively to gather information on their topic and then share what they have learned about their assigned theorist with each other. The extent to which students are provided with guiding questions and the teacher's specific instructions for each student depend on the level of the class, student ability, and the goal of the activity.

The groups then reform with one member from each of the original groups in every new group (e.g., one person who learned about Freud's views on personality, one person who learned about Skinner's views, etc.). Students in the newly formed groups now teach the others about the theorist they studied. Groups continue to mix with one expert on each theorist in each group.

Everyone's learning depends on the effort and success of every other student because students are responsible for teaching and assessing each other. As the groups change members, everyone becomes more knowledgeable about all of the theorists. This activity can be concluded by having students make comparisons among the theorists and by asking them to respond to particular case studies using several theoretical frameworks.

Individual Accountability

Every student's learning is assessed individually. There is disagreement in the literature about the desirability of individual accountability, but I believe that it alleviates a major problem commonly found in group work — inequitable distribution of the work load. Generalizing from my personal experience, every classroom has at least one student who thinks loafer is not just a type of shoe. Consider the jigsaw example just described. Individual accountability can easily be incorporated by grading each student's paper separately or by giving individual exams of any type.

Some professors like to take a middle-ground on this issue and mix individual grades with bonuses or other grading plans that depend on the performance of all group members.

For example, instructors who want to assess gains in students' knowledge or skills might give a pretest at the start of the semester. For long term assignments where groups remain intact for most of the semester, it would be easy to provide a bonus (e.g., an additional 10 percent of total possible points) to everyone in those groups where every student shows a pretest-posttest gain of at least 20 percent.

In this way, students are motivated to assist each other in showing educational gains, but the major portion of their grade depends on their own work products.

When CL activities incorporate frequent self-assessment and informal assessments by other group members, students become better at making judgments about what and how much they know. Practice tests and problem solving groups provide practice with self-assessments, especially when they are reviewed and discussed as part of a CL activity.

Appropriate Assignment to Groups

Heterogeneous groups allow stronger students to model their thinking and learning processes for weaker students. Instructors can create heterogeneous groups by frequently using group work and assigning students to groups in ways that ensure many different mixings of group members. Statistics classes present a good opportunity to follow standard lecture-type instruction with group problem solving. Positive interdependence can be fostered by stipulating that the group assignment is not complete until everyone in the group can solve the problems.

As students teach and learn from each other, the students who are modeling the thinking process must actively reflect on the strategies they are using to solve problems. In this way, the usually tacit process of solving problems is made explicit. The use of heterogeneous ability groups is consistent with Bandura's classic studies of self-efficacy, in which he found that modeling by someone who is similar to you can shape beliefs about your own ability and can increase motivation to achieve a goal.

Teacher as Coach or Facilitator

The instructor's role changes when she moves from in front of the podium to walk around the room and work with students on their CL activities. With CL, the teacher is a valuable member of a learning community who assists students in becoming more independent learners. Student-teacher interactions increase because instructors need to monitor the progress of small groups to determine that they are on track.

I find that the enhanced personal involvement with students is one of the most important benefits of CL. As students become better at assessing their own learning, the instructor becomes more like a learning coach and less like a judge and (sometimes) executioner whose sole purpose is to grade students.

Attention to Social Skills

Expectations about behavior in learning groups are made explicit and often are graded. I have used signed contracts as a way of emphasizing my belief that the ability to work well in groups is an important educational outcome in psychology classes.

Every class member must agree to allow others to state their views without interruptions; disagreements must center on the content of the statement, not the speaker; and conclusions need to be examined for sound reasoning and evidence.

Social and cognitive skills operate jointly in the real world that exists outside the classroom; they need to be practiced together in the classroom. Many psychology classes are minefields for social and political controversies. Why are there group differences on intelligence tests? Is homosexuality normal? How could criminal behavior be inherited? Students must grapple with alternative points of view. CL activities make the thinking and learning process more visible and shared, often forcing students to see alternative ways of constructing meaning and interpreting information. The collision of world views, especially among heterogeneous group members, can reduce the powerful effects of confirmation bias and offers the hope of reducing prejudices.

Interactive Problem-Solving and Discussion

CL activities are responsive to group members. Learners do not act in parallel or respond sequentially to each other. The dynamic interaction among group members is critical, so that the action of one student provides direction for the response of another. The changing nature of technology has created changes in how students learn and challenge our older notions of face-to-face interaction.

CL groups are forming on Web sites and via other media so that people in distant places can function as a cooperative group, without occupying the same room or even working at the same time. Web-based learning sites now allow CL groups with members from different countries contributing solutions to problems or adding information to a data pool.

Cognitive Principles Applied in Cooperative Learning

Cooperative learning is not a unitary technique; there are endless varieties and possibilities for cooperative learning activities. They all work because they utilize basic principles in learning and thinking. These are the same principles that we teach about in many psychology classes (e.g., cognitive psychology, learning, motivation, intellectual development, group processes, and developmental psychology) then ignore when we teach about them.

Increased time on task. This is a basic principle in learning: the more time and effort students put into learning, the greater the probability that quality learning will occur. In general, students spend more time working actively with cooperative learning groups.

Increased motivation. In general, students are more motivated to succeed. Students depend on each other to complete an assignment, a fact that usually increases motivation to achieve at a high level.

More immediate feedback. Students receive more feedback on their learning and thinking and they receive it with more immediacy than in traditional learning settings.

Thinking and learning are modeled as processes. The process of how to think about a complex issue and how to learn is modeled and practiced. Thinking and learning become dynamic processes instead of learning outcomes.

Shared knowledge and skills. When tasks are complex, the knowledge, skills, and experiences of group members can be shared so that the collective knowledge of the group can achieve goals that would elude any single member.

Connected knowledge structures. Information is processed more deeply when students are required to process it in a meaningful way. Cognitive psychologists conceptualize meaning as constructed within a web of related concepts. A concept or idea becomes meaningful when it is connected to many other concepts in memory. When students are required to elaborate information that is being learned, the result is improved comprehension and a greater likelihood that it will be recalled successfully with appropriate retrieval cues.

A Sampler of Cooperative Learning Activities

Once faculty become comfortable with using cooperative learning, almost any learning activity can involve CL. You can start with short activities that adhere to a subset of the six critical features listed above. As you become more comfortable with CL, you'll wonder why you didn't try it sooner. Here are some brief suggestions to get novices started and to encourage you to give CL a try.

A good CL activity with which to begin is a simple but effective activity that can easily be incorporated into any large lecture class. Stop in the middle of class and have students summarize the topic to another student who checks on their comprehension. Then have the student who was the comprehension *checker* present a brief summary to a third student. This is something every instructor can do in his or her next class session in eight-10 minutes. Students can feel the difference in learning when they generate a summary. Active retrieval of information from memory is an excellent learning activity. There is no need to grade short activities like this.

Present a brief problem to solve. This approach is a natural in statistics classes where lecture-type instruction can be followed by small group problem solving. Correct solutions can be put on the board by the entire group which then explains the problem solving process and solution to the rest of the class. Be sure that students are providing clear and complete explanations so that they practice oral presentation skills along with shared problem solving.

Use jigsaw groups in a library assignment in which students need to find information about a complex topic. Consider, for example, the question of how to treat alcoholism. Groups of students can be assigned different treatment methods and asked to find information about each — abstinence programs, family interventions, drug treatment programs, behavior therapies, etc. Given the complex nature of alcoholism, most undergraduate students will need careful guidelines on how to find appropriate information, what makes information credible, what the underlying assumptions are for each approach, and how to read original research. Each group could be asked to suggest one or two readings on their topic that everyone in the class should read. After gathering and summarizing information within each topical group, new groups are formed consisting of one member from each original group. Information is synthesized in these mixed groups and then with the entire class. The instructor needs to carefully monitor and guide the activity and bring it together with questions and summaries contributed, in part, by the students.

Post and respond to questions via listservs, bulletin boards, e-mail, Web sites. We need to take advantage of the new multimedia possibilities for CL. Group learning activities can be found on many psychology-related learning sites and instructors can create their own on the Internet. Instructors can pose a question every week on a class listserv and require that every student respond to some number of them. Listservs require their own set of social skills that need to be developed and practiced. Students can be required to respond to postings from other students as well as the one from the instructor. This sort of CL seems best suited for pass/fail grading, but almost any grading scheme could work depending on the nature of the question and the time and effort requirements.

Use strategies that generate creative responses such as brainstorming, stating a problem in multiple ways, and listing pros and cons. Many psychology instructors want to enhance their students' abilities to think critically. One way to do this is to teach them how to recognize and approach problems. For example, instead of asking for a solution to a problem, present a scenario and ask small groups of students to state the problem in several different ways. Compare their responses with that of other groups who are asked to brainstorm (provide an uncensored list of ideal solutions) and others who are asked to list interesting aspects of the problem. Compare the types of responses that were produced with these different approaches to problem solving. Finally, provide another complex scenario and ask them how they went about devising a solution.

Present an applied problem and have students list three questions they would like to be able to ask about the problem to guide their thinking. Have students form into small groups to discuss the questions they listed and then, as a group, rank order all of the questions in terms of their importance and explain the reasons for their rankings. This sort of attention to the process of thinking critically can reveal unstated assumptions and biases in the thinking process.

For any of psychology's many controversies, assign different perspectives on the controversy to different groups of students. For example, students in a course in organizational development could take different roles on how to handle the problem of declining profits in a large company (e.g., chief executive officer, union leader, employee who is near retirement, local politician, consumer).

Teach students how to draw concept maps in which information that is conceptually related is drawn close to and linked with other similar topics. Groups can then draw maps of their knowledge of a content area before learning about it, (for example, a group map of what students know about mental illness at the start of a course on abnormal psychology). At the end of the course, put students back into their original groups and have them redraw their concept map and then compare the two. How has the information been reorganized? What was added and deleted? How has the nature of their understanding changed over the course? This activity works well as a group contribution to individual grades where outstanding concept maps at the end of the course can be worth additional points toward each group member's grade.

Conclusion

Why should we use cooperative learning? The answer is clear: CL activities result in better learning and retention, enhanced accuracy and creative problem solving, and better critical thinking for learners. But there are also advantages for lecture-weary instructors — class is more interesting and more fun for us as well.

References and Recommended Readings

Angelo, T. A., & Cross, K. P. (1993). *Classroom assessment techniques: A handbook for college teachers* (2nd ed.). San Francisco: Jossey-Bass.

Davis, B. G. (1993). *Tools for teaching.* San Francisco: Jossey-Bass.

Halpern, D. F. (1996). *Thinking critically about critical thinking.* Mahwah, NJ: Lawrence Erlbaum. (This is a critical thinking work book with numerous learning activities that can easily accommodate collaborative learning.)

Hamilton, S. J. (1997). *Collaborative Learning* (2nd ed.). Indianapolis, IN: Indiana University Center for Teaching and Learning.

Johnson, D. W., Johnson, F., & Smith, K. A. (1998). Cooperative learning returns to college. *Change, 30*(4), 26-35.

Storytelling in Teaching

MELANIE C. GREEN
University of Pennsylvania

Tell me a fact and I'll learn. Tell me the truth and I'll believe. But tell me a story and it will live in my heart forever.

— Indian Proverb

ONCE UPON A TIME, long ago and far away (or perhaps not so long ago), teachers did not use fancy PowerPoint presentations, overhead projectors, or even chalkboards. They simply shared their knowledge through stories.

Think back over your years of sitting in classrooms. What are the moments that you most remember? For me, one of those moments was my professor in introduction to psychology spinning the tale of Rosenhan's pseudopatients, perfectly sane individuals who checked into a mental institution and proceeded to act in normal ways. It seemed like an amazing adventure — what was going to happen to these people in the mental hospital? The class was hanging on his every word.

The odds are that your memorable moments, too, have to do with stories — not theories or definitions or dates, but an unfolding narrative, complete with suspense, drama, or humor, or perhaps a personal anecdote shared by a favorite teacher. Of course, a classroom narrative may be linked to a major discovery, study, or figure in psychology, but it is not always the importance of the discovery alone that allows it to stay fresh over the years. Rather, the means of presenting the information can make it exciting and unforgettable.

The power of stories has been recognized for centuries, and even today, in Hollywood and beyond, storytelling is a multimillion dollar business. Stories are a natural mode of thinking; before our formal education begins, we are already learning from Aesop's fables, fairy tales, or family history. Indeed, some researchers have even claimed that all knowledge comes in the form of stories (Schank & Abelson, 1995). Although this strong claim has been questioned, it is generally agreed that stories are a powerful structure for organizing and transmitting information, and for creating meaning in our lives and environments.

Nature of Stories

What is a story? In essence, a narrative account requires a story that raises unanswered questions or unresolved conflicts; characters may encounter and then resolve a crisis or crises. A story line, with a beginning, middle and end, is identifiable. In Bruner's (1986) words, "[Narrative] deals in human or human-like intention and action and the vicissitudes and consequences that mark their course. It strives to put its timeless miracles into the particulars of experience and to locate the experience in time and place" (p.13). Stories can bring abstract principles to life by giving them concrete form. We cannot always give students direct experience with psychological concepts, but stories might come close.

A story tends to have more depth than a simple example. A story tells about some event — some particular individuals, and something that happens to them. Stories engage our thinking, our emotions, and can even lead to the creation of mental imagery (Green & Brock, 2000). Individuals listening to stories react to them almost automatically, participating, in a sense, in the action of the narrative (e.g., Polichak & Gerrig, 2002). Bringing all of these systems to bear on the material in your course helps student learning. Students are awake, following along, wanting to find out what happens next and how the story ends. Bruner (1986) has contrasted the paradigmatic (logical, scientific) and narrative modes of thinking, but these modes need not be mutually exclusive in the classroom.

Purpose of Stories

Stories can serve multiple functions in the classroom, including sparking student interest, aiding the flow of lectures, making material memorable, overcoming student resistance or anxiety, and building rapport between the instructor and the students, or among students themselves.

Stories Create Interest

As an instructor, you can capitalize on the inherent narrative structure of research as the quest for knowledge. Science is the process of solving mysteries; in fact, writers of journal articles are often advised to make their findings into "a good story." Psychologists often start out by confronting an intriguing problem. For example, why are bicycle riders faster when they are racing against another person than going around the track by themselves? Researchers also encounter and overcome various obstacles in their quest to understand a phenomenon. For example, when researchers tried to replicate social facilitation effects, sometimes the presence of others improved performance, and other times it harmed performance. Why would that be? Take advantage of the suspense that this chain of events can create. Telling the story of how researchers became interested in a particular issue, without immediately providing the resolution, will motivate your class to think of their own approaches to solving the problem. They can share in the sense of discovery. Understanding the process of solving a research problem can generate excitement, as well as an increased appreciation for the "detective work" involved in psychology.

Characters are an important element of any tale, and indeed, stories can also make material concrete and memorable by putting a human (or animal) face on theories and issues. Students may remember the peril of H. M., the patient who could not form new memories, long after they have forgotten other details of brain anatomy or memory research. They may have a vivid mental image of Harry Harlow's orphaned monkeys interacting with cloth or wire "mothers." If they remember the concrete elements of the story, they may then be able to reconstruct the abstract lessons illustrated by the story. Furthermore, listeners may identify with the protagonists of your stories, and thus might be better able to relate course material to their own lives. Making the material personally relevant can lead to increased thinking about the material and a greater ability to apply the new knowledge.

Similarly, giving some background about the researchers who developed particular theories can help engage student interest by humanizing the research process, and may even provide role models for students who may be interested in pursing research themselves. (This approach can be used to excellent effect in history of psychology courses.) Stories can convey the passion, enthusiasm, and curiosity of the researchers. Sometimes psychological research can seem divorced from the real world, but in the process of developing his theories about compliance, Cialdini actually went through training programs to becomes a salesman of encyclopedias, dance lessons, and the like. He also went "on the inside" as a particiapnt-observer to study advertising, public relations, and fundraising agencies to learn about their techniques. Students studying social influence love to hear about Cialdini immersing himself in the world of compliance professionals.

Stories Provide a Structure for Remembering Course Material

Coherence is the hallmark of a good narrative. Remembering a list of isolated concepts and definitions is difficult, but recalling the flow of a research story may be easier for students. As mentioned above, stories may also help create vivid mental images, another cue for recall. Because stories provide natural connections between events and concepts, mentioning one part of the story may help evoke the other parts of the story, just as hearing one bar of a familiar tune may bring the entire song to mind.

Stories Are a Familiar and Accessible Form of Sharing Information

Because they have this engaging quality, they may help overcome student anxiety or resistance. Some students may be intimidated by abstract concepts, or may doubt their ability to master or understand the material. A story may provide a nonthreatening way to ease students into learning. A narrative opening may seem simple and straightforward, allowing students to relax and grasp a concrete example before moving into more technical details of a theory or finding. Sometimes stories can even be about the learning process; tales of previous students who struggled but then succeeded might serve as inspiration for current students. (It probably goes without saying that telling stories that mock or disparage previous students may do more harm than good.)

Telling a Story From Experience Can Create a More Personal Student-Teacher Connection

This rapport can lead to a positive classroom climate. Perhaps you are a clinical psychologist who has seen a patient with a particularly compelling presentation of the disorder you're discussing in class. Or maybe you're a social psychologist who has had your own brush with bystander intervention and diffusion of responsibility. Sharing these experiences gives the class a new tone, and makes the subject come alive. As long as every class session isn't another chapter from your autobiography, students enjoy seeing a glimpse of the human side of their professors. As an added benefit, in discussion classes, providing this kind of opening may inspire reciprocity and help create an atmosphere where students are more willing to share their opinions and experiences.

Finding and Selecting Stories

There are a wealth of sources for teachable stories — current events, history, television programs, classic literature or drama, and personal experience (your own and others). Some instructors find it useful to have a folder or notebook for teaching stories; make a habit of clipping relevant newspaper stories, or making notes about events that are perfect illustrations of some psychological concept that appears in your course. These don't have to be current events to capture student interest. A colleague uses a scene from the book *Killer Angels* (Shaara, 1974), about the Battle of Gettysburg, to demonstrate the power of perception over reality. In the book, the Confederate General Longstreet is portrayed as sitting calmly before the battle. A foreign journalist infers that he is composing himself, thinking of strategy and so forth. In reality, he is weeping, knowing his men will die because he asks them to, knowing what the day will bring.

And remember, research results need to be true, but stories do not. Do not be afraid to use stories from fiction, especially well-known fiction. For instance, the children's story "The Emperor's New Clothes" demonstrates social influence principles; the interactions between Iago, Othello, and Desdemona in Shakespeare's play *Othello* provide a powerful illustration of the importance of perceptions over objective reality.

Textbooks may also be sources of stories; some books use stories to introduce or frame chapters, while others (such as Aronson's *Social Animal*, 1995) intersperse narratives throughout. Readers may want to consider books with "inside stories." Such stories have been collected by Brannigan and Merrens (1995) in their Research Adventures series. Other recommendations for sources of stories include:

- *A History of Geropsychology in Autobiography* (Birren & Schroots, 2000).
- *Case Studies in Abnormal Behavior* (6th ed.) (Meyer, 2003).
- *Classic Studies in Psychology* (Schwartz, 1986).
- *Disordered Personalities in Literature* (Harwell, 1980).
- *Forty Studies that Changed Psychology: Explorations into the History of Psychological Research* (4th ed.) (Hock, 2002).
- *Pioneers of Psychology* (3rd ed.) (Fancher, 1996).
- *Portraits of Pioneers in Psychology* (Kimble, Wertheimer, & White, 1991).
- *The Story of Psychology* (Hunt, 1993).

Think about common experiences that your students have likely had — stories about leaving home, dealing with roommates, handling relationships, and the like may be especially relevant to a college-age audience.

The case study method, frequently used in business schools, is a popular means of introducing stories into the classroom. Cases typically set up a problem by giving background information about a situation (for example, the history of a company), and end with a current dilemma faced by an individual or organization. They are often designed to illustrate a particular point or demonstrate certain analytic procedures. Students are encouraged to generate possible solutions and consider the consequences of those solutions. This method encourages active learning, and in essence, puts students in the role of writing the ending to the story.

A related method (which can be more or less narrative in form) is *role-playing*, where students actively create or take part in a mini-drama in the classroom. McKeachie (1999) gives the example of students taking the perspective of Freud or Skinner in responding to a treatment situation. Role-playing is another means of merging the power of stories with the benefits of active learning.

Stories may also be integrated with technology. You may be able to locate computer-based or interactive stories that relate to your course content. (If you are programming-savvy or have time on your hands, you may even be able to develop these kinds of applications.) Teaching Web sites can also be rich sources of stories. And you don't always have to be the storyteller; films and Web sites may also be effective means of delivering psychology's stories.

Telling Stories in Class

The lecture itself may be structured as a narrative, or a story can simply be an illustration of a key point. Taking advantage of the natural drama of research stories can help the pacing and flow of your lectures. Imagine yourself as a storyteller, perhaps with your students gathered around a campfire. Rather than marching through the material, fact by fact, you can add storytelling flourishes. Let the suspense build — pause for a moment before revealing the results of the study, to draw in students' attention. Stories can also be a natural way to introduce humor into your lecture.

One way to learn about how to tell a story is to listen to master storytellers at work. National Public Radio provides some wonderful examples: Garrison Keillor, for instance, enthralls thousands of people each week with his tales of Lake Wobegone. You may also know people in your own life — relatives, friends, and colleagues — who can spin a marvelous tale. Take note of how they involve their audience, and use those techniques as you develop your own style. Do they pause at key places? What information do they give early on to draw listeners in, and how do they maintain suspense? Do they bring characters to life with vivid descriptions or unique voices? Just as you develop your own style of teaching, so too can you develop your own style of storytelling that draws on role models, but fits your own personality.

As with any example, a story should be a clear illustration of the principle you're trying to demonstrate. Because listeners have their own interpretations of the point of stories, it is your responsibility as an instructor to make the message of the story clear, and draw links between the story and the abstract principles it demonstrates. Beginning students, especially, may not be able to make these connections on their own, or they may remember peripheral aspects of the story rather than the main point. Students should be aware that classroom stories are part of the learning experience, not a tangent from it. Keep the story clean and to the point. Furthermore, if a story doesn't quite match the concept you are trying to demonstrate, you may be better off omitting it. At exam time, students who remember a story from class should not be misled by its conclusions.

When is the best time to tell a story for it to have the maximum impact? Schank (1990) suggest that stories should come after surprises, or expectation failures. When individuals have recognized flaws in their existing models of the world, they are open to correcting those models. Individuals are especially open to learning when the expectation failure and story are relevant to their goals. For example, suppose you had just come back from teaching a particularly frustrating day of class, where students' minds were wandering and you couldn't seem to engage the class. If at that moment, your colleague told you about how she had transformed her classroom environment by starting each lecture with a story that presented a real-world problem or mystery, and working through it over the course of the class session, you might be especially open to learning from that tale. For your students, framing stories with relevant problems (succeeding at a job, getting along with roommates) may help make them more likely to be attended to and recalled.

Along the same lines, stories can be told from different points of view. Think about perspective when you're designing your lecture. You could describe an experiment from the researcher's point of view, but you might instead begin by telling the story of what a participant in that study experienced instead, to draw students into the situation. Imagine, for example, being a participant in the Asch conformity studies, with rising levels of confusion and doubt as your fellow participants continue to give wrong answers to a line judgment task. Stories can encourage empathy, and putting themselves in participants' shoes can sometimes help students understand the power of experimental situations. Varying the presentation of research to focus on a researcher versus a participant perspective can also help add spice to your lectures.

In some types of courses, particularly smaller seminars, it may be appropriate to have students share stories from their own lives, and indeed, students may spontaneously do this even in larger courses. This is another form of active learning, and students may be even more attentive to a story told by their peers. An instructor's role might then be to link aspects of these narratives to theories or principles in the psychological literature. (Students may become frustrated with a course that appears to consist only of sharing individual experiences, without links to theory or research.) If individuals are likely to be sharing stories that may be sensitive — for example, struggles with psychological disorders, experiences with stereotyping or prejudice — ground rules about respect for others, not discussing personal revelations outside the classroom, and the like should be established early.

Can there be a downside to using stories in the classroom? One issue that psychology instructors sometimes face, especially in introductory and social psychology courses, is helping students to understand that personal experience isn't everything, and that psychological questions can be tested scientifically and evaluated with data. Your use of stories should be integrated with reference to empirical evidence, so that students do not come away with the impression that a single story, even an especially vivid and compelling one, should be understood as proof for a particular position.

You may also want to solicit student feedback on your stories, especially if you are telling a particular story for the first time, or if you are new at introducing storytelling into your teaching. You might ask students to list stories that they found to be interesting and useful, and alternatively, note whether any stories seemed to wander or create confusion. At the end of class or after telling a story, you might take a minute or so to ask students to summarize the point of a story you told, to make sure that your message has been conveyed.

A Concluding Note

Stories can serve another function that goes beyond the classroom. Shared narrative can be a force in creating community. Stories tie current students to traditions and people from the past. If an important event or discovery took place on your campus or in your town, let students know about it. Tell stories that embody the values of your discipline and your campus. Share your teaching stories with colleagues.

And may you and your students live happily ever after.

References and Recommended Readings

Aronson, E. (1995). *The social animal* (7th ed.). New York: W. H. Freeman.

Birren, J. E., & Schroots, J. J. (Eds.). (2000). *A history of geropsychology in autobiography*. Washington, DC: American Psychological Association.

Brannigan, G. G., & Merrens, M. R. (1995). *The social psychologists: Research adventures*. New York: McGraw-Hill.

Bruner, J. S. (1986). *Actual minds, possible worlds*. Cambridge, MA: Harvard University Press.

Fancher, R. E. (1996). *Pioneers of psychology* (3rd ed.). New York: Norton.

Green, M. C., & Brock, T. C. (2000). The role of transportation in the persuasiveness of public narratives. *Journal of Personality and Social Psychology, 79*, 401-421.

Green, M. C., Strange, J. J., & Brock, T. C. (Eds.). (2002). *Narrative impact: Social and cognitive foundations*. Mahwah, NJ: Erlbaum.

Harwell, C. W. (1980). *Disordered personalities in literature.* New York: Longman.

Hock, R. R. (2002). *Forty studies that changed psychology: Explorations into the history of psychological research* (4th ed.). Upper Saddle River, NJ: Prentice-Hall.

Hunt, M. (1993). *The story of psychology.* New York: Anchor.

Kimble, G. A., Wertheimer, M., & White, C. L. (Eds.). (1991). *Portraits of pioneers in psychology.* Hillsdale, NJ: Lawrence Erlbaum.

McKeachie, W. J. (1999). *Teaching tips* (10th ed.). Lexington, MA: D.C. Heath & Company.

Meyer, R. G. (2003). *Case studies in abnormal behavior* (6th ed.). Boston: Allyn & Bacon.

Polichak, J. W., & Gerrig, R. J. (2002). Get up and win: Participatory responses to narrative. In M.C. Green, J. J. Strange, & T. C. Brock (Eds.), *Narrative impact: Social and cognitive foundations* (pp. 71-96). Mahwah, NJ: Lawrence Erlbaum.

Schank, R. C. (1990). *Tell me a story.* New York: Charles Scribner's Sons.

Schank, R. C., & Abelson, R. P. (1995). Knowledge and memory: The real story. In R. S. Wyer, Jr. (Ed.), *Advances in social cognition* (Vol. 8, pp. 1-85). Hillsdale, NJ: Lawrence Erlbaum.

Schwartz, S. (1986). *Classic studies in psychology.* Mountain View, CA: Mayfield Publishing.

Shaara, M. (1974). *The killer angels.* New York: Ballentine Books.

Entrances and Exits: Making the Most of Sixty Key Seconds in Every Class

CATHY SARGENT MESTER
Pennsylvania State University-Erie

"DID YOU HEAR THE ONE about the dog and the hot air balloon?" In reading that question, you decided whether to read more or not. This article, like every public act of communication, can succeed or fail with the impact of just a few precious seconds, those at the beginning of the message and those at the end. The importance of those seconds is especially critical when the public communication is oral, rather than written because listener attention is very lightly held overall. When we listen we are much more susceptible to physical and mental distractions than when we read. The good news, however, is that listeners are at the peak of their attentiveness at the opening and at the closing of an oral message. These are golden opportunity times.

With a strong beginning, we capture the listeners' attention and interest. With a strong ending, we help the listeners to remember the main points just covered and make them interested in returning for more.

The classroom is just such a public communication event. As instructors, oral communication is our stock in trade and the students are our audience. Thus, whether the class is planned as a lecture or an interaction, the beginning and ending are critical components that should be specifically created in relation to the class goal and overall instructional design.

Students as Audience

In our dreams, we envision students eager to learn, excited about our subject, mentally focused and well-prepared for each day's work. Some students live up to our dream, but many do not. Often, they are mentally distracted by their other classes or even their out-of-class responsibilities to jobs and families. Some are physically drained by the demands of rushing between classes and dealing with a plethora of emotional stresses. As a result, they are not ready to learn the moment class begins and they start to think about their next set of responsibilities or problems well before the class ends. Consequently during those golden seconds at the beginning and end of class, our listeners may not even be tuned in.

Knowing such communicative challenges of the classroom, many instructors have been propelled into creative action. They find techniques that entice student attention in the class's beginning and enable remembering the day's lesson in the closing.

A Grand Opening: Dramatic Options

Remember the sense of anticipation experienced when listening to the crescendo music of "Thus Spoke Zarathustra" as the opening credits of *2001: The Space Odyssey* rolled on screen? That's strategic drama. It makes the listeners' eyes rivet to the front of the room, their ears tuned to nothing but those sounds of the speaker's creation, their whole being waiting to find out what comes next.

Though limited by the classroom logistics a bit, we can still use a variety of dramatic devices to open a class and generate a similar degree of eager anticipation in our students. Props displayed, the instructor appearing in a role-playing costume, music playing, an opening humorous anecdote or unexpected rearrangement of the classroom furniture can all have the effect of capturing the students' attention instantly upon entering the room.

Props are noted as enhancements to attention no matter when used in a lesson, but if incorporated at the very beginning of the class, they can instantly grab the students' curiosity and help them be focused. Of course, props should never be displayed until they are relevant to the point being made. But an opening point that can be enhanced with a prop *should* be. Whether the item is as large and active as a live animal or as small and static as a coin, showing it to the students as a lead-in to the first point takes their random thoughts and transforms them into a perceptual set for understanding the day's material. For instance, when teaching students about the impact of attention and prioritizing on memory, one professor begins by displaying enlarged, incomplete pennies and asks the students to "fill in the blanks." The question is actually a stumper, which serves both to make the point about memory and to start their brains for the day's lesson.

Nearly everyone has used props but few instructors have experience with full-fledged role-playing, though many of us have tried it to a limited extent. One professor reports that just throwing on a bathrobe and entering class acting old and confused is a great way to capture the students' attention for a discussion of dementia. Others, who have created entire costumed characters, complete with music and props, include instructors in the sciences, literature, politics and social sciences. They all report the characters' success in generating rapt attention from the students — a great state for them to be in as class begins.

As for opening anecdotes, suffice it to say that they are sure winners — even if the students don't laugh. It is in the attention-getting department that they are winners because our human nature makes us attend to a story. So, the students who hear your story are, at the very least, putting irrelevant thoughts out of their minds for those important opening seconds as they listen to your tale of the dog and the hot air balloon (or whatever the topic may be). They are focused, and that's good.

We can even get students focused without saying a word. Classroom spaces, including chair arrangement, are subject to unwritten rules of uniformity. Even without assigned seats, students come in and sit in the same seat day after day. That physical routine sets them up to expect that each day is going to be the same as the last. So, surprise them by rearranging the chairs one day and you will instantly convey that they should expect something different from this day. A simple tactic, for instance, is to rope off the last row or turn all the seats to face one another instead of the front of the room. You will have their attention and their curiosity without having to say a word.

A Grand Opening:
Initiating Interactive Learning

For a class intended to be interactive, it is best to begin with some kind of teacher-student dialogue. The classic example is in the foreign language classroom where the calling of the roll is accompanied by specific questions for each student asked in the language being studied. The same methodology can be applied in any discipline, including psychology.

In order to be effective as discussion-starters, the questions need to be guaranteed to be answerable. Your question should not require recall of a specific point in the previous night's reading since the student may not have completed or understood the reading. If that were the case, your opening question just adds to existing stress rather than inviting curiosity about the day's material. Instead, ask an unintimidating personal question such as "What did you eat for breakfast this morning;" "What model is your family car;" or "What color was your most recent clothing purchase?" Such questions could lay the groundwork for a discussion about subliminal impacts on judgments, for instance. Collectively, the questions will engage the students and make them wonder about the connection between the information elicited by the questions and the day's stated topic. Although they may be confused as to the motivation for the questions, they are nonetheless intellectually engaged. Attentive and curious — now you've got them.

Similarly, we can successfully lure the students into discussion by opening with a case study. If the day's focus is on the psychology of aging, you might begin with the story of the 90-year old master swimmer, holder of several age-level sprint records, who is worried about the "younger girls" coming up. Just the juxtaposition of the words "90-year old" and "sprint" should improve the reception on the students' listening antennae. We can then build from there to entertain student perspectives on the assigned reading as well as their own experiences.

You might even open by creating your own case study as in the classic thief-stealing-teacher's-briefcase scenario opening a criminal justice class. That demonstration has been used to elicit attention in many a class dedicated to selective perception, stereotyping, selective memory and other topics.

In the same vein, many instructors in the sciences and engineering find success by opening the class with a problem — no prelude, just a small problem to get them thinking. The same process works well for one award-winning psychology professor who begins a class about statistical probability by displaying a casino-style Plinko game and asking the students where to drop the chips in order to win. The problem turns on the students' brains — they are ready for learning.

A Grand Opening: A Technical Caution

Given the current infatuation with instructional technology, a word of caution is needed about opening a technologically-assisted class. Many instructors have put together remarkable computer-assisted presentations of material that are carefully planned to fill the class period with vividly graphic, informative images. As impressive as that content is, we still need to have the students' attention *before* dimming the lights. We must have piqued their curiosity at the start if we expect them to be receptive in the darkened room throughout the remainder of class. If that is not done, the first slide had better be Zarathustra-like!

The Big Finish: Mnemonic Devices

"Great is the art of beginning, but greater is the art of ending." When Longfellow wrote those words, he was not a teacher. He had no knowledge of our experience of finding our closing eloquence disrupted by the sounds of papers, books, pencils and calculators being repacked in bookbags while last sips are noisily drained from cups and mugs. Yet his insight is well taken; ending a message is a great art.

We must *plan* to end, not have it thrust upon us by the clock. No matter how long the class session, wrap up the lecture or interactive activity at least five minutes before the class officially ends. Use those five minutes for some mnemonic strategy that provides a specific way for the students to remember what was most important in this class hour.

Many faculty find that some version of a "parting paper" accomplishes this goal very effectively. Usable in a full range of disciplines, the assignment is for the students to write a summary of the lesson's key points in under a minute or two. The papers are handed in and are awarded some credit towards a grade, so there is incentive for the students to be reasonably reflective and coherent. By writing such a summary, the students' ability to remember the material weeks later is greatly improved.

One variation on the "parting paper" is to ask the students to write three questions for a pending exam based on the day's material. Again, some credit is awarded, the students' memory has been strengthened and you have a head start on writing the exam.

Another writing option for the closing minutes of class is for the students to make brief notes summarizing their own participation during the class period. The participation could have been outward, such as answering or asking questions. But participation could also refer to the students' mental processing of what others have said. In that case, the assignment calls for the student to articulate personal reflections on the topics covered which not only aids individual memory of the material but also engages the student in very meaningful metacognition.

Oral versions of these kinds of closing summaries also are possible. Some instructors report doing a "lightning round" of quick review questions on the day's material. Being highly interactive, the oral "lightning round" definitely heightens student attention and crystallizes their mental focus on the class material, not what they have to do before their next class.

Finally, a very effective mnemonic device is to return to the questions or cases raised at the beginning of the class, asking for a post-analysis of that opening issue. This strategy "ties up" the class into a tidy package easily filed in the memory for later recall.

That's what a good ending does — it makes the middle memorable.

The Big Finish: Building Suspense

Unlike the stand-alone character of most oral rhetoric, the classroom lesson is part of a continuing rhetoric. So, one function served by the lesson's ending is the creation of interest in succeeding lessons. In the best theatrical tradition of "Who shot JR" and every successful Friday soap opera episode, we must "leave them wanting more."

The suggestion here is still to use those final seconds of class for some form of summing up, but also plan a "teaser" relating to upcoming material. We could, for instance, describe another case study whose relevance appears mysterious, or pose a question that can only be answered by putting together today's material with some not yet covered. In educational psychology, one instructor ended class with the question, "So, if individuals' cognitive processing varies, what hope is there for learning in a class of 500 students?" Since many of the students were in classes that large, they were quite interested to come back the next class and consider the question.

Some instructors create suspense with an amazing quote or visual image that is interesting, memorable but not completely clear. For instance, you might summarize an introductory lesson about cognition and pose the question "what does thinking look like?" while displaying thermal images of brains at work. Looking something like colorful Rorschach tests, the puzzling images are rather dramatic. The strategy has the effect of making the students think about the image and the concept during the days in between class meetings and return with great opening questions.

The Big Finish: An Overall Caution

All the ending strategies just mentioned work well — but only when the students are accustomed to paying attention at the end of class. It is imperative that each of us establishes something of a time-management contract with the students from day one of class. We agree to end class on time, every time; to remind them of coming assignments without rushing at the end of each class and never to try to cram in one more segment in the waning moments of class. For their part, students agree to keep their notebooks open and coats on the chair backs until it is clear that the class is finished for the day.

Speaking of Finishing

Still wondering about the dog and the hot air balloon? This is the true and very comical and dramatic story of one Labrador retriever's frustrated attempts to leap to the noisy, colorful balloon sailing over his fenced-in yard. Like the optimistic dog, we, as faculty, are leaping for something seemingly beyond our grasp — in our case, student attention and memory. Unlike the dog, we actually have a chance of succeeding. If our efforts to create strong class entrances and exits are specifically and strategically planned as suggested here, even the most noisy and colorful students will be ready to learn and ready to remember — our "balloon" retrieved!

References and Recommended Readings

Chizmar, J. F., & Ostrosky, A. L. (1998). The one-minute paper: Some empirical findings. *Journal of Economic Education, 29*(1), 3-10.

Cooper, P. J. (1988). *Speech communication for the classroom teacher.* Scottsdale, AZ: Gorsuch Scarisbrick.

Maier, M. H., & Panitz, T. (1996). End on a high note. *College Teaching, 44,* 145-148.

McKeachie, W. J. (2002). *McKeachie's teaching tips: Strategies, research and theory for college and university teachers* (11th ed.). Boston: Houghton Mifflin.

Tauber, R. T., & Mester, C. S, (1994). *Acting lessons for teachers: Using performance skills in the classroom.* Westport, CT: Praeger.

Hitting a Nerve: When Touchy Subjects Come up in Class

RETTA E. POE
Western Kentucky University

IN YOUR SOCIAL PSYCHOLOGY course you have reached the section on prejudice and stereotyping, and you invite comments on the material you have just presented. One of your students begins to share a personal experience as a victim of stereotyping, and as she talks, her voice becomes stronger and louder. It is clear to everyone that she is very angry, and there is an embarrassed, awkward silence as she finishes speaking.

In another course on abnormal psychology you have divided the class into small groups to develop summaries and critiques of the major theories of depression. As you walk around the classroom to observe and offer suggestions, you notice that one student is visibly upset. Something in the assignment has clearly touched him, and the other students in his group have noticed that he looks as though he might cry.

Teaching About 'Touchy' Subjects

"Touchy" subjects — topics that provoke an emotional response in both students and instructors — can come up in classes in many disciplines, but they seem especially likely to arise in psychology courses because of the subject matter: ourselves! Most of our courses focus on understanding human behavior, and although we may attempt to present the data objectively and dispassionately, our and our students' responses to those data may involve our feelings and values.

Thus, as instructors, we may face a dilemma: On the one hand, we don't wish to offend students or deny students' rights to their values and opinions, but on the other hand, we believe that psychology research has much to contribute to an understanding of many sensitive topics. We may feel that we aren't doing our jobs if we don't challenge some of our students' beliefs, but we don't want to seem to be telling students that their values are wrong. There may be times when we deliberately raise a value-laden topic because we may believe that discussing values and their role in behavior contributes to critical thinking ability and thus is an important aspect of the learning experience. However, when we have students with polar opposite views in the same class, trying to manage class discussion so that it is accepting and non-confrontational can seem nearly impossible.

Whether the "touchy" subject comes up on its own or is raised deliberately by the instructor, it is important to be prepared and plan ahead so that we can handle these issues with sensitivity and appropriate concern for the welfare of our students and for our obligations as instructors. These obligations include treating students with respect for their feelings and their dignity, and providing optimal conditions for learning.

Courses and Course Topics Most Likely to Elicit Emotional Responses

Perhaps a good generalization would be that we (students and instructors) are most likely to have strong feelings about topics that have something to do with religion, sexuality, aggression, and issues related to gender and ethnicity. If this is true, instructors should probably anticipate that students may respond emotionally to topics such as corporal punishment (spanking), child abuse, sexual orientation, abortion, rape, euthanasia, reproductive technologies, capital punishment, gender roles, religion, evolution, ECT (shock therapy), pornography, racism, stereotyping, animal rights, rights of the mentally ill, masturbation, divorce, parenting, drug use, aggression, prejudice, and sexual relationships.

Although strong emotional reactions can occur in about any course, the content of certain courses may make them more likely to generate heat: developmental courses, social psychology, abnormal psychology, psychology of gender or women, psychology of sexual behavior, cross-cultural psychology, and psychology and law. However, even though it may seem as though instructors of certain courses are safe from having to worry about "touchy" subjects, it's probably a good idea for all instructors to be prepared, just in case.

Three Teaching Challenges

Loss of Composure

Sometimes students or instructors burst into tears or lose their tempers. Sometimes the loss of composure is a group phenomenon, such as when two or more students gang up on another student. For example, one student may express a pro-choice viewpoint on abortion and several other students with pro-life views begin to criticize the lone pro-choice student. Tempers flare, and everyone is aware of the tension in the room. There is also the situation when you, perhaps unknowingly, bring up a sensitive topic for discussion; your usually vocal class is uncharacteristically quiet, and the silence in the classroom makes it abundantly clear that everyone is anxious and uncomfortable.

Inappropriate or Too Frequent Self-Disclosure

Students may need help in learning how to self-monitor. For instance, in a discussion of alcoholism one student begins to give a detailed account of her own or a relative's abuse of alcohol. Perhaps another student goes into detail in describing a personal or family problem, or maybe one particular student always contributes some personal story, often somewhat tangential to the topic.

Opinions Students and Faculty Express

A student may state as fact something that is objectively wrong, such as "Most women could resist being raped if they really wanted to." In a similar vein, perhaps a student confuses opinion or personal experience with fact; one example is the student who reports that his father used to whip him with his belt whenever he got out of line, and since he (the student) is fine now, that means that spanking doesn't have any harmful effects.

Most instructors have had to deal with a related problem: a student states an opinion that differs significantly from the instructor's. For instance, you are convinced that affirmative action laws are necessary to address past discrimination against particular groups, but a student pronounces all such laws as mere political correctness. You may have one or more students who monopolize discussion, thereby preventing others from stating their views, such as when one student with strongly-held views about animal rights uses every opportunity to express them, and eventually seems to be the only one talking.

Finally, you may discover (or perhaps even intentionally create) some cognitive dissonance in students as certain topics are discussed; sometimes class discussion has the effect of making students question long-held personal or religious beliefs. For instance, you may discuss evolution as scientifically recognized and empirically supported, thus challenging the religious beliefs of some students.

Strategies for Preventing Problems and Resolving Conflict

Anticipate problems and be prepared. There are several things you can do in advance to head off problems. First, you might find yourself an experienced colleague to serve as a mentor to help you foresee and resolve problems. Second, it is a good idea to inform students at the beginning of a course that sensitive topics may be addressed. Ideally, this information would be presented both in the syllabus and orally. You don't necessarily have to label the topics as sensitive; just listing some of the topics that will be covered may be sufficient either to warn students or prepare them. Thus, students can make an informed choice about staying in the course, and if they do decide to stay, they know what to expect. Third, when you know in advance that a certain topic will be coming up, announce that fact to the class a couple of class periods ahead. This will give the students who might be overly upset by a certain topic the opportunity to come to class more emotionally prepared. Fourth, with the class, develop and discuss "ground rules" for class discussion. Examples of good rules to have are:

- ♦ Treat others' opinions with courtesy and respect.
- ♦ Maintain confidentiality of experiences shared by class members.
- ♦ Don't monopolize discussion.
- ♦ Attack ideas rather than persons.
- ♦ Don't tell things that are too personal.
- ♦ Exercise your right not to share your thoughts and ideas if you are uncomfortable talking about something.

A final suggestion is to insist that if students wish to describe people and events from their own experience, they should protect the identity of the persons they are describing. For example, in abnormal psychology students will often share their observations of unusual behaviors in others; the instructor should make it very clear at the beginning of the course that no identifying information should be provided.

Respect Students' Feelings

Be cautious about using role-playing techniques in teaching about certain topics. Having students role-play situations that relate to "touchy" subjects may result in their losing objectivity and, possibly, emotional control. Also, don't force students to participate by calling on them to share personal experiences about certain topics; give them the option to decline to disclose their reactions. Third, consider giving explicit "permission" for students to skip a certain class if they perceive that the topic will be too upsetting for them to handle. Finally, if a student loses composure, dismissing the class may be your best option to minimize the student's embarrassment. You can then take the student aside, have a private discussion, and, if appropriate, make a referral.

Remember Your Role and Responsibilities

Having controversies and conflicts come up in class can be distressing, but such events can also be opportunities for growth. Try to find a way to make a difference of opinion into a learning experience, perhaps by using research findings about human behavior to explain class dynamics. Also, don't bring up a sensitive topic just for the sake of doing so, but instead have a specific, legitimate purpose that is related to your instructional goals for the course. Third, make yourself available outside of class for a student who wants or needs to talk further about a topic, and be prepared for the occasional student who doesn't say anything in class but instead shows up during office hours, wanting to talk or complain. When that happens, the best approach is to listen respectfully to the student's feelings and focus on finding ways to foster the student's intellectual and personal growth. However, remember that you are the student's instructor, not his or her therapist, so be aware of the need to have some boundaries, and be prepared to make a referral to your institution's counseling center.

Ideally, you might use a situation as a "teachable moment," but sometimes just handling your own and your students' feelings in a sensitive way and without undue embarrassment can be a challenge. For example, in the event that you lose your composure in class, you may need to adjourn class immediately if you are too upset to continue. However, you can model appropriate emotional management skills by apologizing promptly (perhaps at the beginning of the next class meeting) and pointing out that faculty, too, have attitudes and feelings that they bring with them into the classroom.

Ethical and Practical Issues to Be Considered by Instructors

A number of authors have addressed the ethical concerns raised by the discussion of sensitive topics; for example, see Keith-Spiegel, Wittig, Perkins, Balogh, and Whitley (1993), Murray, Gillese, Lennon, Mercer, and Robinson (1996), Matthews (1991), and Keith-Spiegel and Koocher (1985). At a minimum, it is important to make a commitment to deal with sensitive issues in an open, honest way and to convey an attitude of acceptance and tolerance of divergent beliefs and values. It is really important for the instructor to model tolerance; for example, the instructor might specifically ask a student who has expressed a divergent view to explain it further, while the instructor uses nonverbals (head nodding, etc.) to communicate attention and respect. If possible, present the major arguments for both sides of an issue before starting a discussion; this may have the effect of "legitimizing" the views of students on both sides of an issue. Finally, try to help students recognize and — ideally — value a diversity of viewpoints. Insist that it is unacceptable for students to make disparaging remarks (or roll their eyes, or snicker) about another student or the student's ideas. Here are some suggestions.

Plan ahead. Having clarified what your goals are in bringing up a sensitive issue for discussion, you might then plan activities or questions designed to make the best use of the controversy implicit in the issue. For example, when you think you might have difficulty getting students to discuss a sensitive topic (such as racism), you might plan a short "writing to learn" exercise so that all students will have the chance to jot down a few ideas about a specific question. Then you can go around the room and ask students to share what they have written. Hearing others' responses may help students to feel more comfortable in discussing the topic.

If your goal is to develop critical thinking skills, you might develop an exercise designed to help students learn to distinguish between fact and opinion and to recognize the value of opinion that is based on evidence. As an example, Keith-Spiegel et al. (1993) describe a critical thinking approach designed to deal with students who make offensive remarks (such as those that are sexist or racist); they suggest that the instructor might ask other students to comment and then guide the discussion toward a questioning of the offending student's remark. However, be prepared to handle particularly offensive remarks by stating clearly that certain language or the expression of certain views is unacceptable (Keith-Spiegel et al., 1993). Ideally, you should make this point before a potentially touchy subject is discussed, rather than after inappropriate language is used.

Know yourself. To the extent possible, be sure that you have resolved your own personal issues related to the topics under discussion. Doing so may help you to avoid imposing your views on students. Also, clearly identify your opinions and biases on the issues being discussed. Students may have trouble recognizing when you are stating your personal opinion and when you are presenting information based on empirical evidence. Try always to remember the very great power differential between instructor and student. Because of your power over students, they may feel personally vulnerable in expressing views that differ from yours.

Know your students. Become aware of the developmental level of traditional-age college students; some of them may have less sophisticated ways of thinking about moral issues and other areas in which people may have differences of opinion. For example, a student may have difficulty perceiving that more than one legitimate opinion about an issue may exist.

Conclusion

In this area as in other areas of teaching, it is important to acknowledge individual differences: what works for some instructors in particular courses with certain students may not work in other situations. Different classroom personalities call for different styles. In addition, the size of the class may be an important factor to consider in planning one's strategy for dealing with sensitive topics. For example, C. Poe (personal communication, July 3, 1998) suggests that in small classes, which are more likely to be informally structured, values issues are often brought up by students, but in larger, more structured classes, values issues may be more likely to be identified and framed by the instructor. Instructors of large classes can probably more easily avoid having to deal with students' emotional responses during class, but those instructors should nonetheless be aware of the potential for students to be upset by certain topics and be prepared to respond in appropriate ways.

References and Recommended Readings

Bronstein, P. A., & Quina, K. (Eds.). (1988). *Teaching a psychology of people.* Washington, DC: American Psychological Association.

Keith-Spiegel, P., & Koocher, G. P. (1985). *Ethics in psychology: Professional standards and cases.* New York: McGraw-Hill.

Keith-Spiegel, P., Wittig, A. F., Perkins, D. V., Balogh, D. W., & Whitley, B. E., Jr. (1993). *The ethics of teaching.* Muncie, IN: Ball State University.

Khan, S. R. (1999). Teaching an undergraduate course on the psychology of racism. *Teaching of Psychology, 26,* 28-33.

Lusk, A. B., & Weinberg, A. S. (1994). Discussing controversial topics in the classroom: Creating a context for learning. *Teaching Sociology, 22,* 301-308.

Matthews, J. R. (1991). The teaching of ethics and the ethics of teaching. *Teaching of Psychology, 18,* 80-85.

Murray, H., Gillese, E., Lennon, M., Mercer, P., & Robinson, M. (1996). Ethical principles for college and university teaching. In L. Fisch (Ed.), *Ethical dimensions of college and university teaching: Understanding and honoring the special relationship between teachers and students* (pp. 57-63). San Francisco: Jossey-Bass.

Online Teaching: Problems and Solutions

T. L. BRINK
Crafton Hills College

WHETHER YOU ARE A
Web master or a neophyte, you have heard the buzzwords: distance education, Internet delivery, online teaching, Web based courses, cybereducation. There is no one formula for what such a course includes, but it usually involves some combination of e-mail, message boards, multi-media, learning drills, virtual simulations, and online testing.

If you have been waiting for all this to just go away or get really easy, the time has come to stop waiting and get on board. I have heard or experienced most problems with, objections to, and hurdles of distance education, and this article reviews them and suggests solutions. Some of these problems are technical, and involve limitations of hardware or software, while others tend to be rooted in human nature or organizations. My experience is that there is a way around every glitch, hurdle, and objection, and the fruits of distance learning make the effort worthwhile.

Philosophical/Administrative Objections

There are many segments of the college community who look upon online education with genuine fear, but the fears are based upon misunderstanding.

OBJECTION: Concern about instructional quality.

ANSWER: The hallmark of a good learning experience is interaction between instructor and professor. Whether or not this is accomplished will be determined primarily by variables such as instructor skills and class size, not whether interaction is mediated via computer. One-way communication is poor quality education, whether it be a in the form of a boring lecture, talking head video, or "lecture" notes published on the Web. My experience is that computer facilitated distance education permits ongoing interaction not limited by space or time, and is therefore potentially superior to classroom seat time (although maybe not in every discipline, with every student, or with every instructor).

OBJECTION: Professors are worried about loss of jobs.

ANSWER: Their fear is that at some point in the future, one big computer will "teach" all the world's students, and professors will be automated out of their jobs. This was a real concern in the 1950s with telecourses (which failed pedagogically because of the lack of interactivity). Computer facilitated distance education is labor intensive: instructors must build and maintain Web sites, respond to e-mail, monitor message boards, and stay abreast of ever-changing technology. Class sizes must be smaller, not larger.

OBJECTION: Economically disadvantaged students cannot afford a computer or Internet service.

ANSWER: Computers are a great equalizer. Poor students are less able to go away to college and live in a dorm, but now the great universities can come to any inner city housing project or out of the way rural area forgotten by economic progress. Institutions such as libraries can provide public access to terminals. Free e-mail providers now abound. The price of used computers powerful enough to surf the Web gets cheaper every year. One of the challenges is to make sure that the instructor's latest materials are retrocompatible with the older machines. (At home I have maintained an older machines and versions of Windows just to make sure that my drills and simulations will run on them.)

OBJECTION: Disabled students cannot access some computer features.

ANSWER: On campus lecture based classes provide more barriers for students with limitations of mobility, sight or hearing. Think of computers as motor and sensory prostheses. The trick is to design materials so that they will meet the needs of these students. In general, stick with pure ASCII text as the best way to assure that something can be translated into another sensory modality.

Technological Hurdles

HURDLE: The administration says we must build the wiring backbone before we can do online courses.

SOLUTION: Some administrators are still in this "railroad model": we have to lay track before we can run the trains. Online courses use a trucking model: the trucking company does not have to build the highway, it uses what is already there. Universities do not have to build Web sites or e-mail systems. The Internet already exists, and as long as instructors and students have a computer and Internet connection at home, that is all that is needed. Providing students and professors Web access from many points on campus is helpful, but not essential.

HURDLE: It takes too long to build great Web sites.

SOLUTION: Too many Web masters use the medieval cathedral model: each city had to spend a hundred years building its own, and tried to make it better than the other cities' cathedrals. But clicks are quicker than bricks: just link to another Web site. Perhaps post-Gutenberg professors heard a similar objection: how will you have time to write all the books we need for a library? After the printing press, you did not have to write all the books, you just had to get a cheap copy. In the Web age, you don't have to skirt copyright laws by copying things onto your Web site, just link to somebody else's.

HURDLE: Download times are too long.

SOLUTION: This is a genuine concern. Prepare files in such a way as to reduce download time. One backup solution is to offer the students some of the materials on disks or CD-ROMS.

HURDLE: Attached files get corrupted or carry viruses.

SOLUTION: Forbid students to send attached files. Require all e-mail from students to be in the form of pure text in the body of the letter. This can be as simple as writing something in a generic word processing program (such as Notepad), putting it on the clipboard, and then pasting it into the body of the e-mail message.

HURDLE: Our institution's server is unreliable.

SOLUTION: Right, and that is why Delphi, and Juno, and Yahoo do not use your college's server, but you do not have to either. In general, have at least two ways to do everything, and then any one server's failure is no great obstacle. If you just need a site where students can download files or programs, consider ecircles, egroups, idrive, xdrive, driveway or ureach (my favorite). Go to www.ureach.com/tlbrink and click on My Public Files to download some of the drills or simulations I use. For example, try the psyc folders and download the self-administering personality test, PERSONAL.EXE; remember that it is a program to be run and not a file to be opened, so just click on it. If you like anything else you see, go ahead and store it on your server for your students.

Practical Problems

The biggest problem with online teaching is forgetting that the goal is to create materials to facilitate student learning (simple and easy to use), instead of showing off one's technological prowess.

PROBLEM: Some Web sites look like mini textbooks.

SOLUTION: Correct, and there is no need to make such Web sites, since students can and should still have textbooks. Online material should be more interactive than that typically found in a printed textbook.

PROBLEM: Students report problems with plug ins and sound cards necessary for audio visual.

SOLUTION: Forget the streaming AV, especially talking head videos. This problem will resolve itself in about 24 months as soon as some new standard forges a stronger link between the Internet and portable players. One alternative would be to distribute video or audio cassettes. I especially recommend the latter for students to use while driving or cleaning the house. My audio cassettes have a one hour, all semester review of the most important part of my lectures. My video cassette has no talking heads, just moving diagrams. The pace would be too intense for the classroom or broadcast TV, but the student has the pause and rewind buttons to control the pace.

PROBLEM: Chat rooms are real wastes of time.

SOLUTION: True, but they can be replaced. A useful tool that would answer 90 percent of chat room questions would be a terms list keyed to the textbook. See my terms file geared to Coon's Essentials of Psychology, 8th edition. Check out the public file cabinet at: www.ureach.com/tlbrink public file cabinet. Go ahead: copy and edit it to your course and textbook. What is the advantage over the glossary in the back of the book? You can customize it to the way you teach the course and the student can search a term electronically with a CONTROL-F command in Word.

PROBLEM: Instructors are barraged by too many e-mails.

SOLUTION: Pre-empt most of the e-mails by giving students an electronically searchable FAQ (frequently asked questions) file. See my FAQ file at ureach for the answers students seek in most of their e-mailed questions: When is the final? Where is the final? What is on the final? Is it essay? Is it open book? Check out www.ureach.com/tlbrink public file cabinet for my FAQ course file. You can copy it and edit it to suit your course.

Human Frailty

Most everyday frustrations with online teaching do not occur because of the inherent limitations of technology but due to the degree of variability in the human capacity to interact with technology. These can be limited by wise policies but never eliminated.

PROBLEM: Students "accidentally" delete messages and want them resent.

SOLUTION: Require students to have at least two e-mail addresses. If one server is down or the message is deleted, the other is a backup. This means that the instructor sends to both of the students' e-mail addresses, but with an e-mail list it makes no difference if there are 20 addresses on the list or 200. Also, all material sent out e-mail can be backed up on a Web site.

PROBLEM: Professors "accidentally" delete student e-mails.

SOLUTION: Professors also need to have at least two e-mail addresses.

PROBLEM: Students send unidentified e-mails.

SOLUTION: Right, and it is hard to remember that sexything666@aol.com is not the punk rocker in row five but the retired army supply sergeant. One solution is to require all students to put their names (and section) at the top of each e-mail, or else it will not be credited. Another solution is to assign each student an e-mail address corresponding to the name.

PROBLEM: Students are cluttering the discussion with irrelevant points and flame wars.

SOLUTION: That happens on any unmoderated list or message board, even those of professionals and scholars. Think of these unwanted comments as weeds among the flowers. You are the gardener, and you cannot avoid the work of weeding out the bad. Any e-mail list must be monitored by you. Any message board must be edited by you. How much extra work will this take? That depends upon how fussy you are about the appearance of your garden. To delete the few flames and badly written e-mails is easy. To go into each student e-mail and correct the grammar and formatting takes hours.

PROBLEM: Students forget their passwords and cannot log on.

SOLUTION: The use of passwords reflects the classroom security model: lock the door so that someone does not get in and steal something. On your Web site, what can be stolen? Your brilliant ideas that someone else may use? Where possible, get rid of the passwords. We need to replace the culture of secrecy with a culture of sharing.

PROBLEM: Students do not check their e-mail.

SOLUTION: This is the equivalent to not showing up for class or not reading the book. Online courses are more convenient to attend, but nothing is a cure for laziness.

PROBLEM: Cheating will be easier.

SOLUTION: The risk is that someone else other than the student registered in the class could be on the terminal doing the work, but unless you check picture ID's in your lecture classes, how do you know that John Doe is really not Don Cho? Electronic submission of assignments actually makes it easier to catch cheating in the form of plagiarism. Just look at the similar formatting and typos.

Fear of the Unknown

PROBLEM: If we do away with passwords, anyone can enter my virtual classroom.

SOLUTION: Yes, and they do, and it is great! My students in abnormal psychology have interacted with dozens of psychologists, psychiatrists, and social workers around the country, even with a Venezuelan psychoanalyst. A Jungian analyst in private practice lurking on my list gently corrected my misunderstanding of a term. What are you afraid of? Unruly students? I maintain more control over a proctored e-mail list or message board than I have over an unruly student in the physical classroom.

Conclusion

Technical, organizational and philosophical barriers can be overcome. Start with something small and simpler if this allows you to enter the online world of teaching. If some or much of what you have just read sounds too complicated, I urge you to sit down with colleagues on campus who use some of the teaching techniques and processes discussed above, and ask them what the most exciting thing is that they do that was not done five years ago. Be prepared for some hard work, a little frustration, and a great deal of satisfaction in becoming a more effective educator.

References and Recommended Readings

Hanna, D. E., Glowacki-Dudka, M., & Conceicao-Runlee, S. (2000). *147 practical tips for teaching online groups: Essentials of web-based education.* Overland Park, KS: Atwood.

Ralston, J. V., & Beins, B. (1999). Thirteen ideas to help computerize your course. In B. Perlman, L. I. McCann, & S. H. McFadden (Eds.), *Lessons learned: Practical advice for the teaching of psychology* (pp. 73-77). Washington, DC: American Psychological Society.

Part V

Themes Across Psychology

Teaching Scientific Methodology

ROBERT W. PROCTOR
E. J. CAPALDI
Purdue University

Although we construct and justify scientific knowledge on the basis of experimental evidence, the way we do this is much more interesting, and much more problematic, than science textbooks suggest. The suggestion of these textbooks that to adopt a scientific method is to adopt a simple routine fails to do justice to the sophisticated skills which scientists use when they experiment and when they reason from evidence.

— Gower, 1997, p. 11

IN 1960, F. J. MCGUIGAN published a groundbreaking methodology text that set the mold for practically all subsequent methodology texts in psychology. Prior to McGuigan's book, methodology texts tended to deal almost exclusively with substantive topics of experimental psychology, for example, perception, learning, and so on. In contrast, McGuigan organized his book around methodological issues in research design and statistics, emphasizing:

> The point of departure for this book is the relatively new conception of experimental psychology in terms of methodology, a conception which represents the bringing together of three somewhat distinct aspects of science: experimental methodology, statistics, and philosophy of science. (p. iii)

McGuigan's approach to research methodology, which was highly innovative in 1960, has become the standard today. Contemporary methodology texts excel in providing what might be called the nuts and bolts of research: experimental design, proper control procedures, statistics, and so forth.

Lessons Learned Vol. 2 211

However, one of the three cornerstones of methodology emphasized by McGuigan, the philosophy of science, has tended to be neglected in current texts, and this omission has resulted in a failure to provide students with an adequate understanding of contemporary science. As reflected in the opening quote from Gower's (1997) book, *Scientific Method: An Historical and Philosophical Introduction*, this is a general problem that extends beyond psychology.

In point of fact, methodological texts typically provide a view of science that was initially proposed not by scientists but by philosophers of science. Consider a few examples. Up until about 1850, the accepted view of good scientific procedure was to employ induction, a method initially proposed by the philosopher Francis Bacon. Around 1850, the philosopher William Whewell proposed hypothesis testing as a more adequate scientific method than induction. In the mid 1900s, the falsification principle enunciated by the philosopher Karl Popper became popular in science and is often cited in current methodology texts. The impression most methodology texts convey is that science is to be identified with hypothesis testing and falsification of hypotheses, two views that originated as much in philosophic as in scientific practice.

By ignoring the general context in which specific scientific methodologies were, and are, initiated, methodology texts and our teaching fail to adequately provide students with a sufficient methodological background to understand science as it is actually practiced. Moreover, the texts and instructors do little to provide students with the ability to critically evaluate the numerous methodological claims offered by a variety of psychologists and other social scientists who reject science as it is conventionally and, in our view, properly understood. These unconventional approaches, which are in many respects unscientific, go under such names as social constructionism and contextualism and are various expressions of relativism and postmodernism. Some of these unconventional approaches recommend replacing conventional science with such interpretive procedures as narrative, hermeneutics, and dramaturgy (see Capaldi & Proctor, 1999).

We conclude, then, that there are at least two reasons to acquaint students with modern, up-to-date philosophy of science. It will make them better scientists, and it will prepare them to better evaluate the all-too-common antiscientific claims they will encounter in psychology and in the social sciences generally.

Improving Teaching About Science

The teaching tips that follow are intended to improve the teaching of science by remedying various deficiencies in the description of science that appear in available methodology and related psychology texts. Because methodology is often covered in content courses, the tips that follow apply to them as well as to the methodology course itself. The tips were gleaned from two sources: science as it is currently practiced and contemporary philosophy of science.

Emphasize That Contemporary Philosophy of Science Takes a Naturalistic Approach

Naturalism is the view that all statements are to be evaluated as they are in science, empirically. The naturalistic approach to the philosophy of science was first popularized in psychology by Thomas Kuhn (1970a), who suggested that science could be best understood by examining the historical record, that is, how scientists actually behaved in practice. This approach has been refined and developed by a number of outstanding philosophers of science, including Ronald Giere, Larry Laudan, Deborah Mayo, and Dudley Shapere, among others. The naturalistic approach suggests that a methodological principle should be evaluated on how useful it is in practice in giving rise to appropriate empirical and theoretical propositions. Prior to naturalism, methodological propositions tended to be evaluated almost exclusively on the basis of their logical/intuitive characteristics (called foundationism), rather than their empirical adequacy.

Recently, significant findings have been produced by psychologists investigating how science is actually practiced by working scientists in laboratory settings (see e.g., Klahr & Simon, 2001). Various investigators have utilized such techniques as 1) examining the notebooks of practicing scientists, 2) observing the behavior of scientists in the laboratory, and 3) examining scientists' approaches to problems as a function of how experienced they are (e.g., whether they are novices to the field or senior scientists), and 4) examining the behavior of nonscientists when provided with scientific problems in laboratory settings. As one example, Dunbar (1999) has performed extensive cognitive analyses of laboratory meetings of scientists and has identified key components of scientific thinking that are important in generating new models, modifying old models, and solving difficult problems. These components include analogical reasoning, attention to unexpected findings, experimental design, and distributed reasoning among the group of scientists.

Demonstrate the Inadequacy of the Foundational Approach

Consider two widely accepted methodological principles that teachers might employ to demonstrate that methodological principles that seem intuitively reasonable may be false empirically. One example, widely discussed in a variety of philosophy of science sources, is Popper's (1959) proposition that researchers should employ rigid tests of their hypotheses with the intention of doing their best to falsify and thus reject them. Contrary to Popper, however, a variety of philosophy of science sources indicate that 1) in practice scientists do not have the primary goal of attempting to falsify their hypotheses, 2) science would be poorer if scientists routinely rejected falsified hypotheses without further effort to rescue them, and, in any case, 3) all theories are already falsified in one or another respect (e.g., Chalmers, 1999; Kuhn, 1970b). Thus, one can illustrate to students that Popper's popular methodological canon, which he admitted is based solely on logic and/or intuition, is incompatible with scientific practice. Popper provides an extreme example of a philosopher of science who emphasizes how science should be practiced as opposed to the view of naturalism, which attempts to determine how science is actually practiced.

As a second example of the inadequacies of the foundational approach, Kuhn (1970a) demonstrated that the widely accepted methodological principle that successor theories should explain all that displaced theories explain, plus a variety of new phenomena, has never been observed in practice. Kuhn concluded on the basis of historical evidence that if that methodological principle were observed, no new theory would have ever been introduced in science. This certainly applies in psychology to such movements as behaviorism that, when introduced, were not able to explain many of the phenomena which their rival theories successfully dealt with. Historical evidence on this point is available in several sources, including Kuhn (1970a), Donovan, Laudan, and Laudan (1992), and any standard text on the history of psychology.

Demonstrate That Inadequate Methodological Principles May Be Employed if Superior to Available Alternatives

We cite two of many possible relevant examples. The first is the contemporary debate over the merits of statistical null hypothesis significance testing. This approach, still widely used, has been roundly criticized by a number of statistical methodologists because it is has certain logical problems. However, Krueger (2001) suggests that it is proper to employ null hypothesis testing, despite its logical problems, because it is useful in practice.

As a second example, Kuhn (1970a) has shown that scientists are reluctant to abandon a paradigm that is problematic until it is replaced by a better one. In other words, the point that needs to be conveyed is that methodological and theoretical decisions in science are based on pragmatic considerations. Most notably, one attempts to select the best of the available alternatives. This approach, which itself is a methodological principle, applies to both empirical and theoretical propositions.

To be more specific, it appears that scientists, regardless of field, are reluctant to abandon a theory, and generally will not do so, on the basis of criticism of the theory itself, even if that criticism is accepted as valid. What seems to be required in addition is the availability of a better alternative. Kuhn (1970a) put this succinctly, stating that scientists never abandon a paradigm, whatever its problems, until a better one is available. This generalization applies to decisions at any level of science, and the important point to convey to students is that criticism alone is not sufficient to nullify theories and methods.

Discuss Problems Associated With Hypothesis Testing

The considerable virtues of hypothesis testing, which are emphasized in methodology texts, hardly need emphasizing here. What needs to be recognized is that hypothesis testing, as valuable as it otherwise is, has several limitations. Students should be informed that it is exceedingly easy to falsify hypotheses in the beginning stages of a research program. They should also become acquainted with the well-known Duhem-Quine thesis, that failure to confirm a hypothesis may be due to a number of factors other than deficiencies in the hypothesis (see Chalmers, 1999). Among the problems are: the apparatus may have malfunctioned, the deduction from the hypothesis may be faulty, and a minor change in some auxiliary assumption might bring the hypothesis into line with experimental results.

An example of rejecting a theory because of a faulty deduction from its premises is available from the psychology of color vision. Ewald Hering's opponent process theory of color vision, proposed in the late 19th century, was not held in high regard for much of the 20th century because the opponent processes it postulated were incorrectly identified with the photopigments, which showed no evidence of the hypothesized properties. Subsequent evidence revealed that these properties were exhibited by neurons in the visual system.

Inform Students of the Advantages and the Disadvantages of Introducing Auxiliary Hypotheses

Introducing auxiliary hypotheses is almost universally portrayed as a flawed strategy, one that seeks in a more or less self-serving manner to avoid disconfirmation of a pet hypothesis. Yet, as Laudan (1996) emphasizes, the introduction of an auxiliary hypothesis that both rescues a theory and increases its explanatory and predictive power is a difficult task, but one that is very often extremely valuable scientifically. Examples of auxiliary hypotheses from physics having both of these characteristics are discussed at some length by Chalmers (1999) and Lakatos (1970).

Within psychology, two examples of auxiliary hypotheses, which not only rescued the theory but improved it, are as follows. The Rescorla-Wagner model, which was originally suggested to deal with classical conditioning, was subsequently extended to apply to human and animal causal learning. Van Hamme and Wasserman (1994) introduced auxiliary hypotheses that allowed that model to be applied to a broader range of causal phenomena, without changing the fundamental character of the model. In the area of attention, Treisman (1960) revised Broadbent's filter theory from one in which unattended messages were filtered completely prior to identification to one in which unattended messages were only attenuated. This modification allowed the theory to accommodate evidence that meaning of unattended messages sometimes influences performance, without modifying the basic nature of the theory.

Discuss Alternatives to Hypothesis Testing

Limitations of space allow only a cursory description of each of these methods (but see Proctor & Capaldi, 2001a, 2001b, for more detailed treatments). The methods given short shrift in current methodology texts include:

- ◆ *Induction* — Generating general statements from particular instances.
- ◆ *Promise* — Advocating a theory based on the perceived likelihood of its solving significant problems better than its competitors.

♦ *Importance* — Advocating a theory based on the likelihood that it will solve important problems of practical, philosophical, and theoretical significance.

♦ *Explanatory Theory* — Developing a theory that attempts to explain existing phenomena but does not make novel predictions at its inception.

As for induction, Newton's theorizing, at least overtly, eschewed hypothesis testing and emphasized induction, induction being the generally accepted procedure in science until about 1850, at which time hypothesis testing was introduced as an accepted scientific procedure (see, e.g., Laudan, 1996). Regarding promise, Watson (1913) indicated that the evidence for behaviorism was no stronger than for structuralism, but he recommended behaviorism on the basis of its greater promise. This recommendation obviously was accepted within the U.S., as behaviorism quickly became the dominant movement in this country. The tendency to accept theories on the basis of their promise exists not only in psychology but in science generally. For example, Kuhn (1970a) showed that scientists from a variety of areas often accept theories on the basis of their promise. Greene (1999) emphasizes importance in his recent interesting book on string theory, in which he gives numerous instances of theories in physics that when originally suggested seemed far-fetched and improbable, but continued to engage scientists because of their potential importance. This activity ultimately proved scientifically rewarding in several instances in the case of development of atomism from Democritus to Dalton. As regards explanatory theories, there were many such theories in science that were originally proposed on the basis of their explanatory capacity that initially did not entail novel predictions but turned out to be highly useful predictive devices. Two notable examples include plate tectonics and Galileo's acceptance of Copernican theory (Laudan, 1996).

Convey the Idea That Accepted Methodological Principles May Be Modified or Supplanted by Newer Ones

Because methodological statements are empirical statements, it should be expected that they are in a constant state of evolution. After all, science itself, as a clearly recognized activity, is relatively recent. As shown above, some methods important to science at one point in time, for example, induction, are seen as less important at other times. As another example, Popper's falsification principle, as he proposed it, was once heralded in the philosophy of science as a major important innovation, but it is now seen as flawed and in need of substantial modification. As a final dramatic example, it is not inconceivable that the role of hypothesis testing, considered to be of utmost importance today, may decline in influence in the future due to the discovery of a rival, more adequate methodological procedure.

Provide Students With Concrete Examples of How Scientists Have Behaved Under a Variety of Circumstances

It seems useful to provide students with specific examples (case histories and the like) of how particular scientists went about solving significant empirical and theoretical problems. That approach would seem to be as useful with respect to particular subject matter problems as to methodological principles. Fortunately, the various procedures that have been employed to examine science as an empirical activity provide a rich source of material that students can be encouraged to consult. We discussed much of this material previously in the section on taking a naturalistic approach to science. We would especially recommend perusing the excellent case histories provided in *Scrutinizing Science: Empirical Studies of Scientific Change*, edited by Donovan et al. (1992). For examples from the broader history of science, Kuhn (1970a) provides excellent material from a variety of sciences, including psychology.

Demonstrate the Importance of Research Traditions in Science

In dealing with methodological issues, students should be apprised of the importance of research traditions in psychology and science, such as behaviorism, cognitive psychology, and psychometrics. Research traditions define the kind of entities contained in the world (e.g., stimuli, responses, mental images, mechanisms to process information), and they specify what sort of questions may or may not be asked. As shown by Kuhn (1970b), Lakatos (1970), and Laudan(1996), methodological decisions may be seriously affected by the research tradition in which they are embedded. An extended discussion of the role that research traditions play in physics and psychology is to be found in Gholson and Barker (1985).

Conclusion

Successful scientific, and thus appropriate psychological, practice depends to some extent on having a proper appreciation of major issues in contemporary science. Of these issues, few are as critical as those involving methodology. Yet, psychology students' appreciation of methodology does not seem to be as well served by current texts as it might be. In this spirit, the above teaching tips are offered in the hope that following them will improve the science education of psychology students.

References and Recommended Readings

Capaldi, E. J., & Proctor, R. W. (1999). *Contextualism in psychological research? A critical review.* Thousand Oaks, CA: Sage.

Chalmers, A. F. (1999). *What is this thing called science?* (3rd ed.). Indianapolis, IN: Hackett Press.

Donovan, A., Laudan, L., & Laudan, R. (Eds.) (1992). *Scrutinizing science: Empirical studies of scientific change.* Baltimore: Johns Hopkins University Press.

Dunbar, K. (1999). How scientists build models invivo science as a window on the scientific mind. In L. Magnani, N. J. Nersessian, & P. Thagard (Eds.). *Model-based reasoning in scientific discovery* (pp. 85-99). New York: Kluwer.

Gholson, B., & Barker, P. (1985). Kuhn, Lakatos, and Laudan: Applications in the history of physics and psychology. *American Psychologist, 40,* 755-769.

Gower, B. (1997). *Scientific method: An historical and philosophical introduction.* New York: Routledge.

Greene, B. (1999). *The elegant universe.* New York: Norton.

Klahr, D., & Simon, H. A. (2001). What have psychologists (and others) discovered about the process of scientific discovery? *Current Directions in Psychological Science, 10,* 75-79.

Krueger, J. (2001). Null hypothesis significance testing: On the survival of a flawed method. *American Psychologist, 56,* 16-26.

Kuhn, T. S. (1970a). *The structure of scientific revolutions* (Rev. ed.). Chicago: University of Chicago Press. (Original work published 1962)

Kuhn, T. S. (1970b). Logic of discovery or psychology of research? In I. Lakatos & A. Musgrave (Eds.), *Criticism and the growth of knowledge* (pp. 1-23). New York: Cambridge University Press.

Lakatos, I. (1970). Falsification and the methodology of scientific research programmes. In. I. Lakatos & A. Musgrave (Eds.), *Criticism and the growth of knowledge* (pp. 91-196). New York: Cambridge University Press.

Laudan, L. (1996). *Beyond positivism and relativism: Theory, method, and evidence.* Boulder, CO: Westview Press.

McGuigan, F. J. (1960). *Experimental psychology: A methodological approach.* Englewood Cliffs, NJ: Prentice-Hall.

Popper, K. R. (1959). *The logic of scientific discovery.* New York: Basic Books.

Proctor, R. W., & Capaldi, E. J. (2001a). Empirical evaluation and justification of methodologies in psychological science. *Psychological Bulletin, 127,* 759-772.

Proctor, R. W., & Capaldi, E. J. (2001b). Improving the science education of psychology students: Better teaching of methodology. *Teaching of Psychology, 28,* 173-181.

Treisman, A. (1960). Contextual cues in selective listening. *Quarterly Journal of Experimental Psychology, 12*, 242-248.

Van Hamme, L. J., & Wasserman, E. A. (1994). Cue competition in causality judgments: The role of nonpresentation of compound stimulus elements. *Learning and Motivation, 25*, 127-151.

Watson, J. B. (1913). Psychology as the behaviorist views it. *Psychological Review, 20*, 158-177.

Understanding Psychology Deeply Through Thinking, Doing, Writing

Michael L. Stoloff
Sheena Rogers
James Madison University

> *Teaching is an enactment of the teacher's understanding of what it means to know the field deeply — and how that understanding develops.*
>
> — Hutchings, 2000, pp. 2-3

TEACHERS AND STUDENTS alike achieve a deep understanding of psychology in the same way — through doing psychology. We "do" psychology each time we think and write about issues and ideas in our field and each time we act as a psychologist in the laboratory, in schools, in clinical settings, or in the work place. Thus, college teaching, while focusing on central issues in psychology, should give students an "[O]pportunity to engage in the intellectual work of the discipline" (Shulman, 2000, p. 26) alongside their teachers. This chapter attempts to describe what it means to know a field deeply, and what engaging in the intellectual work of the discipline means for the teaching of psychology. We will argue that our students should be doing psychology and not simply "learning" about it. When they begin to think, behave, and write as psychologists, they will begin to understand psychology deeply.

What Does It Mean to Understand Psychology Deeply?

We doubt that all the readers of this chapter will agree on what it means to understand a topic in psychology in depth, but that's OK. People who understand a topic in depth think about what is being said as they read and formulate their own opinions about the subject matter. That's exactly what we would like our students to do as they explore the popular press, read textbooks or journal articles, write essays, listen to our lectures and participate in our seminars. We will argue here, however, that as teachers of psychology we should aim for more than active learning for its own sake. Active learning has many goals. We recommend that opportunities for active learning should be explicitly structured with the aim of helping students think like psychologists. In our conceptual model of understanding psychology deeply, students should embrace certain fundamental assumptions and we should raise and return to these themes in the courses we teach.

- ◆ Behavior is not random, but occurs in patterns. Students must be able to recognize patterns of behavior in themselves and in others.
- ◆ Behavior is predictable if we can identify its causes.
- ◆ Many behaviors can be controlled.
- ◆ The predictions, causes and controls for behavior may not be known, but they are knowable.
- ◆ The ability (or inability) to predict and control behavior raises ethical concerns.

Additionally, to help our students to think, act, and write as psychologists we must assist them in learning how to:

- ◆ Formulate questions in a manner that allows them to be answered.
- ◆ Draw upon their knowledge of theoretical frameworks, systematic methods, and logic to address their questions.
- ◆ Generate and defend the logic of their own theories regarding the causes, prediction, and control of behavior.
- ◆ Make connections among things that are experienced independently, like the facts learned in different courses, or between classroom learning and "real life."
- ◆ Develop their thinking through writing, and write using the conventions of the discipline.

The fundamental question for college teachers is how do we get them to do this?

Promoting Deep Understanding Through the Curriculum

Scholars of the curriculum have been reluctant to identify specific content areas that must be included in the undergraduate psychology major, but all agree on the importance of developing an in-depth understanding. Quality undergraduate programs develop students who think critically and scientifically about behavior, producing graduates who can evaluate the facts of psychology using scientific methodology. They can see relationships among what they know, write with precision about their ideas, and are prepared to make logically sound and ethical decisions. They can do these things because they have practiced them throughout their undergraduate program.

The Capstone May Be Too Little Too Late

Like many undergraduate psychology programs, we restructured our curriculum following the St. Mary's Model (Brewer et al., 1993). Our sequenced curriculum begins with a general introductory course and a methods core, followed by area courses and electives to provide breadth. We had hoped that in-depth understanding would be promoted in a required capstone experience — the culmination of the major. Looking back, we now realize that for most students, the capstone experience is too little, too late. Students who have rarely explored topics in depth prior to their capstone course have little facility with the process, and graduate before they recognize the limits of our understanding of psychology (not just their understanding of what we taught them). Many graduate having barely begun to think, write and act as psychologists do. The capstone experience would be a better culmination if students already knew how to ask good questions when they started the course, and then spent a semester focusing their intellectual and creative energy, using well-practiced skills, on their capstone topic.

We should note that delegating in-depth understanding to the capstone experience alone was never the intention of the St. Mary's Conference attendees. While they said that psychology majors should study at least one topic in depth (hence the capstone concept), they also recommended developing in-depth understanding throughout the curriculum. They suggested covering less in order to study selected topics in more depth. Therefore, what we will say here is not new, but our recommendations go beyond organizing the sequence of courses that defines the curriculum. We advocate changing the way we teach individual courses within the curriculum.

Building Deep Understanding Within Our Courses

Typical students do not begin a class expecting to develop a deep understanding of the subject matter. They do not expect to learn to think like a psychologist; they expect to learn facts and to memorize key terminology and information. They often feel most comfortable with a class when they can take many notes, and they consider class meetings in which they do not take many notes to be less important. Our textbooks and our lectures encourage this focus on content mastery and over time, the volume and complexity of the content requiring mastery in our discipline has increased dramatically.

But should we let textbook coverage define the content of our courses? We tend to think that we do our students a disservice when we do not include this or that important topic in our survey of the field. How many of us have been heard to echo the apocryphal professor who complained, "If we take time to discuss what it all means, we will never get to X by Christmas," where "X" is the topic of Chapter 15 in the book? If we allow the textbook coverage to define the content of our courses, then we must race through the semester to cover as many topics as possible. We will have little time to promote engagement in the intellectual work of the discipline and to work on the development of our students' deep understanding of the subject matter. There will be no time for students to learn how to generate their own questions, to develop strategies for finding answers, to think hard and deeply about the important issues in the field, to write and rewrite thoughtful and well-developed essays, or to make connections across and among disciplines, between the classroom and other experiences of life.

How to Promote Deep Understanding

Change the Course Goals

Abandon the goal of covering the breadth of subject matter now included in the course and drop some topics to allow time to explore those remaining. Be bold! Don't discuss all of the topics in class that you used to, and don't require students to read every chapter in your textbook, or have them read some chapters on their own, that you will not cover in class. Be even bolder. Consider replacing or supplementing portions of the textbook with original sources.

Use Class Time to Promote In-Depth Understanding

Find ways to engage students in active learning during class. Have the class engage in the process of discovery: simulating or conducting research. Have students define critical terms using their own words. Explain the logic of the research that led to findings they will memorize, have students consider the validity of findings, and explore the relationship between one area of study and another. Include informal writing in class.

Technology can help. When you use multimedia technology simply to prepare colorful versions of text transparencies students describe the result as "mind numbing." Used well, however, technology can promote active learning and critical thinking. In my (Stoloff's) large-group Biopsychology class, I explain the theory and procedures of lie detection with materials a former student, Hilary Kissel, helped me develop. Using presentation software and video of a subject in a previously-recorded lie detection session, I present a series of trials during which the subject is either telling the truth or lying. The presentation shows the subject responding to questions, along with a record of their physiological responses. Students decide whether the subject is truthful or not, and report the rationale for their interpretation. While I could more efficiently tell students about lie detection in a straight lecture format, I believe they have a much deeper understanding of the procedures and limitations of the process when they have to think like a psychophysiologist. It is so difficult to distinguish between "truthful" and "lying" trials, students themselves initiate a discussion of the use of lie detection findings in legal proceedings.

Add Out-of-Classroom Activities That Promote In-Depth Understanding

Require students to participate in activities that challenge them to think outside the classroom and consider group activities that inspire discussion of an issue. Require a long-term project. When they write papers, require multiple drafts and revisions. Demand that students go beyond the standard discussion phrase, "more research is needed" to explain the next logical steps that need to be taken to gain a better understanding of the issue addressed in their paper.

In Stoloff's Biopsychology class, students act as psychologists in a semester-long group project applying knowledge about behavior to a "real world" problem. Projects typically are designed to inform a non-technical audience. For example, groups have developed Web sites, videotaped news magazine reports, illustrated booklets, and written children's storybooks explaining a mental disorder and its treatment. The project has five components:

- ♦ Students explore the Web and discover current news stories; post a short synopsis and link to the site on a class Web discussion board where classmates can respond; see the place of psychology in the world; and generate project ideas.
- ♦ Working collaboratively, students formulate the project. Each group member chooses a side of a controversial issue and the group plans a creative project to present and evaluate the controversy. Each group establishes group and individual goals that guide the project through the semester. I ultimately grade students on how well they achieve their own goals.
- ♦ Students read primary source materials and write a brief literature review on their topic.
- ♦ Students evaluate each other's literature review. (I grade the papers after they are revised and rewritten.)
- ♦ Finally, the group develops a single creative product that draws upon the expertise individuals developed during earlier stages of this project.

This project model should work for virtually any psychology course.

Take Time to Build the Skills Students Will Need for In-Depth Understanding

Teach the thinking, writing and other skills you want students to be able to demonstrate by the end of the course. Don't throw students in at the deep end, begin with less complex cases and assignments and raise the challenge level of in-class and homework activities as the course progresses.

Rogers has students write, and receive feedback on, a sequence of increasingly challenging short essays in each of her classes. Many of the papers are limited to one page, a constraint that requires careful planning, deep thinking about content, and judicious editing and rewriting — exactly the skills we wish to develop.

The first essay may require only a careful and precise description of a mechanism or process. The essay is low demand because the student need only understand and report what they have learned.

Later, students will compare and contrast two processes, two experiences or two ideas. This requires that students go beyond the facts learned and think about how the targets are similar and how they are different, make inferences, and draw conclusions.

The next, more demanding task requires analysis and evaluation as they write a critique of a theory or idea.

A research proposal follows, in which students must generate new ideas on a topic they have studied and read about, and formulate hypotheses.

Ultimately, students write a short position paper using all of the thinking and writing skills they have practiced during the semester: thesis development, selection and use of evidence and counterevidence, analysis and evaluation of evidence, synthesis of ideas, drafting, organizing, editing and rewriting.

By the end of the semester, students are very good at this, despite the increasing difficulty of the essays. Have your students save their first essay or paper and their last, comparing and critiquing the two.

Structure Your Evaluation of Student Performance to Reward In-Depth Thinking

Show how much you value in-depth understanding by including graded activities that require more than simple memorization and regurgitation of facts. Expand your grading scheme beyond the multiple-choice format. Short written answers on tests, one paragraph or one-page papers, and Web discussion board postings are great! Reward students for explaining complex ideas in their own words, forming connections, and being creative. Flag these events in student writing and explain why you value them. Even within a multiple-choice evaluation you can reward in-depth understanding by asking questions that require students to apply what they know to a new situation. For example, after studying neuroanatomy in Biopsychology Stoloff uses multiple-choice questions to ask students to predict the behavioral consequences of trauma to a particular part of the brain. Consider having students predict the outcome of an experiment that was not discussed in class but which does have a predictable outcome from the information that was discussed.

Promote These Conceptual Changes Throughout the Psychology Curriculum

To have a powerful impact on student development, we need to instill these attitudes in as many courses as we can. Skills in thinking, acting and writing should be cultivated from the beginning of the program until the student graduates, thinking like a psychologist and like a scientist.

We were going to suggest that faculty select a topic that can be explored from many theoretical perspectives across courses. However, we are rewriting this paper one week after the events of September 11, 2001. Clearly the psychology curriculum at JMU was affected by the events of that day. With a focus on the events of September 11, faculty teaching Personality, Social and Abnormal Psychology began discussing why people behave as they do. Counseling, Clinical and Community Psychology courses focused on people's response to trauma, stress and grief. Developmental Psychology faculty discussed how children perceive traumatic events, and how to help children deal with the events of the day. Perhaps we can teach our students to think like psychologists by exploring significant world events with them, as they unfold. They will learn to think like psychologists as they explore new ground with us.

Summary

When you institute the changes we advocate here, one measure of your success in promoting in-depth learning will be a change in student attitudes. Fact learning and note taking will no longer be their primary expectation of our classes. Students will come to class with questions that are challenging because these will be the same questions researchers in the field are grappling with. Ideally, we will so excite students about the content we teach, that content and its implications will be discussed among students during their "free time." By engaging in the intellectual work of our discipline, in thinking, acting, and writing as psychologists, our students will begin to understand psychology deeply and they will have begun the process of becoming psychologists.

References and Recommended Readings

Benjamin, L. T., Jr., & Lowman, K. D. (Eds.). (1981). *Activities handbook for the teaching of psychology: Volume 1*. Washington, DC: American Psychological Association.

Benjamin, L. T., Nodine, B. F., Ernst, R. N., & Broeker, C. B. (1999). *Activities handbook for the teaching of psychology: Volume 4*. Washington, DC: American Psychological Association.

Brewer, C. L., Hopkins, J. R., Kimble, G. A., Matlin, M. W., McCann, L. I., McNeil, O. V., Nodine, B. F. Quinn, V. N., & Saundra. (1993). Curriculum. In T. V. McGovern (Ed.), *Handbook for enhancing undergraduate education in psychology* (pp. 161-182). Washington, DC: American Psychological Association.

Halonen, J., & Gray, C. (2001). *The critical thinking companion for introductory psychology* (2nd ed.). New York: Worth.

Hutchings, P. (2000). Promoting a culture of teaching and learning. In D. DeZure (Ed.), *Learning from Change: Landmarks in teaching and learning in higher education from* Change Magazine, 1969-1999 (pp. 1-4). Sterling, VA: Stylus.

Makosky, V. P., Sileo, C. C., & Whittemore, L. G. (Eds.). (1990). *Activities handbook for the teaching of psychology: Volume 3.* Washington, DC: American Psychological Association.

Makosky, V. P., Whittemore, L. G., & Rogers, A. M. (Eds.). (1988). *Activities handbook for the teaching of psychology: Volume 2.* Washington, DC: American Psychological Association.

Miserandino, M. (1999) Those who can do: Implementing active learning. In B. Perlman, L. I. McCann, & S. H. McFadden (Eds.), *Lessons learned: Practical advice for the teaching of psychology* (pp. 109-114). Washington, DC: American Psychological Society.

Perlman, B., McCann, L. I., & McFadden, S. H. (Eds.). (1999). *Lessons learned: Practical advice for the teaching of psychology.* Washington, DC: American Psychological Society.

Schulman, L. H. (2000). Teaching as community property: Putting and end to pedagogical solitude. In D. DeZure (Ed.), *Learning from Change: Landmarks in teaching and learning in higher education from* Change Magazine, 1969-1999 (pp. 24-26). Sterling, VA: Stylus.

Various Eds. (1981-1999). *Activities Handbook for the Teaching of Psychology* (Vols. 1-4). Washington DC: American Psychological Association.

Teaching Ethics Across the Psychology Curriculum

DEBORAH WARE BALOGH
Ball State University

Although strategies and approaches may differ, our common goal should be to encourage and inspire students to develop and rely on their own moral compass — despite enormous pressures to the contrary.

— Arthur J. Schwartz
Director of Character-Education Programs
John Templeton Foundation

AFTER READING ARTHUR Schwartz's column on character education in *The Chronicle of Higher Education* (June, 2000), the academic vice-president at your institution announces a new agenda — all departments will incorporate ethics education within the undergraduate curriculum beginning at the start of the next academic year. Suddenly your university begins struggling with issues such as, "The curriculum is already packed, we cannot add another course." "Ethics are so subjective anyway, what values and principles will we teach?" "We don't have an expert on ethics in our department — how will we cover this content?" "It is our job to instruct, not to build character or indoctrinate students with our morals." As a member of the psychology department, you have the good fortune to be associated with a discipline that has been a leader in establishing ethical principles and standards of conduct for its members for several decades.

You grab your copy of *The Ethical Principles of Psychologists* (American Psychological Association, 2002) and immediately add it to the list of required readings for each of your classes. You suggest colleagues who might be well suited to teach an ethics course for your department. You dig out an article from your files concerning an ethical breach in your specialty area and distribute a photocopy to all of the students working in your laboratory. There — you've done it — you are on board with the vice-president's initiative. Or are you? Maybe not. Most experts in the teaching of ethics agree that an intellectualized, point-and-tell approach fails to produce lasting change in awareness and understanding of ethical issues. In addition, many would agree that limiting ethics instruction to a single course within the curriculum is important, but insufficient. Every content area in psychology stimulates numerous teachable moments with respect to ethical issues — the raw material is there, and it is simply a matter of casting course content in terms of its ethical dimension. When ethics content is seamlessly integrated across the curriculum, students come to understand that adhering to ethical principles is the responsibility of all members of the profession and they come to expect to be confronted with ethical dilemmas in many professional contexts.

Starting Out: Establish Goals for Ethics Instruction

Experts in ethics education typically agree that students need to develop their skills in the following areas:

- Sensitivity to ethical issues, sometimes called "developing a moral imagination," or the awareness of the needs of others and that there is an ethical point of view
- Recognition of ethical issues or the ability to see the ethical implications of specific situations and choices
- Ability to analyze and critically evaluate ethical dilemmas, including an understanding of competing values, and the ability to scrutinize options for resolution
- Ethical responsibility, or the ability to make a decision and take action
- Tolerance for ambiguity, or the recognition that there may be no single ideal solution to ethically problematic situations

Using Historical Examples to Introduce Ethical Issues

It is often helpful to introduce ethically questionable practices by describing landmark research studies that raised significant ethical issues, that were heavily debated among researchers, or that stimulated attempts to develop or modify the professional code of ethics. A list of historical references that can be used for this purpose and that raise issues such as the use of deception, informed consent, researching sensitive topics, confidentiality, bias in data collection or reporting, invasion of privacy, risks versus benefits, and unexpected negative effects is provided at the end of this chapter.

The Case Study Technique

The most useful cases are those that are realistic, provoke wide-ranging discussion, and require that a specific question is answered or solution is achieved. Case studies can be simple, focusing on a single ethical predicament (as in Case No. 1 below) or complex, involving multiple interrelated ethical issues (as in Case No. 5). Instructors should consider beginning with relatively brief, clear-cut, and egregious violations of ethical principles. Gradually, cases for which there may be multiple potential solutions can be introduced for discussion.Some cases lend themselves to a format that initially provides minimal information, then adds incremental information that raises new issues or creates additional ethical challenges. Adding variations that change the recommended course of action or that pose competing goals are especially helpful (see Fisch, 1997). Another way to challenge students is through the use of cases that are deliberately ambiguous and are therefore more difficult to resolve.

Nagy (2000), Kitchener (2000), and Koocher and Keith-Spiegel (1998) are excellent sources for case material. The following also are recommended.

Case No. 1: A developmental psychologist is conducting research on physiological correlates of orienting responses in newborn infants. What is his obligation with respect to sharing each child's data with the child's parents? Does it make a difference if the data suggest the presence of neurological abnormality in some participants?

Case No. 2: A major corporation hires a psychologist who has conducted applied research on cognitive errors that result from the way in which a message is presented. Some of her research suggests that consumer brand preferences can be manipulated by techniques that make listeners think they heard something other than what was actually said. The vice president for the marketing division, who is not trained in behavioral research, pressures her to incorporate her research findings in the design of a new marketing campaign.

Case No. 3: A local business is interested in making better decisions about which employees should be encouraged to pursue a career track in management. They ask a psychologist to administer and interpret personality tests that include measures of creativity, ego strength, and introversion/extroversion to a group of new employees. Should he honor this request? What issues are raised if the instruments used by the psychologist were developed using samples of white, middle-class men? What if the psychologist also is asked to administer an integrity test to evaluate each new employee?

Case No. 4: A psychologist who conducts research on jury characteristics has reported that potential jurors with specific demographic characteristics are more likely to render verdicts that favor the defense in certain types of felony cases. An attorney who is defending an accused rapist offers her a position as a consultant. She is asked to advise the defense team about which potential jurors should be eliminated during the voir dire process. Should she accept the position?

Case No. 5: A psychologist is a guest in a weekly radio "call-in" program. Listeners are invited to ask questions. During a show on treatment of depression, a listener calls with a "question" about someone he knows who seems "down." He reports that this acquaintance has been missing work frequently, seems irritable most of the time, and has made comments about "getting out of the rat-race for good." The psychologist, concerned that the caller may be actually speaking about himself, tells the caller that the friend is clinically depressed, is a likely suicide risk, and should be seen by a mental health professional as soon as possible. The psychologist then offers an appointment time in her schedule the following morning if the caller will bring his "friend" to the office for evaluation and referral to a local physician. Has she followed ethical guidelines in handling this situation?

Case No. 6: A psychologist who conducts qualitative research on social support and major life stresses is interested in how parents cope with the death of a young child. He decides to research the use of Internet sources of support. Posing as a parent who has recently lost a child, he subscribes to several listservs and participates in discussions in several chat rooms. He prints postings and discussions for his data analyses and quotes from these transcripts in his publications. What ethical concerns exist? What additional issues arise if the psychologist harvests the lists, not as a participant, but by accessing archives?

Additional Strategies

A media diary is another effective technique for integrating ethical issues within the psychology curriculum. Portrayals of mental health professionals are abundant in film (e.g., *Analyze This*), television (e.g., "Frasier," "Ally McBeal"), and in fiction. Newspaper and magazine advice columns, radio and television talk shows, and news and feature stories are replete with "expert" opinions on applied psychology and psychological research.

Requiring students to keep a media journal or logbook of ethically problematic situations involving actual or fictitious psychologists and to share their observations with the rest of the class usually produces a myriad of ethically questionable practices and reinforces the idea that ethical predicaments are frequent challenges for psychologists. Class discussion can be centered on the actions that could be taken in each situation to remain within the profession's ethical standards and how the profession can and does respond to ethical misconduct among its membership.

Role-playing, skits, and debates are also effective alternatives for teaching students to identify and react to ethical dilemmas. Role playing scenarios that pit self-interest against the interest of others or that involve competing values (e.g., confidentiality versus duty to warn) are especially helpful when students are at the stage of needing to develop awareness of the ethical implications of various choices. When students act out the roles of the key stakeholders in well-publicized court cases such as Tarasoff v. the State of California Board of Regents or Detroit Edison v. National Labor Relations Board (both reviewed in Bersoff, 1995), the ethical dimensions become real to them. For example using this technique the instructor can assign students to the roles of the primary players in the Tarasoff case. Other students are assigned to function as a "Greek chorus," and the instructor serves as facilitator of their commentary.

Debates also are useful and are most effective when the players are required to take the view or act out a role that is opposite to their own point of view. A good topic is the use of animals as research subjects. Another, that introduces competing goals, is psychologists serving as "talk-show experts." Court cases such as those listed above lend themselves well to a debate format. While teams of students debate, the rest of the class can be asked to physically positioning themselves beside the "pro" team or the "con" team. Students are given the freedom to move between the two sides as the debate progresses. The process of literally choosing a side promotes engagement and self-reflection among class members who are not actively debating.

Finally, there is no substitute for students' experience in supervised service learning activities for providing opportunities to confront ethical dilemmas as they unfold in real world settings. Internships and practicum placements are rich sources of material for stimulating discussion of ethical conflicts and competing values. Instructors, supervisors, and practicum/internship administrators can encourage students to regularly consider ethical issues both by modeling ethically responsible choices and by requiring students to reflect on actual professional dilemmas and responsible problem solving. Incorporating a service-learning journal is a helpful technique for encouraging this reflective process.

Promoting and Maintaining Student Engagement

For many undergraduate students, college courses may provide the first opportunity to scrutinize ethically problematic situations, and students are typically anxious to offer opinions about these situations. However, differing developmental levels among students may present challenges in guiding the discussion toward finding responsible solutions to ethical dilemmas. Instructors need to acknowledge that students will not make gains in their ability to critically evaluate and problem solve until they have gained awareness that ethical issues exist. Instructors should be prepared to begin with a discussion of obvious breaches of professional standards. When the majority of students have at least a basic awareness of the issues, cases that are less clear-cut can be introduced.

Students enter college with a wide range of values and views, and some may become concerned that discussion of ethics will eventually threaten their positions on moral issues. It is helpful to differentiate between morals and standards of conduct at the outset. Reminding students that personal criticism is off-limits and that personal religious or ideological principles will be respected creates a safe environment that encourages students to examine the grounds for their beliefs without threatening them or requiring them to adopt the moral values of others.

Students tend to more readily engage in classroom activities when a learning community is created in which students teach one another. Working in small groups is less intimidating and an excellent way to break the ice. The instructor can facilitate the peer learning process by serving as a guide who provides structure. The decision making model provided by Koocher and Keith-Spiegel (1998) offers a useful structural framework for keeping the discussion focused on standards of conduct and avoiding straying into heated deliberation of moral values.

Evaluating Students' Progress

Instructors should consider evaluating students' mastery in: 1) basic knowledge of the ethical standards of the profession and 2) attainment of the goals described earlier. Different grading formats should be used in determining progress in these two areas. Assessing mastery of professional standards can be accomplished by a traditionally graded examination in which students must demonstrate, for example, which practices are ethically acceptable versus which are in violation of ethical standard given a set of parameters or a hypothetical scenario.

Assessment of students' development of ethical sensitivity, critical thinking, and ability to consider alternatives is difficult using a traditional grading format since much of the mastery students achieve is a result of guided reflection. If instructors expect their students to regularly reflect upon ethical issues, then they need to give students opportunities to reflect and they need to provide feedback on how students approach this process. Requiring students to keep a journal or a portfolio of writing assignments in which they engage in self-assessment is, therefore, a good way to monitor and evaluate student progress. Using these formats, a completion grade (credit/no credit; pass/fail) is the preferred method. However, it is important to provide guidance and structure to such writing assignments so that students use them productively.

The Instructor as Role Model

Perhaps it goes without saying that instructors' credibility in teaching professional ethics is greatest when they model ethical conduct. Students recognize when their professors cut ethical corners, bend the rules, or ignore instances of unethical behavior (e.g., cheating) in their classes. Instructors are not immune to ethical lapses. Self-reflection on responsible choices is not just for our students. It is a habit in which each of us should regularly engage to avoid inadvertently sending students the confusing message of "Do as I say, not as I do."

References and Recommended Readings

American Psychological Association. (2002). Ethical principles of psychologists and code of conduct. *American Psychologist, 57,* 1060-1073.

Bandura, A., Ross, D., & Ross, S. A. (1963). Vicarious reinforcement and imitative learning. *Journal of Abnormal Psychology, 67,* 601-607.

Berkun, M. M., Bialek, H. M., Kern, R. P., & Yagi, K. (1962). Experimental studies of stress in men. *Psychological Monographs, 76* (15, Whole No. 534).

Bersoff, D. N. (1995). *Ethical conflicts in psychology.* Washington, DC: American Psychological Association.

Bramel, D. (1963). Selection of a target for defensive projection. *Journal of Abnormal and Social Psychology, 66,* 318-324.

Burt, C. (1972). Inheritance of general intelligence. *American Psychologist, 27,* 175-190.

Darley, J. M., & Latane, B. (1968). Bystander intervention in emergencies: Diffusion of responsibility. *Journal of Personality and Social Psychology, 8,* 377-383.

Djerassi, C. (1991). *Cantor's dilemma.* New York: Penguin.

Feldman, M. (1966). Aversion therapy for sexual deviation: A critical review. *Psychological Bulletin, 65,* 65-79.

Fisch, L. (1997). Triggering discussion on ethics and values: Cases and innovative case variations. *Innovative Higher Education, 22,* 117-134.

Fisher, C. B., & Tryon, W. W. (Eds.). (1990). *Ethics in applied developmental psychology: Emerging issues in an emerging field.* Norwood, NJ: Ablex.

Haney, C., Banks, C., & Zimbardo, P. G. (1973). Interpersonal dynamics in a simulated prison. *International Journal of Criminology and Penology, 1,* 69-97.

Hite, S (1976). *The Hite report: A nationwide study on female sexuality.* New York: Macmillan.

Humphreys, L (1975). *The tea room trade.* Chicago: Aldine.

Kimmel, A. J. (1996). *Ethical issues in behavioral research.* Cambridge, MA: Blackwell.

Kitchener, K. S. (2000). *Foundations of ethical practice, research, and teaching in psychology.* Mahwah, NJ: Lawrence Erlbaum.

Koocher, G., & Keith-Spiegel, P. (1998). *Ethics in psychology* (2nd ed.). New York: Oxford University Press.

Lisman, C. D. (1996). *The curricular integration of ethics: Theory and practice.* Westport, CT: Praeger.

Milgram, S (1963). Behavioral study of obedience. *Journal of Abnormal Psychology, 67,* 371-378.

Nagy, T. F. (2000). *Ethics in plain English: An illustrative casebook for psychologists.* Washington, DC: American Psychological Association.

Piliavin, I. M., Rodin, J., & Piliavin, J. A. (1969). Good Samaritinism: An underground phenomenon? *Journal of Personality and Social Psychology, 13,* 289-299.

Poynter Center, Indiana University, Bloomington. [Online]. Available: www.indiana.edu/~poynter.

Rosenhan, D. L. (1970). On being sane in insane places. *Science, 179,* 250-258.

Scarr, S., & Weinberg, R. (1976). IQ test performance of black children adopted by white families. *American Psychologist, 31,* 726-739.

Schacter, S., & Singer, J. E. (1962). Cognitive, social, and physiological determinants of emotional state. *Psychological Review, 69,* 379-399.

Scharf, B. F. (1999). Beyond etiquette: The ethics of doing naturalistic discourse research on the Internet. In S. Jones (Ed.), *Doing Internet research: Critical issues and methods for examining the Net* (pp. 243-256). Thousand Oaks, CA: Sage.

Schwartz, A. (2000, June 9). Lessons in character. *The Chronicle of Higher Education, 46,* A68.

Taub, E., Ellman, S. J., & Berman, A. J. (1966), Deafferentation in monkeys: Effect on conditioned grasp response. *Science, 151,* 593-594.

Watson, J. B., & Rayner, R. (1920). Conditioned emotional reactions. *Journal of Experimental Psychology, 3,* 1-14.

Beyond the Classroom: Developing Students' Professional Social Skills

MERRY J. SLEIGH
DARREN R. RITZER
Winthrop University

HAVE YOU EVER encountered students whose academic performance is excellent, yet their attitudes are not? For example, you may have known a student who performed exceptionally on assignments but was habitually late to class, argued over class points, and demanded personal exceptions to class policies. One of the reasons students might fit this description is poorly developed social skills.

As teachers, our obligation to help students learn factual information about the field of psychology and to develop cognitive skills is clear. Teaching students critical thinking, written communication, and time management skills also has value. Less attention is given to developing students socially, although social proficiency can be equally critical for future academic and nonacademic success. Most occupational settings require personal interaction, where both performance and personality impact perceptions of employee value. In addition, education is more than the transmission of facts — it is about helping individuals maximize their potential, both personally and professionally. Perhaps the lack of attention to social skill development is because the task is more individually based, more challenging, and less reinforced.

What Are Professional Social Skills?

Professional social skills are those that facilitate interpersonal interaction between individuals or in a group setting. Ideally, professional interactions require having an awareness of the respective positions of the persons involved, the relationships among persons, and the task at hand.

One reason that students may have poorly developed professional social skills is the lack of emphasis on them in a traditional educational setting. A second reason may be that students have not had previous role models of professionalism, either because of limited personal work history or lack of modeling in the home. Third, faculty may feel uncomfortable or have little experience with providing this type of feedback to students. In addition, students who do not realize the costs and benefits of social professionalism may not be motivated to develop those skills.

To clarify which skills are most valued in the workplace, we asked professionals in government, private, and non-profit industries to list the skills they most want to see in their college-educated employees (listed from most frequently to least frequently mentioned):

- ◆ Monitoring one's own emotional expressions and responsiveness (e.g., showing interest in and motivation toward the task at hand)
- ◆ Maintaining composure when challenged
- ◆ Speaking/writing in a manner appropriate to the audience (e.g., different levels of formality in different contexts)
- ◆ Being receptive to feedback and constructive criticism (e.g., a willingness to learn and improve)
- ◆ Awareness of personal responsibility as a listener or audience member
- ◆ Respecting others' professional position, particularly those in authority (e.g., referencing people formally unless instructed otherwise)
- ◆ Being on time
- ◆ Being prepared for the task at hand
- ◆ Being courteous to everyone, regardless of rank or position
- ◆ Appreciating services received and expressing that appreciation
- ◆ Making proper introductions
- ◆ Dressing appropriately

Landrum and Harrold (2003) recently surveyed employers across the United States. They found that five of the top ten most desired skills for psychology graduates related to social relationships (i.e., listening skills, ability to be work in groups, getting along with others, focus on customer or client, and interpersonal relationship skills).

Benefits of These Skills

Many of the benefits of these skills are obvious to those of us in professional circles, and people who behave appropriately are more respected and trusted. More responsibility is given to those who prove trustworthy and reliable. People who express appropriate thanks are, in turn, appreciated. Finally, people often model the respect they receive.

In addition, teachers often learn of opportunities (e.g., internships) that can be extended to students. Who do we select for these opportunities? If you are like us, you select the students who are capable, but also the students who can create a positive impression. Thus, socially skilled students open themselves to additional educational experiences.

On the other hand, a lack of social skills may be a contributing factor in student-faculty conflict. In one study, students' perceptions of faculty behavior and their own self-reported behavior during disagreement reflect a need for improved interpersonal skills (Tantleff-Dunn, Dunn, & Gokee, 2002). Understanding and promoting student professional social skills may be one way to prevent, minimize and resolve conflict.

Developing Social Skills in the Classroom

We can help students both develop skills and appreciate their value through slight modifications to the classroom, resulting in ongoing benefits to the student.

Syllabus Construction

When we see students failing to meet expectations, the first question we must ask is whether the expectations were clearly conveyed. The syllabus is an ideal place to formally present expectations, emphasize valued skills, and initiate relevant discussions.

On their syllabi, teachers should specifically outline their approach to fostering professional social skills. They can include their reasoning for emphasizing social skills, how social skills will be emphasized, and how students will get feedback on their progress. For example: "Part of this course will emphasize professional social skills. The ability to function professionally and to communicate in an appropriate manner is critical to success in any career field. Throughout the semester, students will be given examples of professional social skills, opportunities to practice professional skills, and feedback on their performance."

Teachers also can include specific statements regarding social expectations in the classroom. For example:

- Please be on time, as a display of professional courtesy and respect.
- Demonstrate sensitivity and respect towards other classmates, particularly when personal experiences or differing opinions are being shared.
- Class participation is essential for a complete educational experience. Oral defense of ideas is as important as written presentation of ideas.

Similarly, you can indicate how you prefer to be addressed and the rationale behind your request. When we spoke to non-academic professionals, they expressed concern over the trend for incoming college-educated employees to use an informal interactive style, which can be misinterpreted as disrespect. Thus, we encourage students to assume formality unless instructed otherwise. We prefer to be addressed by our title, because of the benefit it offers to students, not for any benefit to ourselves.

Facilitation of Student Interaction

Many articles have discussed the value of student interaction in the classroom (e.g., Fassinger, 2000), one benefit of which is improving social skills. When the entire class is interacting, teachers should simultaneously model and facilitate. Using names helps students learn to address each other directly and models networking skills. For example, a teacher might say, "Tommy, it sounds like you agree with the position Susan just expressed." Teachers also need to be quick to use disagreement as a chance to practice social skills. For example, a teacher might rephrase a comment so that it focuses on the issue rather than the people involved.

Teachers also can create smaller groups in which students interact. Because the teacher is not always present during group work, providing feedback about social skills requires additional effort. One way is to solicit feedback from all members of the group about the participation of its members. Doing so anonymously usually provides the most accurate information. If consistent themes emerge, either positive or negative, the teacher has the option of addressing those issues with an individual student, privately, of course.

Using Psychology to Teach Social Skills

Psychologists study behavior, and most behavior occurs in social settings so class material can be tied to social interaction and social skills. The following topics, in addition to many others, might provide a launching pad for discussions related to personal development.

- ♦ Impression management
- ♦ Social reinforcement
- ♦ Fundamental attribution error
- ♦ Social development in young and middle adulthood
- ♦ Decision-making heuristics
- ♦ Body language
- ♦ Persuasion

In addition to using class topics to facilitate social skill development, entire courses sometimes have social skills as their primary focus. Many departments offer courses that teach counseling skills or focus on the development of "helping skills" (see Korn, 1980). Developing rapport, listening carefully, and clarifying communication parallel some of the social skills that employers want to see. Teachers of these courses might want to emphasize the broad applicability of these skills beyond counseling settings.

Developing Social Skills Through Guided Activities

In addition to using typical classroom activities, teachers and departments can create specific activities that target skill improvement.

Formal Student Presentations

Student presentations are often used because they offer practice at oral communication. A second benefit is the opportunity to develop professional demeanor. Teachers may choose to require appropriate professional dress and technical language, and a presentation that reflects an awareness of the status, experience, and education of the audience. Students also may be asked to invite questions from the audience, a situation that will help them practice calm and thoughtful responsiveness. If handled with care, teachers can allow classmates to provide feedback not only about the presentation's content, but the presenter's style as well. We recommend having students submit their feedback to the teacher who can then screen any unhelpful comments and type the remaining comments to ensure anonymity.

Community Speakers

Another way to develop students' professional social skills is through recruitment of a guest speaker for the classroom. We divide students into groups of two to seven, depending on the overall size of the class. Each group recruits a professional from the community to speak on a course-related topic, creating an excellent opportunity for polishing their social skills inside and outside of the academic arena. Each group is required to identify a course-relevant community organization or business; discuss its choice with the instructor; solicit a speaker from that organization; prepare the speaker for the presentation; introduce the speaker to the class; send a note of thanks; and gather feedback from the class.

Regardless of who invites the speaker, teachers can use the presenter as a launching pad for a discussion of professional behavior (see Mullins, 2001). Before the presentation, students can be encouraged to show interest and ask thoughtful questions. If the speaker is controversial, the class may want to discuss appropriate ways to behave and respond. Afterwards, the class can discuss what impression the speaker made. Was he/she professional, prepared, appropriate and what impact did that have on his/her message? Did the way the speaker presented him/herself add to or take away from the content? Did they exhibit any behaviors worth adopting for the students' personal use? As students become more aware of how they form impressions of others, they will gain greater ability into how to monitor the impressions they convey themselves.

Facilitated Expressions of Thanks

Students often fail to express appreciation that they feel, which is unfortunate, because offering thanks helps the recipient feel valued and appreciated. Typically, we are willing to work harder for a student when our efforts are appreciated, a social reciprocity that is often mirrored in the workplace. We can encourage this social kindness by facilitating formal expressions of thanks. One simple way is to listen for students to compliment other students or teachers. When this happens, help the student consider ways to pass that compliment directly to the recipient. Another idea is to have a day devoted to expressing thanks. For example, Psi Chi might sponsor a faculty and staff appreciation day. Departments can make a point of inviting students to events where members of the campus community are honored, to involve students in the formal recognition of performance.

Career Building Workshops

Students may view social skills as more valuable when they are linked directly to future outcomes, such as job hunting and career building. Teachers or organizations, such as Psi Chi can organize workshops that address professional behavior. Speakers can include representatives from the job placement office on campus, community leaders, and alumni. Faculty may also be invited to share their perspective on the student behaviors that impress or frustrate them. In our experience, students respond well to this information when it is provided as an adult-to-adult conversation, rather than in a didactic manner.

One simple workshop activity is to distribute sample graduate school or job application forms to undergraduates. Most of these forms ask faculty to rate students on factors such as oral communication skills, ability to work in groups, willingness to learn, motivation, and professional demeanor. In addition, recommendation forms typically ask for a letter that comments on the applicants' strengths and weaknesses. Students are often surprised to learn that they are evaluated on personal behavior as well as academic accomplishments.

Similarly, students can be asked to imagine themselves as a supervisor who has just given feedback to an employee. Ask students to comment on their impressions of an employee who responds by asking for ways to improve his performance versus one who argues over the evaluation. This situation offers a nice analogy to a classroom setting where a student can look over a test with the goal of improving performance, or to argue a point here and a point there. At times, we have directly addressed this issue, assuring students that exhibiting maturity, assuming responsibility, and communicating carefully are far more valuable skills than is a point on any one exam.

Last but certainly not least; examples of professional social behavior can be distributed in handouts. For example, we offer students a guide for how to ask for letters of recommendation, including the following items:

- ♦ Ask teachers, "Would you feel comfortable writing me a letter of recommendation?" This question provides an option for faculty who cannot write a strong letter to decline the invitation.

- Communicate with recommender in person, rather than by e-mail or phone.
- Provide at least a month for the letter to be written.
- Organize all materials, remembering to complete the student's portion of the recommendation.
- Provide stamped envelopes.

Similar guides could be created for other social situations, such as approaching a faculty member in her office. Suggestions could include:

- Ask the faculty member if he or she is currently available. Do not make assumptions based on your cursory observation. Do not interrupt if a faculty member is talking with someone else.
- Introduce yourself and remind the faculty of your relationship to him or her.
- State the reason for being at the office.
- Be prepared and direct about the nature of the issue. If a problem is being addressed, be ready to offer solutions.
- Listen carefully. Maintain eye contact. Think before speaking.

Professional Community Interaction

While the classroom offers one perspective of the field of psychology, students also can benefit from involvement in the professional community outside of the classroom. Teachers should encourage students to gain such experience through community service or internships, making sure to advertise opportunities, working with students on funding sources to help students become involved, and providing opportunities for students to present their own work.

Similarly, teachers should be aware of special events for students at professional conferences. Many conferences offer awards and sessions that are geared directly toward undergraduate students. Following the conference, help students learn by reflecting on their experiences. Ask questions such as, "From whom did you learn the most, and why?" Or, "Was there anything you would do differently the next time?" Posting conference presentations in the department may also be an avenue for continued interaction between students and between students and faculty.

Creating Professional Experiences

For many reasons, it may be difficult to get the majority of psychology students to attend professional conferences or to write grants, so these experiences should be created in the local environment when possible. Departments or institutions can hold mini-conferences to showcase student work. To make the event successful, teachers need to support it and be willing to draw students into discussions about their process and product. Teachers can offer both compliments and suggestions. Perhaps even more helpful is to challenge students to target strengths and weaknesses of their own work, and to practice communicating that information in a comfortable manner.

Developing Social Skills
Through Personal Example

Modeling is a powerful teaching tool. Teachers should be aware of every opportunity to show the behavior they wish to see from students by being on time, respectful, and courteous. Similarly, listening carefully when students speak or handling disagreement calmly provides excellent role modeling of frequently needed skills.

Be on time for office hours and respectful towards students, even when they are not being respectful in return. The goal is not to make office hours a formal, uncomfortable event. In fact, we know that accessibility is important for student success in the classroom (Anaya, 2001). We believe that teachers can be highly accessible while still expecting and modeling respect and appropriateness.

Another way to model a professional skill is to refer to colleagues as you expect students to address them. For example, we do not recommend "Bob's class" to a student, but instead "Dr. Smith's class." Remembering to consider the student's perspective is easier in some settings that others, and teachers might want to consider how to handle addressing one another when students are present.

Besides referring to colleagues in an appropriate manner in front of students, it is important to avoid disrespectful actions or attitudes when interacting with colleagues. The debate of ideas should be handled with a focus on the issues rather than the persons, and teachers should avoid sharing opinions of colleagues with students. Students learn what it means to be a professional by watching the professionals around them.

Providing Feedback

Providing reinforcement for positive behavior and constructive feedback for negative behavior is easily neglected but may be vitally important. The latter can be uncomfortable, but may have a huge impact on a student's future success. A teacher who can provide unpleasant feedback in a gentle, calm, and kind manner is modeling professional behavior in a challenging situation.

Teachers should focus on the issue and not the student. Teacher also should describe the behavior and its consequences. For example, it is appropriate to say, "I feel frustrated by your tardiness, because I will not have enough time to help you now." Or, "It seems as though you are more concerned with your grade than what you have learned. Is this an accurate perception?"

Emphasize that your feedback is designed to help the student succeed, rather than criticism without a clear purpose. For example, "I'm giving you this feedback, because this is a safe environment in which to receive it. The consequence for making mistakes is relatively minimal in comparison to the workplace where mistakes can cost you your job. Here, mistakes are an opportunity to learn and improve." To be appropriate, teachers need to examine their own motives. If strong emotions are expressed during the feedback, teachers are not only ineffective; they are modeling what they do not want to see.

Often, students are adept at working through solutions to problems when scaffolding is provided. When students are part of a problem, allowing them to be part of the solution can be a valuable learning experience. For example, we might say, "You chose not to take the third exam. I cannot allow you to take a make-up, without being unfair to your classmates. What do you think we should do about this situation? What would be fair to you, me, and your classmates?" This scenario allows students to view situations from others' perspectives and to practice their problem-solving skills in a social setting.

Conclusion

Helping students understand the value of professional social skills will benefit both your students and department. Both undergraduate and graduate students are representatives of our schools, and their success in the job market is often reflected in enrollment figures and alumni contributions, and in further job opportunities for future graduates. The facts that we teach may be soon forgotten, but developed social skills benefit students long beyond their academic tenure.

At a more global level, one of the goals of an undergraduate liberal arts education is to prepare students for active and effective participation in society (Barker, 2000). Being a useful and well-rounded citizen requires both technical expertise in a chosen career and also the professional skills necessary to function within that realm. Students master the technical knowledge, skills, and abilities through traditional classroom activities such as reading, writing papers, and taking exams. However, given the unprecedented pace of change within disciplines, specialized techniques and training (i.e., technical skills) quickly become outmoded (Barker, 2000). The ability to cope with this change, the capacity for critical thought, and a professional demeanor may have far more lasting value. In fact, professional social skills transfer across, and are valuable in, all domains and settings.

References and Recommended Readings

Anaya, G. (2001). Correlates of performance on the MCAT: An examination of the influence of college environments and experiences on student learning. *Advances in Health Sciences Education, 6,* 179-191.

Barker, C. M. (2000). *Liberal arts education for a global society.* Meeting summary of State of American Liberal Arts Education, Carnegie Corporation of New York.

Fassinger, P. A. (2000). How classes influence students' participation in college classrooms. *Journal of Classroom Interaction, 35*(2), 38-47.

Korn, P. R. (1980). An undergraduate helping skills course: Skill development and career education. *Teaching of Psychology, 7,* 153.

Landrum, R. E., & Harrold, R. (2003). What employers want from psychology graduates. *Teaching of Psychology, 30,* 131-133.

Mullins, P. A. (2004). Using outside speakers in the classroom. In B. Perlman, L. I. McCann, & S. H. McFadden (Eds.), *Lessons learned: Practical advice for the teaching of psychology* (Vol. 2) (pp. 119-126). Washington, DC: American Psychological Society.

Tantleff-Dunn, S., Dunn, M. E., & Gokee, J. L. (2002). Understanding faculty-student conflict: Student perceptions of precipitating events and faculty responses. *Teaching of Psychology, 29,* 197-202.

Part VI

Tests and Grading

Grading for Optimal Student Learning

MARTHA S. ZLOKOVICH
Southeast Missouri State University

MOST OF US ENJOY OUR roles as teaching faculty, but that does not mean every pedagogical task is enjoyable. One of the most troubling tasks, possibly second only to finding a parking place on campus, is grading. Yet the vast majority of faculty must summarize their students' knowledge and abilities — however multi-faceted and rich — into grades. This process takes time and effort, and is seldom described as fun, but more often as a job that must be done. However, there is more to grading than assigning a letter grade. Attention to grading practices can improve not only the reliability and validity of a final course grade, but equally or more importantly, faculty teaching and student learning.

So where should conscientious instructors start to improve the quality of their teaching and grading, as well as their students' learning? Faculty must recognize that grading is an integral part of the teaching and learning process, so consideration of assessment must be interwoven within careful course planning and viewed as part of teaching, not as an unpleasant "add on." Planning, teaching, and assessment are all necessary elements of instruction that must be coordinated in order for grading to be reliable, valid, appropriate and meaningful for both students and teachers.

Many faculty think of teaching as a linear process, with planning occurring first, teaching second, and grading third; however, a more complicated relationship that involves bi-directional influences is probably more accurate. "Assessment can and should be integrated with instruction and should inform both instruction and ongoing course planning" (Brookhart, 1999, p. 2). In reality, effective grading begins with a clear vision of the kinds of learning we value for students, and helps them to achieve this learning and skill development.

Planning

The first step in addressing both learning and the grading process is planning. Planning for effective grading should begin well before the syllabus has been finalized and the course starts. This means that instructors must do the following:

Articulate the Learning Goals of the Course

Keeping in mind the level of the course and anticipating who the students will be in terms of major, year, and interest level, instructors must decide what is most important for students to know. What should they be able to do? How should students be different by the end of the course?

Make Informed Choices About Grading

Faculty should start with themselves and try to answer questions such as:

- Why do I use the grading methods I do?
- Are these methods accomplishing what I want them to?
- What do I really know about grading?

Faculty can then read about grading and talk with colleagues. These discussions should avoid the trap of the typical discussion of "hard grading and standards versus easy grading and standards" which avoids important issues. Ask colleagues, especially those teaching other sections of your courses, or courses at similar levels, questions such as:

- What grading schemes do they use and why?
- How well do these grading schemes work?
- Do they change their grading processes depending on the type or level of class?
- Do they drop the lowest grade in a course or weight early tests less than later ones? Why have they adopted these grading processes and do they work?

Talk with students about grading. Find students from a course you just finished teaching. Ask questions such as:

- What did you think and feel about the grading?
- Did you understand the grading criteria used?
- Was the grading fair?
- Did you know what to do to earn a good grade?

After the first week or so of a course, ask students whether they understand your philosophy and system of grading. If you try new grading schemes, ask students for feedback during and after the course to see how well they worked. Finally, you may want to look at the grades students earned on course assignments and their final grades and see how these would change if you altered your grading. For example, would the student who started off poorly but showed great improvement have been better served by a different approach to grading? Questions about grading also could be included in course evaluations for future reference.

Choose Grading Methods Once Course Goals Are Clear

Avoid being locked in to one grading method for all course assignments, exams, and the final grade. Some different methods that may be used for different assignments throughout the course include:

Criterion referenced grading. Student achievement is measured with respect to a specified standard of performance, and each student's grade is assigned independent of other students' grades. Advantages of this method are that it promotes success in later courses that build on the content learned in the current course, allows performance to be measured against a standard rather than other students' achievements, focuses on learning rather than relative ranking against other students, and it may motivate students because there are no limits to how many people can earn high grades.

Norm referenced grading or "curved grades." Each student's grade is based on her or his relative position compared to the other students. The meaning of any one score is derived from a comparison with other scores in the norm group. This method promotes a normal distribution with a small number of "A" and "F" grades and makes assigning letter grades easy for the instructor. Curving has problems, however. It creates a relative standard that varies with the performance of the particular group, and does not describe how proficient a student is with respect to the material covered, but with respect to other students' performance.

Mastery learning. Every student is given access, time, varied instruction, frequent feedback, and encouragement to persist until information is mastered. This method can be time consuming for faculty because it requires extensive record keeping and students are not all on the same material at the same time, but there are advantages for the students. These include clear definitions of criteria for specified competency levels, modification of learning activities to achieve mastery, frequent feedback, and ample opportunity for students to display learning. The number of students who can succeed is unlimited since they are given multiple opportunities to achieve mastery.

Pass-Fail. This method is based on the assumption that students will be encouraged to explore course material if they do not have to worry about letter grades, as well as the hope that students are interested in learning for learning's sake.

Plan for Realistic and Appropriate Time Commitments for Yourself and Students

It is important to consider time commitments in terms of faculty and student workloads, as well as the relative importance of particular assignments. A grading plan that requires onerous time burdens for the instructor or the students may not best serve learning goals. In addition, a simple assignment should not count 50 percent of a final grade nor an extensive term paper 10 percent. Balance a given assignment or requirement with the amount of work required both in and out of class, and with the percentage of the course grade associated with that task.

Decide Which Assignments Will Receive Formative Assessment and Which Summative Assessment

Formative assessment, such as students obtaining feedback on initial drafts of papers from peers or the instructor, allows students to learn from their mistakes and to improve their grade when summative assessments are made. Summative assessments allow students to demonstrate what they have learned, but without the opportunity to further affect their grade on that particular performance. Formative assessments are important for encouraging learning and skill mastery, summative for indicating previous learning.

Communicate the Method of Grading Clearly to Students

This should be done in the syllabus, on the course Web site, and in initial class meetings. An important part of this information should be a clear connection between the goals of the course and the grading methods you describe. Students should be reminded of the grading methods throughout the course, especially close to due dates for assignments and exams.

Putting It All Together

Let me suggest the following outline. As you plan a new course or think about one you have taught many times, list each course module and assignment. Next to each, write the goal each is supposed to meet (e.g., learn facts, improve writing skills, critical thinking).

In a third column write why this goal is important to you as an instructor and to the course.

In a fourth column enter the grading procedure you will use for each assignment and exam (e.g., letter grade, points — criterion referenced grading, curving).

In the last column, list how students can do well on each assignment/requirement to be graded (e.g., read the book, active learning, use of tutors, come to class for reviews, turn in paper for formative review).

Once this table meets the goals you have for the course share it with a colleague or two, and several students for their feedback.

When it is completed, add a column with due dates and include it in the materials you distribute to students at the beginning of the course. You may even want to leave a blank that can be checked off next to each assignment so students can note when they are completed, and so you can point out to students how the course is developing (e.g., we have now completed the second writing assignment, or we have now completed the third of four modules emphasizing the facts, theories, and people in this subdisciplinary area).

Teaching

The second step is teaching the material and skills related to the course goals you have communicated to your students, making sure that the time you spend in class corresponds to the emphasis you gave each topic in your goals and grading procedures.

Teach What Students Need to Know for the Test

This does not mean teaching the test, or handing students the test and going over the answers with them; this means that what students need to know and how they will be evaluated should not be a mystery to them. Teach to the criteria by which you will evaluate the test (Walvoord & Anderson, 1998). For example, if you are giving an essay exam that you will grade based on content, organization, and critical thinking, spend time in class on all three. You could point out the relationship between different ideas, group them by common elements, and have students meet in small groups to analyze and critique. In other words, do not expect students to be able to organize and think critically if you have not taught these skills. Help them develop these skills through your teaching. The points emphasized during class time, the assigned readings, and the explanation of grading criteria should make it clear what students must know for the tests.

Choose How Class Time Will Be Used and Use Various Methods of Teaching

Choose whether class time will be devoted to initial (first) exposure to material or the processing of material. Traditional lecture frequently provides first exposure to material, unlike process-oriented teaching, which allows for face-to-face inter-action between the instructor and students as they attempt so-phisticated thinking (Walvoord & Anderson, 1998). Keep in mind that many class activities require students to have completed a first exposure to the material, some reading or studying before class, on their own time. Class time can then be used to provide feedback on work or learning done outside of class. Active learn-ing methods such as small or large group discussions, manipu-lation of materials, or interaction with the instructor, help stu-dents to approach the material they are trying to learn from multiple perspectives.

Assess Learning Regularly

Find out what students have learned before they complete exams or other graded work. Frequent learning checks allow for ongoing planning and instructional changes in response to what students are learning — or not learning. These checks need not be time or labor intensive for the instructor and might include:

- ♦ Stopping after 20 minutes to have students summarize their notes so far and ask about anything they don't understand.
- ♦ Having students take one or two minutes to discuss their notes with a partner.
- ♦ Giving a quiz that can easily be graded by the instruc-tor or other students.
- ♦ Asking students to contribute to a Web discussion on the topic outside of class.

Adjust Teaching During the Course as Needed Based on Student Understanding

These adjustments are especially important when later classes build on earlier material. You may have to give up some course content if students are not learning what they need to early on.

The feeling that you have to cover "X" amount of content can be the enemy of good teaching.

Be Thoughtful and Supportive About Grades

Grades are important to students and affect their future plans, feelings, and motivation. Be available and supportive in talking about their course performance and grades. Be sure to have criteria to explain the assignment of grades and be patient with students who think you have made an error — we all make mistakes and the student may be correct. Be prepared to suggest how students can improve their grades in the future. With sensitive support, even a student who fails your course can learn important skills from you that can help that student succeed in later courses.

Assessment

Measure Learning Several Different Ways

Students should have the opportunity to exhibit their knowledge in different ways. These might include multiple-choice tests, essay exams, papers, various forms of oral communication, portfolios, or research projects.

Provide Ongoing Feedback so Students Can Adjust Their Studying Before It Is Too Late to Affect Their Grade

In-class assessments such as those mentioned above that inform instructors about their teaching can also inform students about their comprehension of the material, and help them manage their study time most effectively.

Give Prompt Feedback on Exams, Papers, and Other Work

Students deserve and appreciate prompt feedback. Such feedback provides optimal opportunities for students to learn from their successes and mistakes.

Make Testing Authentic

At least some of the time, real world performance must be attempted, especially if application of knowledge was an important goal identified in course planning (Brookhart, 1999). Real world performance may be assessed by essay or multiple choice exams, or by performance of an activity. Exams, however, must be well-written in order to ensure that students have learned underlying concepts, not just strategies to pass exams. Testing should focus on assessing whether students have met learning goals, rather than having simply figured out how to spit back information from the text or class. This can be accomplished by demonstrating how a particular concept applies to a variety of situations. Then on a test, students are better prepared to think about how the concept applies to a new situation. If a concept such as operant conditioning, for example, is only presented in the context of Skinner's pigeons, students may learn how to spit back the application of the concept only in that particular situation. If however, operant conditioning is explained in terms of Skinner's pigeons, potty training young children, lottery players, and maintenance of sustained relationships, students are more likely to develop a comprehensive understanding of operant conditioning, and therefore be better able to apply that understanding to new situations presented on exams.

Consider Retesting

The possibility of retaking a test applies especially to criterion-referenced or mastery learning grading methods. The grading policy should specify at the outset what will happen if a student fails to meet the minimal standard. Questions to consider when constructing a retest policy include:

- If a second chance is given, how does the instructor treat students who performed satisfactorily the first time?
- How many chances to pass should be allowed?
- Will students start to regard the first attempt as a low-effort trial run?
- How much more work will this entail for instructor (different versions of test/additional papers)?
- Is the maximum possible grade on an assignment lowered on a second or third effort and if so, by how much?

Summarize Each Student's Work
Into a Course Letter Grade

There are several choices for aggregating grades across the semester into one letter grade. The method of aggregation has to be communicated to students early in the semester and should influence course planning and teaching. Points to consider when choosing a method of determining the letter grade are whether students can overcome poor performance early in the course, and whether high performance in one area can make up for low performance in another.

Weighted letter grades. The weight of a grade refers to its proportion of the final grade. This method is based on the assumption that different performances and different kinds of excellence are differently valued (e.g., when class participation is weighted less than a term paper), and that the instructor applies a value judgment in assigning weights.

Accumulated points. This method defines each letter grade by the percentage of total points available. For example, an "A" might be defined as earning at least 90% of the total number of points available. This method is based on the assumption that good performance in one area can help make up for low performance in another area, that it allows for developmental progression throughout the course, and that it allows students to decide where to concentrate their effort. A potential problem is that students who did well early in the course may have accumulated enough points that they decide to put their effort into other courses.

Definitional assessment. This method requires students to meet or exceed particular standards for each category of assigned work, for example, requiring an "A" on tests and at least a "B" on papers for an "A" in the course. It is based on the assumption that each category is important and one category cannot make up for poor work in another. This method is less common and will need to be carefully explained from the outset.

Median grading. This method is useful when grades tend to fluctuate widely or when scores are based on only a few assignments. The final grade is determined by arranging the grades in order and picking the middle grade. One exceptionally low or high grade does not affect the median as much as it would the mean.

Holistic grading. This method involves the use of formative assessment across the semester, with the final grade determined primarily or completely by summative assessment of a final project at the end of the semester. It is particularly appropriate when the goal of the course is to produce a final product. The method may include more than one category of accomplishment, similar to definitional assessment. An advantage of this method is that it allows ongoing instructor feedback on students' work toward that final product to aid them in learning, without penalizing early errors at the end of the course.

Conclusion

Faculty should focus on being a teacher first and a gatekeeper second, because student learning is the primary goal of an education (Walvoord & Anderson, 1998). If grading practices can encourage a learning-centered rather than a grade-centered motivation among our students, then we will have progressed toward that goal. Equally important, as faculty learn about grading, talk about it with colleagues, think about what they want it to accomplish, and talk about it with students, the number of problems related to grading should decrease, and the quality of their teaching, as well as their feelings of efficacy as teachers, should rise.

References and Recommended Readings

American Association for Higher Education.(1989). Assessment forum: *Nine principles of good practice for assessing student learning.* [Online]. Available: www.aahe.org/assessment/principl.htm

Black, P. (1998). *Testing: Friend or foe?* London: Falmer.

Brookhart, S. M. (1999). *The art and science of classroom assessment: The missing part of pedagogy.* Washington, DC: The George Washington University.

Hammons, J. O., & Barnsley, J. R. (1992). Everything you need to know about developing a grading plan for your course (well almost). *Journal on Excellence in College Teaching, 3*, 51-68.

Milton, O., Pollio, H. R., & Eison, J. A. (1986). *Making sense of college grades: Why the grading system does not work and what can be done about it.* San Francisco: Jossey-Bass.

Walvoord, B. E., & Anderson, V. J. (1998). *Effective grading: A tool for learning and assessment.* San Francisco: Jossey-Bass.

Returning Graded Assignments Is Part of the Learning Experience

SANDRA GOSS LUCAS
University of Illinois Urbana-Champaign

1. THE CLASS PERIODS when quizzes, exams, and graded assignments are returned to students are _____

Fill in the space with the best answer:

a) low points in the semester.
b) adversarial, with students arguing for points and higher grades.
c) a waste of time, since little content is covered.
d) all of the above.

If you answered "d" you are in the majority, and often right. As Stephen Brookfield (1990) put it, "Teaching is the educational equivalent of white-water rafting" (p. 2). He was referring to the teaching ups and downs typically experienced by college instructors. Seldom is there a "lower" point in the semester than when we hand back graded assignments.

The Importance of Feedback

What makes the experience so painful? Whether we like it or not, many students are motivated by grades, and attempt to obtain as many points as possible from each assignment. Lowman (1987) argues that instructors encourage this Grade Orientation when they place more emphasis on the external reward of a grade than on an internal reward of learning (Learning Orientation) or when students are not given specific feedback on what they missed and the correct answer. Without structured feedback procedures classrooms can become battlegrounds or, at the very least, unpleasant. As Lowman (1987) so eloquently summarizes, "Evaluation is the single most important topic to the interpersonal rapport of a college class" (p. 71).

Some instructors try to avoid the situation by not providing feedback, saying they cannot take valuable class time to go over a quiz, exam or paper. This is not a good solution. Feedback is the best way to make a test a learning experience, a confirmed essential of learning. Students should be able to see how they performed on each question, what they got right as well as what was wrong. In this manner, students can see which topics they mastered, whether any problems exist, and whether their methods of study are effective (Jacobs & Chase, 1992, p. 7).

Students are entitled to information about their performance and Chickering and Gamson (1991) list feedback as one of their "Seven principles for good practice in undergraduate education." As they point out, "Knowing what you know and don't know focuses learning. Students need appropriate feedback on performance to benefit from courses. ... [A]ssessment without timely feedback contributes little to learning" (p. 66).

McKeachie (1999) concurs, saying tests "are important tools for learning and discussion of the test is a worthwhile use of class time" (p. 193). He adds that students also learn from their corrected papers.

The Best Offense Is a Good Defense

As with most teaching issues, advance planning is the key. By careful planning of your overall evaluation strategy; by meticulous development of your quizzes, exams, papers and other assignments; and by establishing procedures to deal with handing back graded assignments, the evaluation process can become a positive learning experience for both you and your students.

Using a diversity of evaluation instruments including essay and multiple choice exams, short writes, longer papers, group projects, mini-assignments, homework, oral presentations, and so forth provides a more valid evaluation of each student, especially given our diverse student populations. By including a variety of graded components, students with different learning styles and strengths have an opportunity to perform well on at least one component of the final grade. Students also should be less anxious about each individual assignment. I will concentrate on returning graded exams and papers.

Maximizing the Student's Learning Experience

Relieve Student Anxiety

Exams and other graded assignments should not be cast as "adversarial" activities. It is not the instructor versus the student. Graded assignments should be presented in the context of the course, as essential feedback and evaluation tools. This means that students need to feel that the assignment was fair. As Svinicki (1999) puts it, "Testing should not be a game of 'Guess what I'm going to ask you.' Students don't mind 'hard' tests as long as there are no surprises and they can recognize the relationship of the test to the course" (pp. 245-246). There are many ways to achieve this goal.

Relieving student anxiety surrounding taking quizzes and exams and writing papers has an impact on student views and emotional reactions when graded assignments are returned. Therefore:

- Do *not* make each assignment a huge percentage of the student's grade.
- Make the first assignment relatively easy.
- Avoid pop quizzes (Davis, 1993).
- Help students learn how to study; encourage study groups.

Be accessible before graded assignments are due so students have an opportunity to ask questions (Brookfield, 1990; Davis, 1993). This availability could include extra office hours, online office hours, or an extra review session.

Provide students with practice exams or practice questions, as often as each class period. This allows them to understand how the quiz and exam questions are written and to try to "think through" an exam question in a non-stressful environment. Practice questions can cover new material or be used as a review. By asking students to explain both why an answer is incorrect as well as why an answer is correct, they learn to monitor their thinking during test taking. Ask students to revise the question to make each incorrect answer correct. This is an excellent technique requiring them to analyze the material in more depth than just recognizing the correct answer.

Writing assignments or papers should be clearly explained and a scoring grid, or outline of how the assignment will be graded, should be attached. Students should know specifically how their assignment will be graded.

Provide Optimal Feedback: Exams and Quizzes

If your quiz/exam was developed following psychometric guidelines, if you look at how the items performed on the exam, and if you allow students a civilized forum in which to voice their concerns, handing back quizzes/exams can become a critical thinking, learning experience — for both students and teacher.

Pick the 10 or 12 most missed items. This feedback does not take an entire class period. Enlarge these items and print them on a transparency. Go through them as you do your practice questions, talking about why the correct answer is correct and the incorrect answers are not. Show the students the item analysis for the question. By explaining those items, the majority of student questions are answered and students learn how to better think through exam questions, increasing the likelihood that they will do better the next time. Students can then be invited to go over the entire exam during office hours.

Break students into groups (Davis, 1993) to discuss the answers among themselves with "questionable" questions referred to the instructor for discussion by the entire class. This process often requires less time than going over each item in class and students report enjoying it more.

Offer students a post-exam review session during the next class period. Addison (1995) found that students who attended such reviews when the exam items were explained performed better on later exams than those who did not. While a cumulative exam was given in the classes Addison (1995) studied, students in courses with non-cumulative exams may learn material important for understanding later course content and something about their own thinking process during the testing situation. Although Addison could not infer a direct causal link between receiving such feedback and later test performance, the "findings offer further support for the value of feedback in learning" (p. 23).

Discuss common errors. When returning graded assignments ask students questions such as "How many of you made silly mistakes?" or "How can you avoid such mistakes in the future?" Students often will mention that they did not read the item carefully or they worked too quickly, common problems. Then ask, "What can you do to better prepare for the next exam?" Students will often come up with the idea of forming study groups or other good ideas for optimizing study time.

Deal with ambiguous exam questions. Questions that are ambiguous or could be interpreted as having more than one correct answer can occur no matter how carefully you have

Fig 1   Strutured complaint routes, like this Request to Review a Quiz/Exam Item form, allow students to make coherent arguments, and eliminate the teacher stress of evaluating student arguments in front of the class.

developed and proof read the questions. It is important to encourage students to engage in critical thinking by having a structure in place that allows them to make a case that either there is no correct answer to the question, or another foil also is correct. Such a structure not only decreases negativity, but it empowers students by encouraging them to analyze a question and research potentially correct answers, many of which they will discover are wrong, ending their appeal with no effort expended on your part. Consider a Request to Review a Quiz/Exam Item form available whenever an exam or quiz is returned. It is important that these forms be placed so that students have access to them without having to ask an instructor for one. The form is an organized way of asking for useful and necessary information. The form (Figure 1) allows students to make coherent arguments, and eliminates or decreases the teacher stress of evaluating student arguments in front of the class.

When going over the exam in class, students often want a decision about a particular item on the spot — not a smart teacher decision based on what we know about stress narrowing cognitive functioning! It is much less stressful to say, "You might have a valid point. Be sure to pick up a form, fill it out and return it at the next class period."

It is important to review all the forms. If necessary, reread the textbook explanation of the concept, consult other instructors, and review the item analysis. Then make a decision about the validity of each argument.

This process really helps students correct misperceptions. Since they must find supporting evidence for their argument in the textbook, many will figure out why their answer was incorrect before they finish the form. Others will not understand why they missed the item, but their argument will suggest a pattern of incorrect thinking that can be corrected by pointing out flaws in their arguments and noting textbook pages that explain the concept. Some times the argument is excellent and the question is indeed bad. Then the quiz/exam is re-scored and students are not penalized for instructor error.

Many teachers worry that a structured complaint route produces numerous forms to review but this does not happen. Seldom do I receive more than a few forms, most about the same two or three exam questions. Teachers also worry that students will challenge items late in the semester. Putting a statute of limitations on such requests, typically one week, easily handles this problem.

By following the procedures outlined above, class periods when quizzes and exams are returned become much less stressful, and students appreciate the opportunity to be heard in an organized and coherent manner. The whole experience has changed a dreaded, argumentative day into a learning experience.

Provide Optimal Feedback: Returning Graded Papers

A little advance planning not only makes handing back graded papers easier; it actually helps you grade the papers. Every major written assignment that I give follows several guidelines.

Grade papers blindly (McKeachie, 1999; Davis, 1993; Lowman, 1987) to avoid the halo effect. I give specific instructions about how the paper should be organized and actually give students a point for proper organization. Their name appears nowhere on the paper except on a separate sheet at the end.

Provide your scoring grid when the paper is assigned so students are aware of the criteria used to evaluate it. These criteria guide students as they write, helping them decide where to put most of their efforts, and which parts of the paper the instructor believes to be most important. Thus, when I return my graded papers, each student receives a criteria sheet with points in each area, and comments. When papers are handed back, the scoring grid is immensely helpful, conveying to students that I have graded their work fairly and pointing out areas where they have done well and those where they did not.

Provide comments on the paper and summarize them in the comment area of the scoring grid. After I have totaled the points and summarized my comments, I look at the student's name and enter it on the scoring grid. At this time I often add a personal comment to the student.

Provide avenues of appeal: encourage thoughtful student rereading and comments to you. I encourage students to ask me to reread their paper, but students must write responses to my comments on their papers before I will do so. This requirement alleviates fishing for points while allowing students who genuinely believe that their paper was misread an avenue of appeal. I seldom have more than one or two requests to reread papers, and I can almost always see where I missed a point or did not follow what the student was trying to say.

Ensure Student Confidentiality and Follow FERPA Guidelines

One important, and often overlooked, issue is student confidentiality. The Family Educational Rights and Privacy Act of 1974 (FERPA) outlined student rights and institutional responsibility in handling educational records, including grades. These rights include, but are not limited to, how instructors post grades and return graded assignments. Some common procedures are actually against the law, such as posting grades by the last five digits of the student's social security number. The only appropriate method of posting grades in a public place (such as bulletin boards or on office doors) is to use a unique identifying number that each student generates. Most universities have moved to random generated student ID numbers or computerized grade books, where students can access their grades and information about the test (means, standard deviations, and other statistics) but cannot see other students' grades.

In the past, instructors often passed out papers and exams by sending the whole pile throughout the classroom or putting a pile of graded assignments in the front of the classroom and having students sort through them. It is illegal for students to have access to the grades of others.

Provide Feedback to Students in Large Classes

Setting up a routine for students to retrieve their graded assignments is especially important in large classes. Once students learn the drill, the time it takes to return them diminishes. Ask students to come as early as possible on days when graded assignments are returned. Consider dispensing the graded assignments outside the large classroom, before people from the previous class have vacated the room. Get help from Teaching Assistants, graduate students, and other instructors to decrease the time needed. Having several individuals returning assignments organized alphabetically by the student's last name can greatly speed the distribution process. Lowman (1987) suggests having Teaching Assistants in each corner of the room with part of the alphabet calling out student names. He says such a process can take 10 to 15 minutes in a very large class, but it is essential to return the assignments. He also advocates returning "papers with as much specific feedback and respect as possible" (p. 80).

Another option, requires some advance planning and work, but can considerably speed up the return of graded assignments. Make several sets of labels of student's names at the beginning of the semester. Then when an assignment is to be returned, attach the label to a manila envelope and put that student's assignment inside the envelope. Stacks of envelopes can be arranged alphabetically throughout the room, facilitating speedy retrieval. Because other students cannot see the grade, this is an acceptable method. (Thanks to Missa Eaton, a Psychology 100 instructor at the University of Illinois for this hint.)

It is unacceptable to not return graded assignments or to ask students to come to your office to get them. As Jacobs and Chase (1992) put it, "Unfortunately, too little feedback characterizes university teaching, especially in large classes. Often students are given only the total score and this is not sufficient" (p. 7). Advance planning can reduce the amount of time needed to return exams in large sections. It will take time but it is worth it.

Summary

As teachers, we are "on our students' side," wanting them to be as successful as possible. We can promote student success when we plan our evaluation tools well; spend time developing quizzes, exams, paper assignments and projects; tell students how they will be evaluated; relieve anxiety about being graded;

provide informative feedback; and allow them to question our evaluations.

Days when graded assignments are returned have become positive days. I no longer dread handing back graded assignments or worry that I have unfairly assessed student performance. Students are empowered to defend their work, to respond to teacher evaluations, and to learn from their errors. I do not think we can ask for much more.

References and Recommended Readings

Addison, W. (1995). Consequences of missing postexam review sessions. *Teaching of Psychology, 22,* 121-123.

Brookfield, S. (1990). *The skillful teacher: On technique, trust, and responsiveness in the classroom.* San Francisco: Jossey-Bass.

Chickering, A., & Gamson, Z. (1991). Appendix A: Seven principles for good practice in undergraduate education. In A. Chickering & Z. Gamson (Eds.), *Applying the seven principles for good practice in undergraduate education: New directions for teaching and learning, 47,* 63-69.

Davis, B. (1993). *Tools for teaching.* San Francisco: Jossey-Bass.

Eble, K. (1988). *The craft of teaching: A guide to mastering the professor's art.* San Francisco: Jossey-Bass.

Jacobs, L., & Chase, C. (1992). *Developing and using tests effectively.* San Francisco: Jossey-Bass.

Lowman, J. (1987). Giving students feedback. In M. Weimer (Ed.). *Teaching large classes well: New directions for teaching and learning, 32,* 71-83.

Lowman, J. (1995). *Mastering the techniques of teaching* (2nd ed.). San Francisco: Jossey-Bass.

McKeachie, W. (1999). *McKeachie's teaching tips: Strategies, research, and theory for college and university teachers* (10th ed.). Boston: Houghton Mifflin.

Ory, J., & Ryan, K. (1993). *Tips for improving testing and grading: Survival skills for scholars No. 4.* Newbury Park, CA: Sage.

Svinicki, M. (1999). Four R's of effective evaluation. In B. Pescosoliod & R. Aminzade (Eds.), *Fieldguide for teaching in a new century* (pp 244-246). Thousand Oaks, CA: Pine Forge Press.

Walvoord, B., & Anderson, V. (1998). *Effective grading: A tool for learning and assessment.* San Francisco: Jossey-Bass.

Author's Note: I am indebted to my mentor, Doug Bernstein, since we developed the majority of these procedures when we worked together in the introductory psychology program at the University of Illinois at Urbana-Champaign.

The Final Exam

JOHN C. ORY

University of Illinois Urbana-Champaign

SON: Hey Pops, you want to help me study for my Algebra final?

DAD: Sure thing, we've been working together all semester so why stop now. Did your teacher hand out a review sheet?

SON: Yeah, take a look at this six-page practice test we got today.

DAD: So what's the first problem? Graph the following equations. Hey kiddo, do you remember how we graph absolute values?

SON: Not a clue, we did that six units ago back in September!

DAD: [*Flipping back 200+ pages in the text, muttering under his breath.*] That's just great, you didn't tell me we were taking a *comprehensive* final!

WHY DO SOME INSTRUCTORS administer exams at the end of a course that cover an entire semester of content while others test only the last unit or two? Ask most students and they will tell you that some instructors are simply more mean-hearted than others. Certainly, there must be more behind a professor's testing strategy than a personality disorder. As part of a campus-wide testing office for some 25 years, I have seen hundreds of exams and spoken with almost as many professors about their testing concerns. However, I had never specifically asked faculty about their strategies for giving final course assessments. How do faculty decide on the type of assessment to use at the end of a course? Do they follow any guidelines while making these decisions?

A quick skim of the best-selling measurement textbooks offers very little on the topic. There is a great amount of wisdom available on how to develop classroom exams in general, including some excellent previous offerings in this chapter (See Perlman, McCann, & McFadden, 1999, Chapters 8 and 9). Yet, there are few written words of advice for developing the course-ending assessment known simply as THE FINAL.

To better understand how and why professors develop final exams I went to the streets, or in our case, the campus quad. With clipboard in hand I asked the passing faculty about their final exams. Their responses reflected a variety of assessment purposes and strategies as well as their thoughts about administering final exams. I offer the following listing and discussion of the considerations or questions professors seem to be addressing when developing a final exam.

What Are Some Reasons for Giving a Comprehensive Final?

♦ "I'm afraid students will forget the early material if I don't include it again on the final."
♦ "I test the whole semester of work on the final to make sure the students have it!"
♦ "A final exam should pull together a semester of content — connect the disconnected."

It seems apparent from many of the comments collected that professors have two major reasons or purposes for administering a comprehensive final. Professors either want students to "show" what they know or to "use" what they have learned from the entire semester of work.

'Show' Finals

I categorize under the "Show" heading those faculty who cover a semester of content through a compilation of objective items, often multiple-choice and short answer. "Show" finals are intended to make students study and review all of a semester's content in order to demonstrate student mastery of knowledge. Professors administering "Show" finals often want to prepare students for the next course in a sequence. They believe (or hope) forcing study and review of an entire semester of content will enable students "to-hit-the-ground-running" in the early days of the next course in the sequence. Following this thought, the "Show" final is as much a pre-measure for the next course as it is a post-measure of the current course. Some professors want students to use these post-measures as self-assessments of their ability to continue in the discipline. A poor final exam performance may encourage a student to get remedial help before continuing in the course sequence or major.

Another way of understanding "Show" finals is to think of them as assessments at the initial levels of a learning hierarchy. Benjamin Bloom and a committee of colleagues developed one of the best-known learning hierarchies. *The Taxonomy of Educational Objectives* (Bloom, Engelhart, Furst, Hill, & Krathwohl, 1956) views the learning process as climbing a ladder of learning outcome rungs. A student can only get to the top level by successfully climbing the lower steps. Bloom's Taxonomy has six learning levels, starting with simple knowledge outcomes and proceeding through increasingly complex levels of comprehension, application, analysis, synthesis, and evaluation. The hierarchy is progressive in that achievement of comprehension objectives relies on the mastery of knowledge-level objectives, achievement at the application level requires successful completion of knowledge and comprehension objectives, and so on.

The majority of "Show" finals I have seen through the years attempt to measure student attainment of knowledge, basic understanding of content, and possibly the ability to apply material. Successful performance on a "Show" final demonstrates the foundation for moving up the ladder of learning. Necessary terms, elementary concepts, and core principles need to be mastered before students can perform higher levels of learning such as Analysis and Synthesis. For example, students should not be expected to critique the appropriateness of a given research design until they have learned of competing alternative designs and their respective strengths and weaknesses. "Show" finals are used by professors who are interested in providing a solid foundation of knowledge by encouraging students to study for a compilation of objective and short-answer exam items.

'Use' Finals

Does this mean that comprehensive final exams cannot be used to measure higher levels of learning? The answer to that question can be found in the second category of faculty who give comprehensive finals requiring students to "use" the knowledge acquired in the course. Professors administering "Use" finals typically want students to demonstrate their ability to use a semester's worth of accumulated knowledge by performing at higher levels of learning. There are at least two kinds of "Use" finals: finals that require students to use their knowledge to produce or create an end-product and those that provide problems or tasks requiring a wealth of acquired information to solve. An example of the first type would be an undergraduate senior seminar take-home final requiring students to develop their own theory of personality. Another example is requiring students in a statistics course to collect journal articles wherein statistical procedures are used either properly or improperly, and the students must provide reasons for their selections.

Examples of the second type of "Use" final, which often involves problem solving or task completion, can be found in statistics courses where students are required to perform analyses on a given set of data. These professors are assuming one cannot conduct an ANOVA without knowledge of means and variances. Another example is a final that requires students to demonstrate their knowledge of JAVA programming by finding errors in a given program. For both examples the student is not asked to show knowledge by creating an end-product such as a theory or critique, but instead is asked to apply what he or she has learned to complete a task or to solve a problem.

Again using Bloom's Taxonomy, it may be useful to think of "Use" exams as assessing higher order learning than "Show" exams. Critiquing a journal article or comparing two theories of color vision demonstrate learning at the Analysis or Evaluation levels of Bloom's Taxonomy. Both require an ability to break down material into constituent parts and to identify and evaluate the relationship of the parts. Furthermore, asking students to develop a theory of personality or to design an experiment challenges them to demonstrate an ability to put together elements and parts to form a whole (abilities at the Synthesis level of Bloom's Taxonomy).

In sum, I have learned that professors using comprehensive exams do have a reason for doing so, reasons that are not at all related to a penchant for cruelty to students. The faculty want students to either SHOW their accumulated knowledge by answering a collection of items or to USE their expertise by creating some end-product or by completing a problem/task. Professors seem more inclined to administer "Show" finals when teaching introductory material or the first course in a sequence when they are most concerned about laying a foundation of knowledge. "Use" finals requiring evidence of higher order learning, such as analysis and synthesis, are most often given in courses taught at the end of a sequence, in capstone courses, or possibly at the conclusion of practicum or intern experiences.

Non-Comprehensive Last Exam

Of course, some professors prefer not to give a comprehensive final of either type described. Typically, these professors structure their assessment program (including all exams, papers, and projects) to assess student learning sequentially and have no interest in back-tracking or retesting content through a comprehensive final. For most of these professors the final exam or paper is the last assessment of uncovered material, such as the fourth of four exams. This assessment strategy may be most appropriate for courses whose content stands alone (e.g., the course is not part of a series of courses) or when the course material is not cumulative in nature (e.g., a stand-alone course on laboratory measurement techniques where a different apparatus or tool is covered in each unit).

How Is the Type or Format of the Final Exam Selected?

- ♦ "I always give a multiple-choice final so I can get my grades turned in on time."
- ♦ "My final is an essay exam, just like the other three course exams."
- ♦ "The final exam is the only test I give in my senior courses."

Even with the help of teaching assistants, professors teaching very large classes face a daunting, time-consuming task of grading a large stack of essay finals. Consequently, I believe logistical concerns such as end-of-semester grade submission deadlines as well as holiday travel arrangements dictate many decisions of testing format. While I don't mean to discount practical or logistical concerns, I would hope there are some pedagogical reasons behind our choice of testing formats.

Select a Final Exam Format That Matches the Level of Learning Taught at During the Semester

A common student complaint expressed on end-of-course student rating forms is this mismatch between teaching and testing. Students don't think it is fair for professors to ask a series of fact/text-based multiple-choice items at the end of a senior seminar course which has centered on discussion and debate of issues.

Choose More Than One Testing Format and Complement Other Course Assessments

Just as today's experts (Gardner, 1993) are reminding us to attend to differences in our student's preferences for learning, we should also acknowledge student differences in their ability to take tests and to demonstrate learning. Ask a large group of students about their testing preferences and about as many students will prefer essay over multiple-choice as vice versa. For this reason I have always stressed at faculty workshops the use of more than one testing format in a course. The use of multiple formats may mean giving a mix of multiple-choice (M-C), essay, and take-home exams, or having multiple-choice and essay items included on the same exam. The final should be complementary to the other course assessments. In other words, if all hourly exams used both M-C and short answer items so should the final exam, or if the hourly exams used M-C, short answer, or essay items then the final shouldn't use an item type so different from these as to confuse the students.

Use More Than One Graded Assignment

When planning the semester a professor should be considering not only what type of assessments to require but how many. With the exception of courses requiring a major paper or class project, measurement experts suggest requiring more than one or two graded components. We all have a bad day! Students should not fear having their entire course grade rest on a single poor performance. I strongly believe the larger the number and variety of course assessments, the greater the likelihood a final course grade will represent an accurate (valid and reliable) measure of student learning. I felt compelled to include this last pedagogical concern for all of the professors I spoke with who think it is sufficient to give only a single assessment — the final exam.

What Is the Difficulty or the Weight of a Final Exam?

♦ "My exams are pretty easy until I get to the final exam."

♦ "I give a final covering the last four weeks of class but give it more weight than the other unit exams."

Exam Difficulty

The answer to the question of "How difficult?" depends on one's interpretation of difficulty. If difficulty refers to testing achievement at higher rather than lower levels of learning then I would say comprehensive "Use" finals are and should be more difficult than other course assessments. However, if we define difficulty as the number of students answering items correctly, I would argue the difficulty level of "Show" finals or non-comprehensive finals should not differ from the other course assessments. The fourth (or final) exam covering only the last three units of a course should have a similar score distribution as the other three exams. The difficulty indices (percentage of students answering an item correctly, see Ory & Ryan, 1993) for items on a comprehensive "Show" exam should be similar to the difficulty indices for items previously administered on other exams. Just because it is the last exam is not a reason for giving fewer high grades and more lower grades than on previous exams. I have yet to hear of any pedagogical defense for doing otherwise. Unfortunately, most attempts to make a final exam more difficult than the other semester exams often result in the professor using unfamiliar item types, tricky wording, or the testing of trivial information; all of which are obvious violations of sound test construction practice.

Exam Weight

The amount of weight assigned to a final exam depends on the number and type of other assessments used in the course to calculate a course grade. There is no single formula to apply to all classes. Obviously, "Use" finals requiring a major class project or term paper will need to place the lion's share of weight on the final course grade, whereas a final exam covering the last three out of twelve units can be weighed equally with the other three or four exams. While I certainly see the value of large end-of-course projects and papers that account for a majority of the final grade, I recommend using more rather than fewer course assessments. As previously stated, by using three-to-five graded components we can be more confident in our final grade while not placing too great an influence on any one assessment.

Exam Score Distribution

Remember, unless you are using standard scores for each exam, desired weights and actual weights may differ depending on the standard deviation for each exam (i.e., an exam with a larger spread of scores will have greater weight when combining raw scores from different exams, see Ory & Ryan, 1993).

Do You Use Final Exams to Motivate or Reward Students?

♦ "I let students know where they stand before the final and they can either take it or not depending on what grade they want."
♦ "I give students the option of taking a final exam or writing a paper."

Motivation

I believe it is fair to say most professors motivate students to prepare for their final by simply assigning it the highest weight of the graded components. Heavily weighted finals encourage students to continue studying in order to either maintain a high grade or provide hope that a low grade can be raised by a strong performance on the final.

Some professors may also attempt to motivate student performance on the final by allowing students to choose from several assessment alternatives, such as taking an in-class exam, completing a take-home exam, or writing a paper. There are, however, some pedagogical concerns when using an alternative assessment strategy. It is difficult to determine the comparability of different assessments. Is performance on a take-home exam comparable to performance on an in-class exam? Is writing a paper comparable to taking a final exam? It is also difficult to assign grades to alternative assessments when there are uneven numbers of different assessments submitted. If only one paper is handed in, you had better have a carefully crafted rubric for grading papers because there are no other papers to use for comparison.

Reward

Some faculty seem to be more interested in using the final exam to reward rather than motivate students. These professors do not require a final exam but instead offer it as a way for students to reach their desired course grade. If a student is content with their course grade they can skip the exam. I have two concerns with this strategy. The first concern is the previously discussed problem of possibly having an insufficient number of exams submitted for grading comparisons. The second concern only applies if the optional final is the only measure of the last few weeks of class material. If it is, I wonder why a professor would spend days preparing and teaching material that may never get tested. Is the material covered from the last hourly exam to the time of the final any less important to learn? I realize not all students are motivated by grades alone, but I am concerned about the waning interest of our students if we fail to have an assessment of the last few weeks of the course.

Do You Provide Feedback to Enhance Student Learning?

♦ "Students can pick up their final exam results in my office at the beginning of the next semester."
♦ "My students can see what they have learned through their final exam score."

I have heard many professors express the importance of using tests to give feedback to students about what they have and have not learned. However, many of these same professors are unwilling to spend "valuable" class-time reviewing exam results. Instead, students are often told to use the professor's office hours if they have a question about the exam. Failing to spend class-time discussing common errors and misunderstanding is missing an opportunity for further learning. Unfortunately, much the same can be said of faculty who express interest in using finals to provide feedback (for further coursework or study in the discipline) but who make little effort to do so. Student feedback is more than knowing a final test score. But how can we provide useful feedback from a final exam that is given on the last day of class?

Students must have a way to get their exams or papers back, either from the professor or the departmental office. This sounds obvious, but how many professors do you know that merely post final exam scores on their door and don't bother returning individual exams or papers? It is easy to ask students to provide a self-addressed stamped envelope so they can get their papers returned.

Feedback on a paper or written project should be of sufficient detail to allow students to know what the grader did and did not see in the work. A copy of an exam should be posted along with the answers on a locked bulletin board or Web site. Ideally, the correct answers could be presented along with a brief comment, text reference, or the most common mistake made on the problem. Our reluctance to publicly display our exams should be over-ruled by a greater interest in enhancing student learning. We shouldn't use the same exam every year anyway, and besides, we can always use some of the items again in later years.

Make yourself available for student questions and concerns. After these conditions have been met, it is still important (and necessary) to make yourself available for further discussion. Tell your students to use e-mail or to stop by your office next semester if they have any questions. At this point you are probably remembering how few of your students have picked up their finals and thinking that receiving feedback is the responsibility of the professor and the student. I respond to your thoughts by asking how much of your students' lack of interest or irresponsibility has been fostered by our collective failure to offer useful feedback in the past? Why should students bother to pick up their exams or papers if all they find written on the pages is a letter grade or numerical score at the top? Most likely all of us could do a better job of providing useful feedback on our assignments to generate student interest in receiving feedback on the final or any course assessment.

Conclusion

My less-than-scientific survey of our faculty revealed that there are many hows and whys to using final exams. Some of the beliefs and practices described by the faculty follow sound pedagogy and learning theory while others are less supported. Whatever their foundation, I would conclude that final exams should be not just reflections of the personality of their makers but products created from thoughtful attention to several considerations. I have tried to identify some of these considerations within a discussion of pedagogy and accepted testing practice.

References and Recommended Readings

Bloom, B. S., Engelhart, M. D., Furst, E. J., Hill, W. H., & Krathwohl, D. R. (1956). *Taxonomy of educational objectives: The classification of educational goals.* New York: David McKay.

Ory, J. C., & Ryan, K. R. (1993). *Tips for improving testing and grading.* Newbury Park, CA: Sage.

Gardner, H. (1993). *The frames of mind: The theory of multiple intelligences.* New York: Basic Books.

Perlman, B., McCann, L. I., & McFadden, S. H. (Eds.). (1999). *Lessons learned: Practical advice for the teaching of psychology.* Washington, DC: American Psychological Society.

Part VII

Enhancing Student Learning, Performance, and Participation

Encouraging Student Attendance

MERRY J. SLEIGH
DARREN R. RITZER
Winthrop University

WHEN I TOOK MY REQUIRED public speaking class in college, the professor repeatedly admonished us to "know your audience." This rule of thumb served me well during my college class and thereafter. As I have prepared and taught my own classes, I try to make my messages understandable and meaningful to those who will hear them. Of course, this rule of thumb assumes there is an audience. Unfortunately, as teachers, we often spend less time cultivating an audience than we do preparing for that audience.

Ways Students Benefit When They Attend Class

Most teachers would agree that class attendance facilitates learning in a variety of ways. The auditory presentation of material supplements reading assignments. Multimedia classroom presentations, that provide an auditory/visual supplement to reading assignments, target a broader range of learning styles than textbooks alone. Also, students who are in class hear discussion and elaboration of important concepts, including the teacher's perspective on the material, and teachers often offer more current information than that found in the textbooks. In addition to learning from the teacher's explanations of class material, students who are in class hear questions and comments from others, and share their own.

Teachers can use class discussion to enhance students' critical thinking skills. They can ask them to explain the material in their own words, pose questions that require students to make connections between different elements of the class material, or challenge students to relate class material to other areas of psychology or to realms outside of the field. The more students examine and analyze material, the better their retention will be. In general, class attendance also influences course grades (Buckalew, Daly, & Coffield, 1986; Simpson & Nist, 1992) and the development of academic skills (Terenzini, Theophilides, & Lorang, 1984).

The development of academic skills transfers to other realms. For example, to take quality notes, students must prioritize, organize, and synthesize the material being presented, and skills developed in one classroom generalize to other courses. Also, regular class attendance requires discipline and time management. These tools are beneficial no matter what career path students follow. In a broader sense, attending class increases students' personal interaction with a variety of faculty members, raising the likelihood of finding mentors and role models who can help guide their academic, career, and personal development.

Ways Faculty Benefit When Students Attend Class

Good attendance is cost effective to faculty. Most faculty put a great deal of effort and time into their teaching. It is students who provide the intellectual and interpersonal stimulation from being in front of, and with, a class. Only with students can faculty tell whether their ideas are being understood, and whether their questions are evoking good thinking. When parts of a class are missing, it simply does not function as well.

Student feedback is critical to modifying and improving faculty teaching. The presence of students in the classroom is, therefore, a learning opportunity for the teacher. Teachers need student feedback in order to gauge their level of understanding and thus improve how they meet students' needs and help them learn course material. The classroom is a faculty's chance to share and renew enthusiasm for psychology. When teachers share excitement about a topic, students often reflect back the same level of enthusiasm. In addition, contact with students allows faculty to get to know those who are struggling, talk with them, increase rapport, schedule meetings with them out of the classroom, and help them improve their course performance. With good attendance, faculty receive a positive return on their investment.

Is Attendance Important to Students?

Students seem to agree that class attendance is important. We surveyed over two hundred students, both upper-level and lower-level, at George Mason University. Only 8 percent reported that getting class notes from a missed class is as useful as attending class. Those who thought borrowed notes were as good as attending class had significantly lower reported grade point averages than those who valued attendance more than borrowed notes. Most students also reported a strong relationship between number of absences and the final course grade.

Although the majority of students reported that attending class is important, about two-thirds indicated that they would miss more classes if they could get the missed notes from a professor. Students miss class for a variety of reasons, most frequently because they need to complete other course work, find the class boring, are ill, or have social obligations (Van Blerkom, 1992). Although we have limited control over some of these situations, we do have control over the structure and content of our classrooms. These elements deserve further attention.

Improving Student Attendance

Teachers have little to lose and much to gain by implementing strategies for motivating students to attend class. Keep in mind that what you do to increase and maintain attendance may differ for courses with primarily lower- versus upper-level students, and for large and small courses.

Class Structure and Content

One approach is to structure class so that those who attend experience obvious benefits, such as better grades, personal growth, and "informative entertainment."

- Test on material covered in class. All material presented, including class discussion, video clips or guest speakers, should be fair game, conveying that class time is of value, whether the instructor is lecturing or not. In a recent survey in our classes, the number one factor that influenced student attendance was the amount of in-class material that would be on the test (Sleigh, Ritzer, & Casey, 2002).
- Avoid repetition of the textbook or assigned readings. If students have access to the same material covered in class, they often perceive little reason to be there.

- Notes provided to students from a remote location, such as a Web site, should not be a transcript of class.
- Recognize that being informative and being entertaining are not mutually exclusive. Using performance skills to convey information captures students' attention and interest. For a detailed discussion of this topic, see Mester and Tauber (2000).
- When the subject matter is made personally relevant, understanding and comprehension are deeper and more meaningful. Students will be more motivated to attend lectures that reflect elements of their background, interests, or future.
- Structure class meetings so students who must be in class for one activity, such as an in-class writing activity, also participate in another, like reviewing feedback on an exam.

Policies

Because college students are adults or on the cusp of adulthood, some faculty believe they should be free to decide whether to attend class. Others believe attendance should be mandatory. Regardless of your perspective, expectations regarding attendance should be clearly explained and attainable because students are often more willing to comply with policies when they understand the reasoning behind them. Such communication also conveys a level of adult-to-adult respect between faculty and students. Present your policies in oral and written formats, and follow through with established consequences. Students learn to ignore policies that are not enforced.

Require attendance and attach it to grades. But think carefully before adopting this policy because it can be controversial. First, some schools prohibit attendance-based grading. Second, this level of control may not be appropriate for adults. Third, providing external justification for attendance may diminish a student's intrinsic desire to learn.

If students are penalized for missing class, they are going to want an opportunity to explain their absences. Teachers can find themselves in the position of trying to evaluate the validity of a range of excuses, which can create a difficult situation.

Some faculty with an attendance policy do not try to validate excuses. They ask students to tell them if they are going to miss class or to inform them as soon as possible after missing one. In the working world, one cannot just stay home and not inform someone. They ask students not to lie. The message is that the faculty member understands that life is complex and knows that students cannot always make it to class. But an attendance policy can communicate that a faculty member values student attendance.

Grade class participation. On the positive side, grading participation makes students more conscious of their presence and behavior in class. Students who are concerned about their grade may try to be actively involved in class, which will theoretically facilitate learning. On the negative side, students may dislike this level of control. Forced participation may be less authentic, waste valuable time, and provide false feedback to the teacher. Teachers are then placed in the awkward position of evaluating "quality" of participation. Students who are quiet by nature may be particularly uncomfortable in a class that rewards extraverted behavior. Finally, it is difficult to keep track of participation in classes larger than about 12 students.

Use in-class quizzes or assignments. We know from the field of learning that unannounced quizzes, on a variable interval schedule, increase attendance. The downside would be students perceiving a lack of control and predictability in the classroom.

Use policies that explain the consequences for missed exams or late assignments to encourage attendance. If a faculty allows students to drop one test grade, a missed exam automatically becomes the dropped grade. When policies are in place, students can make informed choices about attendance, and faculty reduce the need for judgment calls about an absence.

Model the Behavior We Wish to See

In teaching, as in parenting, we should examine our own behavior. We may be unintentionally modeling the very behavior that we deem undesirable in students by arriving late to class, being unprepared, and not keeping appointments, including office hours.

Classroom Atmosphere

The atmosphere in the classroom may be more influential in drawing students than the material presented. Students are more willing to spend time in a place where they are comfortable and valued.

Require respect among students and model this behavior by respecting your students. Create a classroom that has a sense of community where each member has something to contribute and where disagreement is tolerated.

Consider creative, fun ways of rewarding attendance. Elementary school teachers know the value of a smiley face sticker for encouraging student effort. You might translate this strategy to the college population by using age-appropriate incentives. Use attendance as the price to enter a raffle to win a free cup of coffee or soda. These raffles could be spaced across the semester in accordance with the faculty member's budget.

Individual Accountability

Individual accountability is more difficult to accomplish in a large classroom but is worth the effort. We know from social psychology that students are more conscious of their behaviors when they perceive themselves to be individually identifiable and accountable for those actions. One teaching tip that has proven valuable to us is to learn student names as quickly as possible. Calling a student by name demonstrates that you have an interest in the individual as well as the group. Students rate "showing interest in them" and "knowing students' names" as the fourth and fifth most common behaviors teacher can exhibit to develop rapport (Buskist & Saville, 2004). In the same study, students reported that a positive effect of rapport was "to motivate them to come to class more often, and to pay attention in class." While it is difficult to learn students' names in large classes, an earnest attempt and even moderate success doing so, is extremely salient to students.

When you know students by name, you also can reinforce good attendance in ways other than assigning grades. You can provide individual praise and express your concern to absentees. The benefits of this personal attention extend well beyond encouraging class attendance.

Conclusion

Teachers can view their role as that of a strict, authority figure and utilize strategies that penalize for absences or may adopt a laissez-faire attitude and not address attendance at all. Perhaps, the best position is between these extremes. In order to reach an audience, there must be an audience present. To have an audience present, teachers must cultivate an audience by creating policies, lectures, discussions and other uses of class time, and environments that encourage attendance. Once the policies for attendance are established, focus on rewarding good attendance rather than punishing poor attendance.

The critical task for teachers is to know their audiences well enough to create classes that meet students' needs and to modify their pedagogical approaches to fit the situation. Ultimately, encouraging attendance is a critical teaching task. Without students, there is no need for a teacher.

References and Recommended Readings

Buckalew, L. W., Daly, J. D., & Coffield, K. E. (1986). Relationship of initial class attendance and seating location to academic performance in psychology classes. *Bulletin of the Psychonomic Society, 24*, 63-64.

Buskist, W., & Saville, B. K. (2004). Rapport-building: Creating positive emotional contexts for enhancing teaching and learning. In B. Perlman, L. I. McCann, & S. H. McFadden (Eds.). *Lessons learned: Practical advice for the teaching of psychology* (Vol. 2) (pp. 149-155). Washington, DC: American Psychological Society.

Mester, C. S., & Tauber, R. T. (2004) Acting lessons for teachers: Using performance skills in the classroom. In B. Perlman, L. I. McCann, & S. H. McFadden (Eds.). *Lessons learned: Practical advice for the teaching of psychology* (Vol. 2) (pp. 157-164). Washington, DC: American Psychological Society.

Nilson, L. B. (1998). *Teaching at its best: A research based resource for college instructors.* Boston: Anker.

Simpson, M. L., & Nist, S. L. (1992). A case study of academic literacy tasks and their negotiation in a university history course. *National Reading Conference Yearbook, 41*, 253-260.

Sleigh, M. J., & Ritzer, D. R. (2001 January). *Students' perceptions of the process of taking class notes and obtaining missed notes.* Paper presented at the National Institute on the Teaching of Psychology, St. Petersburg Beach, FL.

Sleigh, M. J., Ritzer, D. R., & Casey, M. B. (2002). Student versus faculty perceptions of missing class. *Teaching of Psychology, 29*, 52-55.

Terenzini, P. T., Theophilides, C., & Lorang, W. G. (1984). Influences on students' perceptions of their academic skill development during college. *Journal of Higher Education, 55*, 621-63.

Van Blerkom, M. L. (1992). Class attendance in undergraduate courses. *Journal of Psychology, 126*, 487-494.

Using Textbooks Effectively: Getting Students to Read Them

Denise R. Boyd

Houston Community College

SOMEWHERE THERE IS A college where psychology professors motivate students to use their textbooks simply by putting statements such as "this text is required" and "exam 1 will cover the first three chapters" in their syllabi. Upon being dismissed from the first class meeting, the students at this college go immediately to the college bookstore, where they gladly spend the money they had allotted for concert tickets on the required text and begin reading Chapters One through Three as they are walking from the bookstore back to their dormitories, the bus stop, or to their cars. For those of us who do not have the good fortune to teach in such an institution, creative strategies are required to motivate students to obtain and use their textbooks effectively.

Obviously, the first step to effective textbook use is motivating students to get one. Anecdotal reports from faculty and publishers' surveys of college bookstores suggest that about 20 percent of students do not buy books. In my own experience, the rate ranged from 10 to 25 percent per semester before I started using strategies that require students to have a book and to bring it to class. I also noticed that the particular course seemed to influence students' decisions about textbook purchasing. My introductory psychology students were less likely to buy books than those enrolled in more advanced classes such as life span development. Predictably, too, my statistics students rarely if ever tried to get through a course without a textbook. This phenomenon probably reflected student experience. Students who have taken more courses may be more realistic about the necessity of a textbook. Moreover, based on their pre-college educational experiences, most students know that a math course typically requires students to work problems from the textbook.

When we speculate about why students do not buy books, the reason we most often propose is that they are unable or unwilling to pay for them. To find out whether this assumption was accurate, I surveyed my students about their textbook-buying attitudes. Responses suggested that 1) students have little understanding of the reasons behind the cost of textbooks, and 2) they are more concerned about how a book is used than about how much it costs.

For example, when asked to respond to the statement "Textbooks are expensive because they are costly to produce," less than half of students agreed or strongly agreed. An approximately equal proportion disagreed or strongly disagreed. Ironically, perhaps, a large proportion of respondents expressed a preference for books possessing features that add to a textbook's cost (e.g. figures, marginal key terms, end-of-section questions). Further, three-quarters of students responding to the survey agreed or strongly agreed that "Textbooks are expensive because of free instructional aids provided to professors."

With regard to how books are used, 98 percent agreed or strongly agreed with "It helps when a professor makes connections between lectures and the textbook." Likewise, about three-quarters indicated that they regarded the textbook as the most important source of information in the course. Perhaps for this reason, more than 80 percent said that spending money for required textbooks was a higher priority than spending on leisure activities. In addition, only 13 percent agreed or strongly agreed with "Sometimes I decide not to buy a textbook because I can't afford it."

Motivating Students to Purchase Textbooks

The survey findings suggest a number of strategies for increasing the likelihood that students will buy required textbooks: take student preferences into account (e.g. key terms defined in margins), consider cost, and offer choices. My introductory psychology students have three options: purchase the required text, purchase an earlier edition of the text, or purchase any introductory psychology book of their own choice. I tell them that they can check out introductory textbooks from the college or a public library; if they prefer, they can buy them for very reasonable prices at used bookstores or even at thrift stores such as those operated by Goodwill Industries. Of course, they are responsible for correlating the content of their chosen book with the required reading assignments. The overwhelming majority chooses the first option, but they feel it was their own judgment that buying the required text was the best of the three choices given.

Be Tight With a Dollar

Professors can also introduce the notion of choice by making students aware of the many Internet sites where textbooks can be purchased at discounted prices. For example, both Amazon.com and Barnesandnoble.com offer student-to-student listings of used books. I found used copies of the text for my introductory psychology class offered for as little as $24.75, a far cry from the campus bookstore's $65. There are a host of other sites that specialize in discount textbooks, and a few others that will even search these sites and compare prices. When I used the Textbookland.com search-and-compare service, I found my introductory text priced from $82 to $97 for a new copy. The larger outlets also frequently offer earlier editions of best-selling college textbooks for very reasonable prices. For example, an earlier edition of my intro text goes for less than $50 new and $37 used on Amazon.com.

Explain the High Costs of Texts

The survey results also suggest that it can be helpful to educate students about the textbook production process and what the price of a textbook includes, such as the free companion Web sites now available for most books. I also like to direct students' attention to the list of reviewers in the preface. I tell students about the author(s) and the reason why they have credibility due to their record of published research or long-standing respect for superb teaching. I point out that the reviewers are all experienced psychology instructors who helped to make the book more useful. Further, I encourage them to think of the textbook author as a tutor who has provided them with explanations that other expert instructors (i.e. the reviewers) have helped to shape and with effective study aids such as end-of-section review questions. The goal of my mini-lecture on textbooks is to help students understand the value of a textbook in relation to its cost. I hope that they see their textbook as something more than just 600 pages of printing, so that they begin their course feeling good about having purchased a book.

Motivating Students to Read Textbooks

Once students have purchased a book, the next challenge, of course, is to get them to read it. The survey results indicate that there are several instructor characteristics that may help.

For one, I have found it useful to explain at the beginning of a course that I do not lecture on everything in the assigned readings. I assure them that my lectures will be much more interesting if they are not just lists of details they can read for themselves.

Following through on this statement by testing students as thoroughly on required reading material as on my lectures builds on their belief, as expressed in the survey, that the textbook as the most important source of information in the course.

Using the book frequently in class is also important. For example, I have students turn to the charts, graphs, and tables in the book when I am lecturing rather than using the corresponding transparencies or Power Point slides provided by the publisher. When students don't have a book, they feel uncomfortable and sense they are missing something. To avoid that feeling in the future, they bring their book to class (This is a good example of negative reinforcement for my lecture on operant conditioning!)

Another helpful strategy is to explicitly point out the book's pedagogical features. For example, guiding the class through reading a short section and then answering the questions at the end can help them realize how the questions can be useful in assessing their understanding and memory of the text. This practice also helps illustrate that the book's section headings and end-of-section questions provide them with a framework for a useful text-reading strategy, that of breaking the text into manageable parts

In-Class Assignments and Exams

I have found that there has to be some kind of immediate material incentive to get students to keep up with reading assignments. My strategy is to offer them an opportunity to earn a grade with nearly 100 percent chance of success.

One such technique is called a "Course Overview" exam (5 percent of course grade). On a certain day early in the course, students must bring to class the book, syllabus, and student supplement (a study guide for our department final at Houston Community College), all of which they use to answer 85 true-false questions about these materials (e.g. Syllabus: Research papers are penalized five points for each day late; Student

Supplement: The term "working memory" is on the department final; Textbook: The principles of operant conditioning are explained in Chapter 5).

This technique ensures that all students will get a book early in the course because they will understand that this is likely to be a very easily obtained good grade. Typically only one student per semester shows up without a book for the overview exam. Although they all believe they are going to get 100 percent of the questions right, in reality, the average is typically around 85 with a very small standard deviation. And, yes, some do fail.

Another of my strategies is to reward students for attending class and for bringing their books with surprise in-class assignments or homework that require use of the textbook (usually 10 percent of course grade). I strictly adhere to a must-be-present rule regarding these assignments, so students who are absent receive a "0" for a missed assignment.

Of course allowances must be made for absences resulting from illness, a death in the student's family, or college-sponsored activities such as student government association functions, athletics, debate tournaments, and the like. Typically, I manage this problem by dropping two or three assignments at the end of the semester. One way of managing the absence problem is to drop each student's two or three lowest grades, including any zeros resulting from absences, without regard to the reasons for absences. This might be called the "absolution" solution or, in the case of some students, the "unmerited grace" approach. Another solution, which we might call the "penance" technique, and one, that might be more consistent with the goal of motivating students to read, would be to provide text-based assignments only to students who have legitimate excuses for absences

When a make-up assignment is absolutely necessary, one type of activity I have found to be useful for this purpose is a true-false quiz for which students have to provide textbook documentation of their answers. A response of "true" must be justified by a quotation and page number, and a response of "false" must be accompanied by both a quote and a restatement of the item that renders it true. Course support software, such as Blackboard and WebCT, provides a way of managing make-up assignments that helps instructors avoid the problems such as keeping up with which students need which assignments, which of them have completed the assignments, the various individual time limits for completing the make-ups, and so on. Once I post an assignment on my course homepage, with a pre-set time limit, it is the student's responsibility to get it done. Whatever approach is taken towards absences, obviously it should be thought out in advance of implementing the in-class assignment technique and appropriate notice of the policy provided to students in the syllabus or verbally.

In-class assignments such as these provide intermittent reinforcement for attending class. In a typical semester, there is some kind of assignment in about two-thirds of class meetings. Predictably, this strategy dramatically increases attendance. This is interesting because these assignments count so little toward students' course grade. It seems likely that their power to shape student behavior lies in the students' beliefs that they are opportunities for success that are very much under their control.

Application Exercises

In addition to influencing attendance, all of these assignments provide students with opportunities to actively process and rehearse text information. Most of my in-class assignments are application exercises (either group or individual) where students have to classify behavior according to developmental stages, types of defense mechanisms, psychological disorders, or personality traits. Exercises that require them to use brief scenarios to distinguish between independent and dependent variables or punishment and negative reinforcement are also useful.

Consensus Groups

I also use a variation on "The Great Debate" technique described by Thiagarajan (1988), which I call the "consensus group." In groups of three to four, students read brief stories pitting one character against another with regard to a psychological principle. For example, one story involves a three-year-old boy whose grandmother paints his fingernails with red polish at the boy's request. The grandmother and the boy's father disagree about the potential effects of this event on his gender role development and sexual orientation. Each group must come to a consensus about which character they believe to be right, find justification for their position in the textbook, and collectively write a one-page essay explaining their position.

Activities that require readers to apply the knowledge they gain from reading a text in this way have been shown to facilitate learning (Hynd, Holschuh, & Nist, 2000). And, reading a text under mild time pressure, as happens when students have to use the text to complete these exercises within class time, increases both comprehension and memory for text (Walczyk, Kelly, Meche, & Braud, 1999). Further, students usually enjoy participating in them, especially the consensus groups.

Take-Home Exams

Perhaps the most powerful application of the notion that students will read if they believe they have virtually 100 percent chance of succeeding on a test or assignment is the take-home exam. To facilitate maximum student effort, ideal questions for a take-home exam are those that require a lot of reading and weighing of one alternative against another. Answering such questions increases the amount of text students read, the number of times they re-read, and the degree to which they engage in active processing about what is read (Bruning, Schraw, & Ronning, 1999).

Students also ask an enormous number of questions about the items on the take-home exam, each of which is an opportunity for me to expand upon whatever is the subject matter of the item. And I am doing so in response to an expressed desire-to-know on the part of the student. Thus students are more likely to attend to and remember what I say than if I deliver a lecture based on what I think they want or need to know about a topic to better understand it. I have also found that using very difficult questions discourages students from copying each others' answers; they seem less likely to trust another student's judgment with regard to difficult questions than questions that require them to do nothing more than look up definitions of terms. The distribution of grades on my take-home exams is highly similar to my conventional tests, but with a higher average (usually in the low 80s). I usually have four exams in a 16-week semester, one of which is a take-home.

Conclusion

As we all know, all the time that goes into choosing a book goes to waste if there is not some follow-up mechanism for getting students to read it. And again, as we all know, we cannot take students' reading for granted just because we test on the text. We should think of textbook use as a two-fold process. First, we have to adopt the best book we can find, balancing cost against students' preferred features and our own priorities. Second, we need to be good motivational psychologists and use both cognitive and behavioral approaches to increase the chances that students will read their textbooks. On the cognitive side, we can provide information about the value of books, try to persuade students that textbooks are good investments, and model the importance of the book by referring to it in class. On the behavioral side, we can immediately and tangibly reward students for reading by using strategies such as the course overview exam, surprise in- and out-of-class assignments, and take-home exams.

References and Recommended Readings

Bruning, R., Schraw, G., & Ronning, R. (1999). *Cognitive psychology and instruction.* Upper Saddle River, NJ: Prentice Hall.

Dewey, R. A. (1999). Finding the right introductory psychology textbook. In B. Perlman, L. I. McCann, & S. H. McFadden (Eds.). *Lessons learned: Practical advice for the teaching of psychology* (pp. 25-28). Washington, DC: American Psychological Society.

Hynd, C., Holschuh, J., & Nist, S. (2000). Learning complex scientific information: Motivation theory and its relation to student perceptions. *Reading and Writing Quarterly: Overcoming Learning Difficulties, 16,* 23-57.

Klusewitz, M., & Lorch, R. (2000). Effects of headings and familiarity with a text on strategies for searching a text. *Memory and Cognition, 28,* 667-676.

Thiagarajan, S. (1988). Reading assignments: 13 interactive strategies for making sure your students read them. *Performance and Instruction, 27,* 45-49.

Walczyk, J., Kelly, K., Meche, S., & Braud, H. (1999). Time limitations enhance reading comprehension. *Contemporary Educational Psychology, 24,* 156-165.

Going the Extra Mile: Identifying and Assisting Struggling Students

Rebecca D. Foushée
University of Alabama

Merry J. Sleigh
Winthrop University

AT SOME POINT DURING our college and graduate school careers, most of us can remember struggling in a course or two. Although the courses and reasons for our difficulty may have varied, we probably remember our feelings of frustration and anxiety as we worked to grasp a new concept, perform well on assignments, or relate to professors. Unfortunately, when we finally move to the other side of the lectern, it is sometimes easy to forget about the students who struggle in our courses. We need sensitivity to the needs of at-risk students.

Traditional pedagogical styles are geared toward the majority of students, who fall near the middle of the distribution. However, exerting extra effort to enrich the course experience for students who fall below the middle can be personally and professionally rewarding. In this column, we address techniques designed to help teachers target and assist students who struggle in psychology courses. Our definition of "struggling students" encompasses those who attend class regularly (and appear to be trying) but display poor performance on class assignments and exams; those who perform inconsistently; those who appear less than fully engaged in course activities; and those who have life circumstances impeding progress.

To identify successful methods for reaching struggling students, we interviewed several psychology teachers from colleges and universities across the United States who had won Teaching Excellence Awards from the Society for the Teaching of Psychology. To gain students' perspectives, we surveyed 204 undergraduates (94 men, 110 women) from a large regional university. Finally, we interviewed professionals in disability and resource services and college administrative positions at two universities. From these interviews, we compiled a list of techniques for identifying and assisting struggling students that even busy teachers can implement without substantially increasing their workload.

Why Do Students Struggle?

In today's college classroom, you will likely encounter students in introductory and lower-level courses who vary in educational and occupational background, maturity level, interest in psychology, outside commitments, and motivation to perform college work. These individual differences in life circumstances may influence how easily students can process course material, but have little to do with a student's intrinsic ability to learn or perform well in college studies. Instead, other factors may have a greater influence on student success in the classroom (see Perlman & McCann, 2002, for students' perspectives on struggling and success on course exams). When we asked students to list reasons why they struggle, their top responses were 1) poor study habits, 2) poor class attendance, 3) poor time management, and 4) poor teaching.

College faculty and administrators listed these reasons why students have difficulty in college:

Underdeveloped or inadequate study habits. Many students come to college somewhat underprepared for college-level work. They have difficulty studying, taking notes, asking questions, managing time, setting goals, and actively learning. College work presents new challenges and requires a range of unintuitive skills that must be developed.

Poor critical thinking and reasoning skills. Poor reasoning abilities and critical thinking deficits may be due to the cognitive developmental stage of incoming, traditional-age students, or from lack of recent exposure to academic life and work in nontraditional students.

Life circumstances that interfere with learning. These hurdles can include pregnancy and parenthood, inadequate financial resources, stress and anxiety from balancing obligations, dysfunctional personal relationships, working full-time, and poor integration into the "campus network" of fellow students. Unavoidable life circumstances or illness may cause frequent absences from class, compounding other problems.

Individual differences in learning styles. Students often struggle when their learning strategy (i.e., auditory vs. visual learning) does not mesh well with that of a particular professor.

Poor awareness of teacher expectations. Students are often unsure of what is expected in coursework, participation, and performance. Students may have incorrect expectations or beliefs about what constitutes "good work" in college.

Learning disabilities. Many students are unaware that they have a learning disability, even if they have been assessed earlier in their school careers.

Psychological impairments and/or addiction. Mental illness or substance use, abuse, or addiction impairs academic performance, even if students believe otherwise.

Identifying Struggling Students

According to students, 38 percent (range = 5 percent to 95 percent) are struggling in the average college classroom. When asked if they themselves were struggling in any or all of their courses, 29 percent of students said "yes" and 52 percent "no;" the remainder reported being neutral. Students' perceptions largely matched those of faculty and administrators. Faculty perceptions varied, depending on the type of institution at which they taught. Faculty at community colleges and public four-year institutions estimated a larger percentage of struggling students than faculty at private colleges. It appears that many students struggle, so what are some ways you can target or identify these students? Our interviews of faculty, administrators, and college resource center personnel led to several suggestions.

Solicit Information From Students

Taking a baseline inventory of your students' needs at the beginning of the course helps identify those at risk. Informally talk with them during the first week. In large classes have students fill out index cards or questionnaires on the first day. Ask them to list their time commitments and time management techniques, study style and habits, reasons for taking your course and goals for the class, GPA, major, age, work schedule, resource needs, or previous experience taking psychology courses. Some teachers with expertise in their use administer the Motivated Strategies for Learning Questionnaire (MSLQ; Pintrich et al., 1993) or the Learning and Study Strategies Inventory (LASSI; Weinstein, Schulte, & Palmer, 1987).

Provide Opportunities for Students to Self-Identify

Include a statement on your syllabi indicating your willingness to accommodate disabilities and requesting students to self-identify. Often, students will let you know they need extra help if they perceive that you are approachable and sympathetic to their special needs. Public Law 504 — ADA states that at the college level, students are expected to become their own advocates and provide documentation of any disability. However, be sensitive to gender, ethnic, and cultural differences that may influence how comfortable students feel in revealing and discussing a disability.

Monitor Performance or Changes in Performance

Students who change their performance during the semester may be experiencing a change elsewhere in their life. Students often find it harder to return to a classroom after a poor performance or extended absences. In these cases, teachers should quickly contact students regarding their performance and be sensitive to their students' perspectives and problems. Teachers are not expected to solve these problems, but can refer students to appropriate resources.

Techniques for Assisting the Struggling Student

Although some factors influencing whether or not students struggle in your courses are beyond your control, teachers who implement techniques that are under their control may minimize or counteract other forces that impede student success. Beyond using good teaching strategies (see McKeachie, 2002 or Perlman, McCann, & McFadden, 1999 for suggestions), here are some specific strategies to help struggling students.

Show Students You Care

When students perceive that you care about their success, they will be more likely to ask for extra help. Try to get to know your students, within the realities of class size and your personal style, and build a sense of rapport, or positive emotional connection, with as many as possible. Buskist and Saville (2004) argue that rapport helps students feel part of the "community of learning." Learn their names, or at least recognize their faces, respect them as individuals, make yourself readily available, be engaging in the classroom, and make course content relevant to their lives. Reflect a positive attitude that the class is "worth it" for everyone, not just those who are psychology majors or graduate-school bound.

Focus on Skill Development, Not Grades

Struggling students may benefit if you shift your teaching strategy from outcome-focused (i.e., earning grades) to process-focused (i.e., building skills). Chances are that those who struggle initially will not miraculously learn to process course material without someone showing them how. Instead of focusing on course content and grades, try building students' learning skills, expanding their information processing strategies, or changing their cognitive style. Teach them how to use memory strategies, answer test questions, put concepts in their own words, and write logical papers. Good grades will follow their mastery of effective learning skills. Even more importantly, these skills will transfer to other courses.

Be Accessible

Being easily accessible outside of the classroom is important. Today's students defined accessibility in many ways, including through office hours, phone, e-mail, Web sites, discussion boards, and teaching assistants. One-on-one interactions with struggling students provide perfect opportunities to answer questions in a non-threatening and personal manner, to help students work on academic skill building, or to refer students to counselors, writing centers, or tutoring.

Be Sensitive

Be sensitive to struggling students in the classroom. Avoid the question, "Is anyone having trouble?" and replace it with "Would anyone like me to repeat that information?" Make personal contact with poorly performing students immediately after the first assignment. This initial contact may be unnerving for some, as struggling is a sensitive issue for many students. Always ask that students meet with you privately, rather than discussing problems in public. Students who have academic difficulty frustrate many teachers and students are aware of our feelings. Showing students that we are genuinely interested in helping them may alleviate their anxiety in asking for extra assistance.

Encourage Use of Tutors and Study Groups

Struggling students often benefit from studying with other students. Create or encourage students to self-organize into study groups, where active involvement is emphasized. Students can engage in question and answer sessions, divide up material and present summaries to each other, or write sample test questions for the group to answer. You can also facilitate improved studying by utilizing tutors. If your department does not offer tutoring services through Psi Chi or the Psychology club, consider making a list of high-performing students from previous semesters who might be willing to serve as tutors.

Establish Student Management Teams or Student Groups

Helping students help themselves is an excellent way to reach those who are at-risk. Use student groups and teams, which give students control over their own learning process and connect them with fellow students. Consider identifying several students at the beginning of a course to serve on a student management team or create focus groups made up of students who have concerns with the course. These teams advise the professor by relaying concerns, suggestions, and questions on behalf of others. Or, create diverse student groups of five to seven members based on information you gathered from them. Assign students to different roles (e.g., recorder, spokesperson), where each role builds on different strengths and gives students of all abilities opportunities to shine. You can rotate students in roles or have students keep the same role throughout a course.

Provide Clear Examples of How to Succeed

Students are not mind readers. To help them succeed, provide explicit examples of what you expect. Post or read in class good and bad quality papers, provide examples of multiple choice or essay questions, or show them exemplars of projects, exercises, exams, or problems from previous classes. Remember that students of all abilities struggle most when they are unaware of what is expected of them.

Good teaching helps all students, but especially the struggling one. Study guides, workbooks, handouts, and study sessions, as well as clear wording and directions on assignments or tests are particularly helpful. Offer various types of exam questions, review tests when they are returned, create a comfortable atmosphere in the classroom to reduce test anxiety, and work individually with students who perform poorly on assignments.

Teach to All Learning Styles

Paying attention to your students' learning styles by teaching to both auditory and visual learners helps students struggle less. Vary class activities, lectures, and assignments to include multi-media components whenever possible.

Become Technology-Savvy

Familiarity with technology can make you more accessible and responsive to students' needs. For example, most of today's students feel comfortable with electronic communication. Both students and professionals recommended contacting students via e-mail, because this format offers students flexibility in when and how to respond. When using this format, however, remember that emotions behind a message can be misinterpreted. Write carefully and interpret student comments generously.

Encourage Questions

Strive to create an atmosphere were students feel comfortable asking questions. Periodically stop your lecture or class activities to ask if anyone needs clarification. Create a question box into which students can anonymously drop questions. Begin the next class by answering those questions and encourage students to contact you via e-mail, phone, or appointment for further explanation. Come early to class and stay after to help. Again, being readily available encourages struggling students to actively participate in their educational process.

Provide Rapid Feedback and Positive Reinforcement

Struggling students often need encouragement and immediate feedback about their progress. Try to use positive reinforcement for skill building whenever possible, and keep in mind that struggling students may suffer in self-esteem or self-efficacy based on their prior classroom experiences. Providing at-risk students with opportunities to be recognized and reinforced for their achievements and successes helps them believe in their capabilities to achieve their educational goals. Reinforce students by acknowledging effort and improvement in addition to achievement. For example, provide summary information about test scores, but also report how many students improved their exam scores. Individually recognize students through short notes on papers or exams, in e-mails thanking students for obvious effort, or by personal and private conversations after class.

Utilize Creative Assignments

For both in-class and out-of-class assignments, teachers in institutions or courses where students typically struggle should allow room for creativity and individuality in learning style.

Sometimes, students who struggle with traditional assignments excel if they can respond in non-traditional ways. Consider assignments that allow students to build on their strengths and use their talents. Some teachers have students choose their own assignments from an assortment of options. For example, have students choose to write papers or take exams. Suggest that they read and summarize a primary article on a psychological topic, or gather observational data on that concept and report their findings. Other teachers use strategies such as active learning, role-playing, service learning, and journal writing. Many faculty focus on teaching fewer concepts at a deeper level of cognitive processing. Almost all encourage students to use study guides that accompany texts and attempt to relate course material to students' lives.

Inform Students of Available Resources

Most colleges and universities offer courses in learning strategies and study skills. Resources such as writing centers, learning resource centers, and counseling centers, tutoring programs, student support groups, and health and child-care centers, are often provided on campus. Struggling students could benefit from these resources, but have to know they exist before they can use them. Even if you cannot help students with life issues impacting their academic progress, you can point them to whatever resources your college or university provides.

Adjust Expectations

Your struggling students will likely not earn the same grades as other students. However, grades are not always the best measure of success in learning. Good teaching may manifest itself in students who get "C" or "D" grades instead of a "D" or "F," or students who modify their thinking or studying style because of their class experience.

Evaluate Your Teaching Style

The teacher-student relationship is a partnership where you serve as a facilitator of student success. For some students, success comes easily. For others, you may have to implement different methods to help them reach their full potential. Evaluate your "teaching tools" by having colleagues periodically evaluate your teaching for weaknesses that may be particularly detrimental to students with disabilities or certain learning styles. Or, have students develop profiles of "good" and "bad" teachers based on their needs, perceptions, and previous experiences.

Students appreciate teachers who show a willingness to take responsibility for their teaching, so ask struggling students, "What can I do to help you in this class?"

Final Words of Wisdom

Remember that students bring different strengths and weaknesses to the classroom. Striving to maximize the potential of all students regardless of where they fall on the learning continuum can be highly rewarding for both you and your students. Try to inspire students and make course content relevant to their personal lives. Seriously evaluate your beliefs about how and why students learn, as well as what you hope to accomplish in teaching. Actively engage and create connections with struggling students however you can from the beginning of the course. Inform students about campus resources that are available for them. Finally, celebrate the diversity of students and tailor your teaching methods to different learning styles whenever possible.

References and Recommended Readings

Buskist, W., & Saville, B. K. (2004). Rapport-building: Creating positive emotional contexts for enhancing teaching and learning. In B. Perlman, L. I. McCann, & S. H. McFadden (Eds.), *Lessons learned: Practical advice for the teaching of psychology* (Vol. 2) (pp. 149-155). Washington, DC: American Psychological Society.

McKeachie, W. J. (2002). *McKeachie's teaching tips: Strategies, research, and theory for college and university teachers* (11th ed.). Lexington, MA: D. C. Heath.

Pastorino, E. E. (1999). Students with academic difficulty: Prevention and assistance. In B. Perlman, L. I. McCann, & S. H. McFadden (Eds.). *Lessons learned: Practical advice for the teaching of psychology* (pp. 193-199). Washington, DC: American Psychological Society.

Perlman, B., & McCann, L. I. (2002). Student perspectives on grade changes from test to test. *Teaching of Psychology, 29,* 50-52.

Perlman, B., McCann, L. I, & McFadden, S. H. (Eds.). (1999). *Lessons learned: Practical advice for the teaching of psychology.* Washington, DC: The American Psychological Society.

Pintrich, P. R., Smith, D. A., Garcia, T., & McKeachie, W. J. (1993). Reliability and predictive validity of the Motivated Strategies for Learning Questionnaire (MSLQ). *Educational and Psychological Measurement, 53,* 801-813.

Weinstein, C. E., Schulte, A. C., & Palmer, D. R. (1987). *Learning and Study Strategies Inventory.* Clearwater, FL: H & H Publishing.

Teaching Non-Traditional Students

MARY J. ALLEN

California State University-Bakersfield

A FRESHMAN IN 1964, I went to a major university and was surrounded by peers who, like myself, were going to school immediately after high school. We were "traditional" students: predominantly young, White, middle-class, full-time students. Students with learning disabilities were "invisible," and students who worked were rare.

The student body has changed since then. *The Chronicle of Higher Education* annually reports summaries of students at two-year and four-year colleges. Over the last several decades the proportions of students who are women, older, Asian, Hispanic, and part-time have been increasing, while the proportions of students who are male, young, White, and full-time have been decreasing. The "traditional" student is becoming increasingly uncommon, and faculty face a rich mixture of students, diverse in age, gender, ethnicity, and the exclusivity of academics in their lives.

I teach at a small college in the California State University system. Over half of our students are non-White, and many are first generation college students. They include children of farmworkers, refugees from Latin America and Southeast Asia, and descendants of Dustbowl migrants. Almost every student I know works, many full-time. Many are parents, and many help older family members interact with the English-speaking world that surrounds them. They lead complicated lives, and their college degrees will open opportunities for them that many of their parents will never see. How can faculty meet the needs of such a diverse student body?

General Principles

Chickering and Gamson's (1987) widely accepted seven principles of good practice in undergraduate education continue to be relevant. These principles encourage student-faculty contact, student reciprocity and cooperation, active learning, prompt feedback, good time management, high expectations, and respect for differing learning styles. In addition, Chism (1999) has articulated some basic principles for teaching in a multi-cultural environment. All students must believe that they:

- ♦ Are welcome.
- ♦ Can fully participate in their classes and campuses.
- ♦ Are treated as individuals.
- ♦ Are treated fairly.

How do we put these principles into practice? Faculty might find the following teaching tips useful for teaching non-traditional students.

Planning Your Course

Teach by Objectives

Communicate your learning objectives to students. Non-traditional students will appreciate the extra guidance the list of objectives provides. Explicit learning objectives focus faculty and students as they prepare for the course.

Consider the Students' Perspective

As you design the course, consider each element from the perspective of your students. Are assignments culturally relevant, fair, and interesting? Are readings selected to include pluralistic perspectives and relevant research on diverse groups? Diversity materials may not be available for every course, but should be included when possible.

Consider Optional Lessons

Do students have the prerequisite knowledge and skills to succeed in your course? If some may not, consider designing optional learning experiences to develop the prerequisites and schedule them in the syllabus appropriately. Returning students who took prerequisite coursework years earlier may benefit from the focused opportunity to refresh skills and information. For example, you might provide a basic statistics review or an introduction to technology skills required to complete your course.

Consider Community Assignments

Non-traditional students may not have ties to the local professional community, may have trouble seeing themselves as professionals, and may not be aware of the full range of career opportunities available to college graduates. Community service assignments may help them overcome these disadvantages and develop a professional self-image.

Community engagement is not relevant for all classes, but could be integrated fairly easily into such courses as child development, industrial psychology, and community mental health. Also useful would be to have community guest lecturers relate courses to real-world applications and career opportunities and to suggest that students connect with your institution's career/placement center.

Teaching Your Course

Use Classroom Assessment

In the diverse classroom it is difficult for faculty to be aware of each student's progress. Classroom assessment techniques (CATs; Angelo & Cross, 1993) are excellent ways to keep in touch with student attainment of learning objectives. In addition, use CATs to assess prerequisite knowledge and experiences and to provide topics that stimulate productive discussion. Common CATs include the muddiest point (ask students to describe what is confusing at the end of a course session) and the one-sentence summary (ask students to summarize what they just learned).

Require Student-to-Student Interaction

Group work increases student learning, student attitudes toward learning, and student persistence (Cooper & Robinson, 1998), so is well worth the time. In addition, interactions will enrich the experiences of all students by engaging students in the sharing of personal perspectives. Students on my campus are often amazed to hear about their own community through the eyes of people quite unlike themselves. Older students have life experiences related to work, family, and cultural changes that younger students may never have considered; students varying in cultural background often have different experiences and perspectives; and international students can add cross-national information.

Encourage Outside Preparation

Encourage students to obtain their first exposure to materials outside of class time. Readings and assignments can be used to promote student exposure to course content before they come to class, allowing you to spend more in-class time engaging students in active learning exercises, group activities, and consolidating higher-order learning. Students who need more time to digest materials can spend that time outside of class, rather than during class. Journal assignments, quizzes, study questions, and routine integration of pre-assigned readings into class activities may help motivate students to complete readings in time.

Test and Grade Fairly

Unless vocabulary is being tested, use simple, direct language in your test questions, and give students who might have English as a second language time to complete tests. If the goal of the test is to assess student learning, don't confound that with vocabulary size or processing speed. I once had a student who grew up speaking Persian, went to school using French, then came to the United States. She would take exams by translating the English to French, then to Persian. She would compose her answer in Persian, and translate from French to English before responding. Yes, she needed more time to take exams, but her exams demonstrated mastery of course objectives. Use a variety of exam formats so students have various ways to demonstrate learning and consider alternatives to exams, such as student portfolios that document their learning. Grades are important to students, and all students should be given the opportunity to earn a grade that reflects their learning.

Use a Non-Competitive Grading System

Grading on a curve encourages students to compete with each other and makes some students who come from non-competitive cultures uncomfortable. In addition, it discourages students from working together and helping each other because they may reduce their own grades in this way. Have high standards, but all students who meet your standards for a grade should receive it. Non-competitive grading based on absolute standards creates a "community of learners" within your class, and this community includes you because you and the students jointly strive for student success.

Encourage Study Groups

I want my students to be actively engaged with the course and with each other. Encourage study groups by distributing study questions that go beyond "memorize what's on page 82."

American Psychological Society

I'm delighted when groups of students drop by my office before an exam, describe their debate about a study question, and seek more information. In my experience, active participation in a good study group can move a student up at least a grade, and all students develop better understanding when they explain concepts to peers.

Consider Using Technology

Web links can be used to give students options and to expose them to materials not in traditional academic libraries, including international and non-English materials, and e-mail communication allows students to thoughtfully compose questions and receive personalized attention. Non-traditional students who are quiet in traditional classrooms and students who require time to frame statements in English may open up when allowed to communicate electronically, and give those with scheduling problems access to your wisdom.

Avoid Assumptions

Faculty assumptions about life experiences may inadvertently exclude some students from the desired impact of an example, and may alienate students whose values and expectations differ from their own. International students are about 3 percent of students in American colleges, and other students may be first-generation Americans; they may have quite different reactions to your references to historical events, literary allusions, or your implied assumptions about life experiences. A student recently told me about his childhood in Mexico, and how every day he carried a can to the central well to bring water to his household. An example of rewarding a child by buying a new movie or videogame may miss the mark with this student.

Slow Down

Give students time to think during class discussions. Although native-English-speaking extroverts may participate immediately when you stimulate a discussion, other students may need time to process your question, to collect their thoughts, and to phrase them for presentation to the class. Consider asking students to write responses before the discussion begins, and consider a "think-pair-share" strategy in which students share responses within dyads before the whole-class discussion. Although it takes a few more minutes, all students should be able to contribute to the discussion. "Taking the stage" and challenging authority may violate cultural norms for some students, and special sensitivity, encouragement, and shaping of such behaviors may be necessary.

Allow Class Time for Group Projects

Commuting and working students and students with family obligations may have difficulty working on group projects outside of class, especially if their schedules differ from others in their group. Give them the opportunity to participate during class.

Diversify References

Use a variety of ethnic names (e.g., Imelda, LaKeisha, Shoreh, Tran, Rafael, Buford, Ahmed, Jin) in exam questions and examples. For example, I include reference to Dr. Perez as well as to Dr. Jones in exam questions, and I deliberately balance names with roles, so that sometimes the professional has a female name and sometimes the professional has a male name. Students should see opportunities for people like themselves.

Communicating With Students

Communicate Assignments Clearly

Non-traditional students may not know what you want when you assign papers, projects, or activities. Tell students what you expect and describe grading criteria to clarify their task. Communicate assignments in writing, so students can refer back to instructions as they proceed.

Role Model Respect

Show respect for and interest in differences in opinions and perspectives, and correct student misinformation based on stereotypes related to age, ethnicity, sex, disability, religion, sexual orientation, etc. Be prepared to cite relevant literature that undermines stereotypes, or, if relevant, provide students opportunities to explore this literature among their course assignments.

Encourage Office Hour Visits

Nontraditional students may be more comfortable discussing personal issues in private, and you will learn much from them. For example, gay and lesbian students may be uncomfortable discussing their reactions to homophobic or disparaging remarks in class, but may help you recognize and avoid problems in the future. Informal advising during office hours may allow you to help them broaden their educational experiences and deal with barriers to their success.

Show Confidence in Students' Abilities

Non-traditional students may lack confidence in their academic skills. Older students, who often end up with the highest grades, frequently begin with low self-efficacy. Their basic skills and motivation generally are very high, and they need to learn that they can compete with younger students. First-generation college students often feel out of place and inadequate in the academic environment, and they respond especially well to faculty who genuinely believe in their potential for success.

Celebrate Success

An "A" in your class may not be an objective for all your students. I teach statistics and research methods to psychology majors, and for many a hard-earned "B" or "C" is a proud accomplishment that we both celebrate.

Know Yourself

Be aware of your own stereotypes and prejudices, and consciously avoid allowing them to affect how you interact with students. Don't make assumptions about students' background or competency based on how they look. Nurture the talents of students who don't give you positive first impressions; they may pleasantly surprise you.

Avoid 'Tokenism'

Don't assume that a student can speak for his/her group, e.g., "Marta, how do Mexican-Americans feel about this issue?" Students may be uncomfortable when they are singled out, and they cannot respond for their group any better than one of us can respond for all faculty.

Avoid Jokes That Play on Stereotypes

Students who believe they are outsiders in the academic environment may become convinced that they don't belong if they become the source of jokes based on stereotypes.

Don't Patronize Students

Be careful to avoid patronizing non-traditional students. They may be sensitive to subtle differences between genuine concern for their needs and implied assumptions that they are incompetent. Avoid the appearance of "talking louder and slower" to someone who doesn't speak your language.

Socializing Students

Communicate Expectations

First-generation college students and working students may have unrealistic expectations about the time commitment required to succeed in college. If reading assignments early, arriving on time, participating in class discussions, and writing well are important to you, let students know the rewards and repercussions if they fail to meet your standards. Academic dishonesty is increasingly a problem on college campuses, so be explicit about your policies and define key concepts (e.g., plagiarism) to avoid misunderstandings.

Teach English

Non-traditional students may need help developing their vocabularies. Define abstract words (e.g., altruism, anomie) when you first use them, and point out word roots. For example, correlation deals with how two variables co-relate, i.e., relate together (just like cooperate is to operate together) and bivariate means two variables (just like bicycle means two wheels). Written and spoken English will be important in students' academic and professional lives. Give them practice, feedback, and support to develop these skills. Consider allowing students to iterate drafts of papers, with feedback from peers or yourself on writing style.

Teach Math and Graphing

Non-traditional students may "tune out" when mathematical or statistical concepts are discussed or when graphs are displayed. Help them become math and graph literate by carefully explaining related concepts and organizational schemes. Have them do relevant calculations or graphs within groups so that students who understand such concepts can give one-on-one support to work partners.

Encourage Participation in Student Organizations

Encourage non-traditional students to join your Psychology Club or Psi Chi chapter and to take on leadership roles within these organizations. Encourage them to be full participants in the academic community.

Offer Mentoring

Offer mentoring to non-traditional students who may be over-looked by other faculty. Cultural differences may make some non-traditional students appear less responsive to individual attention, but many of these students blossom when receiving opportunities to conduct research or assist in the next session of the class.

Conclusion

Most faculty teach in an environment different from their own educational background, and they face increasing numbers of non-traditional students. Non-traditional students turn our classes into multicultural environments that can enrich student and faculty experiences. Faculty must be aware of themselves and their students when planning and teaching their courses and communicating with students. A variety of learning and testing opportunities, a non-competitive grading system based on learning objectives, and genuine concern for individual students support student achievement. They may be "strangers in a strange land," but with dedicated faculty, non-traditional students can join our academic culture and enrich our lives.

References and Recommended Readings

Angelo, T. A., & Cross, K. P. (1993). *Classroom assessment techniques* (2nd ed.). San Francisco: Jossey-Bass.

Chickering, A. W., & Gamson, Z. F. (1987). Seven principles for good practice in undergraduate education. *American Association for Higher Education Bulletin, 39,* 3-7.

Chism, N. V. M. (1999). Taking student social diversity into account. In W. J. McKeachie (Ed.), *McKeachie's teaching tips: Strategies, research, and theory for college and university teachers* (10th ed., pp. 218-234). New York: Houghton Mifflin.

Chronicle of Higher Education, The 1998-1999 Almanac Issue (1998).

Cooper, J., & Robinson, P. (1998). *Small-group instruction in science, mathematics, engineering and technology (SMET) disciplines: A status report and an agenda for the future.* [Online]. Available: www.wcer.wisc.edu/nise/cl1/CL/resource/smallgrp.htm.

Davis, B. G. (1993). *Tools for teaching.* San Francisco: Jossey-Bass.

McKeachie, W. J. (2002). *McKeachie's teaching tips: Strategies, research, and theory for college and university teachers* (11th ed.). New York: Houghton Mifflin.

Walvood, B. E., & Anderson, V. J. (1998). *Effective grading.* San Francisco: Jossey-Bass.

Teaching Outside the Classroom: Sustaining a Vibrant Psi Chi Chapter or Psychology Club

Peter J. Giordano
Belmont University

Elizabeth Yost Hammer
Loyola University New Orleans

Ashley E. Lovell
Belmont University

IF YOU ASK THE AVERAGE person-on-the-academic-street to free associate to the phrase "academic department," you are not likely to hear words like "vibrant," "energized," or "pulsating" in response. More typically, you might receive comebacks like "staid," "scholarly," or "restrained." Probably somewhere between these two extremes is where the truth lies. Like all institutions, academic departments vary widely in the climate of the departmental culture. Some research labs are highly visible and vibrant with the work of the faculty and students, and this energy pervades the department. In teaching oriented departments, the culture may pulse with lively conversation about teaching or with students "hanging out" before or after classes. It is our contention in this article that one way to contribute to the life and liveliness of your psychology department, regardless of your institutional type, is by empowering your Psi Chi chapter and/or Psychology Club to infuse additional energy into the departmental ethos. Such energy benefits anyone who connects with it.

Though Psi Chi chapters and Psychology Clubs might be seen as functioning outside the traditional arena of "teaching," we believe that significant teaching and learning occur in the context of the activities of these student groups. By participating in these organizations, students learn not only about the scholarship of psychology, but also acquire a number of professional skills that will enhance their intellectual, personal, and career development.

Further, the ideas and tips we discuss in this article are relevant for both sustaining an already active student group or for revitalizing a club or chapter that has lost its momentum. Sometimes, a group that was once thriving may have lost its energy. If your chapter or club is in this situation, we encourage you to experiment with the ideas we present, as a means to restore the vitality of the group.

If your department currently has a Psychology Club but not a Psi Chi chapter, you may wish to consider chartering a chapter of Psi Chi at your college or university. To do so, contact the Psi Chi National Office toll free at 877-774-2441 or go to their Web site at www.psichi.org for information on eligibility and the application process.

The Faculty Advisor Is Important

The role of the faculty advisor is central to the success of the student organization, whether it is a Psi Chi chapter or Psychology Club. Their energy, enthusiasm, dedication, and availability are the foundation on which all else rests. What may be less obvious, however, is that effective faculty advisors are not micro-managers of the student group. In contrast, advisors are intentional about the development of the chapter, but step out of the way to let students take charge, make things happen, and solve the problems that inevitably arise. Ultimately, students should take the credit for a successful chapter or club. One important first step toward a vibrant chapter or club is to help students develop leadership skills.

Leadership Training

Any experienced faculty advisor will tell you that the oscillations in the chapter's effectiveness hinge on the quality of student leadership. When leaders are active and involved, the chapter thrives; when they are not, the group falters. To maximize the payoff of strong student leadership, we recommend five strategies for ensuring a strong student leadership presence. In a nutshell, it pays to be deliberate in mentoring student leaders.

Hold Elections Early and Nurture Younger Talent

To be effective, leaders need experience. It takes time for student leaders to get to know their faculty advisor, their student peers, and the history of the club or chapter they are leading. Therefore, it is important to give officers time to acclimate to their new responsibilities. We strongly recommend holding officer elections early in the semester or quarter when elections are held. The time of elections often is related to the timing of the induction of new members into the organization. In our experience, new student leaders can be recruited from those newly joining the group. Some lead-time is needed to give incoming officers time to observe their more experienced peers. It is a good idea to talk about leadership and the various elected offices at some point during the induction ceremony. For Psychology Clubs, which may not have formal inductions, find another venue to highlight the importance and benefits of these leadership positions. Ideally, the chapter or club should involve a sophomore or junior level student in an officer role. This practice bodes well for developing leadership talent at "lower" offices and ensures a better pool of leaders for key positions, such as president. If a student expresses an interest in holding an office, and there are currently no positions open, do not turn the student away! Find another opportunity (perhaps create a new office) to involve this student in a meaningful way.

Provide Transitions and Training

Keep in mind this truth of academe — when summer hits, most students (and some faculty) disappear into the ether. They reappear later, but during the summer they typically vaporize. Students connect with the next phase of their lives, and faculty cherish the time to focus on research or other scholarly activities. From year to year, if faculty advisors are not intentional about providing helpful transitions from one group of officers to the next, a great deal of momentum may be lost. It is imperative, therefore, to create time for some type of transition between officers. If you hold elections early, you have more time to transition and train new officers. Transition rituals promote open communication between the advisor and student leaders, establishing a productive pattern of relating. We have used an annual breakfast at the end of the spring term as a way to facilitate officer transitions. We use this time to plan the fall semester's meetings, while the new officers can still get help from the old ones. Another tactic that has worked for us is to have each officer maintain an officer notebook with a description of responsibilities and tips that can be passed down as officers change.

Coach Group Dynamics and Conflict Resolution Skills

Throw a few human beings together, add the need to accomplish something, toss in a time-frame within which it all needs to get done, and you have the recipe for some interpersonal lumps in the mix. Psychology Clubs and Psi Chi chapters are no exception to the time-honored tradition of interpersonal conflict. As full-grown adults, many of us have learned, through reading or the proverbial school of hard knocks, what it takes to work through interpersonal conflicts as they inevitably arise. However, most students are less experienced in these matters, and they can benefit from coaching.

Sometimes merely recognizing the reality of difficult group dynamics can be helpful for student leaders. Without knowing that everyone in positions of leadership experiences these challenges, student leaders may feel isolated and inadequate in the face of interpersonal troubles. However, at other times it is necessary to be more active in helping officers work through difficulties. The effective faculty advisor is typically not superwoman or superman flying in heroically to take care of business and make everyone get along. A more successful approach, in our view, is to serve as a guide or coach, to help student leaders work things out themselves. Ongoing, open communication among officers and the faculty advisor is critical in dealing with interpersonal difficulties. At all costs, encourage officers to avoid gossip and talk directly and constructively about problems that arise.

Teach Professional Behavior

It is also important to teach aspects of professional behavior to student leaders. Making contacts with community partners, writing thank you letters as follow ups to speakers, introducing speakers, making requests of department chairs (e.g., for financial support of an event), leading a meeting, serving as mentors to younger students — these are but a few examples of important professional behaviors that students must learn to master. Students may pick up aspects of these behaviors by observing their faculty behaving professionally, but again it is typically desirable to be intentional about teaching these skills. Also, be willing to let students falter and not do things perfectly. At a later point, you can carefully point out where students did well and where they need some work.

Teach the Joy of Delegation

New student leaders sometimes think they must take care of everything through their own effort. We have found it useful to be explicit in teaching officers the importance of delegation. Involving others in the work of the club or chapter not only allows for greater accomplishment but also helps student leaders learn the art of this important leadership skill. Delegation creates in others the feeling of being an integral part of the group, allows new members to become active in the organization, and ultimately builds the leadership pool for future officers.

Provide Essential Services to Your Department

Visibility within the department is one sign of a Psi Chi chapter or Psychology Club that is alive and well. The student group thrives, in part, by making itself useful and by supporting important departmental goals or initiatives. Here we highlight just a few ways to create essential services for your department.

Support Research

Research activities are central to many psychology departments, and a Psi Chi chapter or Psychology Club can make important contributions in this domain. Chapters or clubs often invite faculty from their own institution or nearby institutions to give research talks. This type of event provides a valuable connection for getting students placed into research labs. If students are going to present their research at local, regional, or national conferences, the chapter can host poster preparation or oral presentation practice "parties" and supply food for the students and faculty who attend. Chapters or clubs can also sponsor regular lab meetings where students discuss their current research and share ideas.

In addition, the chapter or club can raise money to contribute to travel expenses for students. Also important may be a service where advanced students serve as research mentors for beginning student researchers. Such mentoring relationships provide perks to both upper and lower level students. Finally, if your campus hosts any kind of research conference (departmental, local, or regional), members of the student organization can serve as hosts and can contribute in other important ways to the functioning of the event.

Publish a Newsletter

Newsletters need not be expensive or elaborate, and they can communicate a heap of important information to students or alumni. A Psi Chi chapter or Psychology Club can take the lead and make sure that a newsletter gets published at least once a semester, if not more frequently. Students can make important contributions to the newsletter by writing or editing the entire publication. A newsletter can include a wealth of valuable information including information on new course offerings, course schedule changes, faculty research and other professional activities, student research, alumni news, a schedule of departmental events (e.g., social events, speakers, visiting scholars), job opportunities for students, advising information, or new faculty hires. After a few semesters of a quality newsletter (produced at a reasonable cost), a department chair will be singing the praises of the chapter or club.

Provide a Tutoring Service

Because of their knowledge of psychology and their experience with the expectations of college courses, advanced students can serve as academic tutors for less experienced students. A Psi Chi chapter or Psychology Club can coordinate this type of service, thereby contributing both to the welfare of student peers and to the life of the department. To establish this type of service, a group of tutors needs to be identified by soliciting students who have some expertise and confidence in particular areas of psychology (e.g., research methods, physiological, social) and who are willing to volunteer a portion of their time to assist others. It may help that teaching to others is one of the best ways to really understand it yourself. Then, students who want help need to be identified and paired with the tutors. It is relatively easy to connect tutors with students by 1) giving student contact information to tutors and letting them arrange the tutoring session or 2) posting sign-up sheets for students to sign up at particular times with tutors in particular areas. We have used Psi Chi meetings to solicit names of both tutors and students who wish to be helped.

Engage in Community Service Activities

Institutions of higher education are increasingly recognizing the importance of moving outside the walls of the ivory tower to connect with the surrounding community. Psi Chi chapters and Psychology Clubs can support this emphasis by engaging in service projects that bring together the institution and the community. Although the community partner will benefit from these activities, the greatest compensation may be to the students who participate. When students link to the community, they broaden their perspectives and are able to put their classroom learning to use in applied settings. These group experiences also contribute significantly to chapter or club cohesion.

Create Annual Traditions

Traditions create a sense of history and continuity for chapters and clubs. By purposely creating such customs, the student organization fashions a legacy that is passed down from one student generation to the next. It is important to let the traditions evolve, however, so that they do not stagnate with time. There is a big difference between a meaningful tradition and an old, tired convention. Always allow students to reinvent and rethink traditions. Some of the most fruitful customs in our departments have come about from the insight and initiative of students.

Central to the success of traditions is effective communication regarding the organization's events. We have already highlighted the importance of ongoing and open communication between faculty advisors and student leaders. Communication also needs to flow from the student group to other students and to departmental faculty who are not advisors. Regarding faculty attendance, sometimes faculty do not understand that their involvement is very important to the life of the chapter or club. By attending the traditional events of the group, the faculty show their commitment to the students and to their intellectual and professional development that occurs in contexts other than classrooms. Faculty presence at these events is a clear symbol that they recognize these events as important. Clear, concise, and timely communication with faculty via e-mail or a note in a mailbox can be effective. For special occasions (e.g., student research presentations or inductions), the faculty advisor may wish to extend a special invitation to faculty, with a rationale for why their attendance is meaningful to students.

Hold an Induction Ceremony

Chief among traditions is the induction ceremony (most appropriate for Psi Chi chapters), which ideally should be held twice a year, although two inductions are sometimes not possible for chapters. Induction ceremony formats vary, but often include a speaker or meal, along with the actual induction of new members. The purpose of the ceremony is to convey to inductees the significance of their accomplishment by recognizing them in this important way. The induction is also an ideal time to mention leadership opportunities and to encourage members to get involved. Invite the entire psychology faculty to the inductions. It is a nice way to build group cohesiveness outside of the traditional classroom or departmental setting. Keep in mind as well that the focus of this ceremony is on the new members and existing members should go out of their way to welcome the inductees.

Travel to Professional Conferences

Another useful tradition is to enlist students to travel to regional or even national meetings to present their research or just to experience the conference environment. Such travel can be expensive but has multiple payoffs, including socializing students into the discipline, exposing them to leading scholars in the field, and providing opportunities to present papers and posters. These experiences prove invaluable to students interested in graduate school. Students make connections with faculty and students outside their institution, see professional behavior modeled, and learn about current research in their fields of interest. Often, trips to conferences will give students a sense of excitement to come back to their school and initiate independent research or further collaborations with student peers and faculty.

Engage in Social Activities

Although Psi Chi chapters and Psychology Clubs should provide more than a social outlet for students, such communal activities are significant in creating bonds among members, bonds that will facilitate the ability to work effectively on other projects. In a recent national survey of Psi Chi chapters initiated by the Psi Chi National Council, an important finding was that active chapters engaged in regular social activities when compared to non-active chapters. Sometimes social activities can be combined with other important functions of the club or chapter. For example, fundraisers can take on an atmosphere of shared fun. A car wash in April when the weather is warmer, for instance, might raise a good deal of money while providing a break from the typical academic grind of the month.

Be Involved With Alumni Events

Once graduation occurs, it can be difficult to maintain contact with departmental alumni. Such connections are valuable to the department and to the university as a whole, however, and, by helping with this type of activity, a Psi Chi chapter or Psychology Club can provide another essential service to the department. Thus, the chapter or club can help coordinate or staff alumni events during homecoming or other similar functions on campus.

Keep a Scrapbook or Photo Archive

A good photo archive takes time to create and maintain. With the advent of electronic photos and scanned documents, however, this type of memorabilia has become somewhat less cumbersome. This kind of historical record connects with other points we have made in this article. For instance, it contributes to the sense of tradition in the club or chapter, and it connects with alumni tracking. The quality of the archive may ebb and flow over time, but the ongoing effort to maintain it is worth it in the long run. Just be sure to take photos of everything!

Show Me the Money

It doesn't take a rocket scientist to understand that traditions and other chapter activities require funds to make them happen. For example, hosting an induction ceremony or traveling to professional meetings can be expensive. In addition to some of the traditional fund-raising activities like bake sales, car washes, or t-shirt sales, chapters or clubs do well to educate themselves about and take advantage of other sources of money. For example, many universities have funds that can be applied for through student government or student affairs offices. Department chairs may also reserve a certain amount of money to help fund important chapter events. It is good professional training for student leaders to apply for university funds or approach department chairs to request financial support. As another example, the national organization of Psi Chi has a grant program designed to help fund local undergraduate psychology research conferences, particularly conferences that are new. From the standpoint of having good programs for students, the value of raising money is clear. What may be less obvious, however, is the importance of including students in the process of financial planning. Experience with fundraising gives students a chance to experience directly this dimension of an organization and to develop this important leadership skill.

Pursue Scholarly Activities

Undergraduates, in particular, may have never considered themselves capable of publishing an article or receiving grant funding to support their research. Faculty advisors know these accomplishments are possible, and they should do all they can to help students achieve in these domains. Psychology Clubs or Psi Chi chapters provide the perfect context for this encouragement to take place because they provide a supportive, peer-oriented environment within which risk-taking is safe. Psi Chi has numerous research grant programs (e.g., summer research grants, NSF/REU research grant partnerships, undergraduate research grants) and research award programs. We strongly encourage faculty advisors to connect students to these programs, because the professional development opportunities for students are so great. *The Eye on Psi Chi*, the magazine of the national organization, has details on all of these programs, as does the Psi Chi Web site (www.psichi.org).

Moreover, the *Psi Chi Journal of Undergraduate Research* is a professional peer-reviewed journal that publishes quality undergraduate scholarship. There are other journals devoted to the publication of undergraduate research, and these journals are listed on the inside back cover of the Psi Chi journal.

Conclusion

We hope we have provided some useful tips for creating and sustaining a dynamic Psi Chi chapter or Psychology Club within your department. Success with these student organizations does not come without its share of blood, sweat, and tears. But the benefits are clear and can be a source of self-efficacy for students and professional renewal for faculty who are involved. Active student organizations can also energize the entire departmental culture, an assertion that brings us full circle to a point we made at the outset of this article.

We recognize that there is no perfect formula for how to make these organizations work successfully and fully appreciate that universities and psychology departments have their own unique heritage, culture, and personalities. We encourage you to experiment with the suggestions we have provided and see which ones fit best for your situation. Better yet, create your own strategies. Experiment, be flexible, and stay innovative. As you learn new and effective tactics, by all means share them with colleagues. Above all, listen carefully to students and work with their suggestions. They typically have the best ideas.

Recommended Reading

Regularly consult the *Eye on Psi Chi*, which is published quarterly by the Psi Chi National Office. It is full of ideas for chapter activities and initiatives, filled with useful articles regarding graduate school and professional issues, and contains information on all of Psi Chi's grant and award programs. If your institution does not have a Psi Chi chapter, you can still access the *Eye* online at www.psichi.org.

Part VIII

Student and Faculty Integrity

Understanding and Preventing Plagiarism

JOSHUA D. LANDAU
York College of Pennsylvania

RECENTLY, I WAS GRADING student papers from an upper level psychology course and as I made my way through the stack, one stood out from the rest. In contrast to most of the others, this paper was easy to read, made several important points, demonstrated analytical and creative thought, was free of misspellings and grammatical errors, and did an excellent job of analyzing a particularly complex area of psychology. The assignment met or exceeded all of my expectations for an undergraduate paper. I knew immediately that something was amiss.

After re-reading the paper several times, I considered the quality of the other written assignments that this particular student had submitted over the course of the semester. This paper was far superior to the student's previous work. Despite my initial suspicious reaction, I tried to give the student the benefit of the doubt. After all, students' writing could drastically improve in a short time span if they carefully follow good advice: create an outline (and use it), obtain assistance from writing tutors and other peers, meticulously edit the paper, and spend the entire semester thinking about and revising the paper. After I quickly dismissed the notion that this student had actually taken my advice, I did some research and discovered that this exemplary paper included several extended verbatim quotations lifted from a journal article. Thus, I had to inform the student that the paper contained a significant amount of plagiarism. At this point, I am sure many readers are thinking, "been there, done that."

What Is Plagiarism?

Plagiarism occurs when people take credit for thoughts, words, images, musical passages, or ideas originally created by someone else. Although many people can recite some form of this definition, it is not clear how to use this information in the classroom. What exactly should you tell students about how much of someone else's work they can use before it qualifies as plagiarism? Is it three words in succession, four words, or five words? Unfortunately, most formal definitions of plagiarism are vague. For example, according to the APA style guide: "psychologists do not present substantial portions or elements of another's work or data as their own, even if the other work or data is cited occasionally" (American Psychological Association, 2001, p. 395). Like most plagiarism definitions, this one has several shortcomings. For example, it does not provide any guidance about what plagiarism actually looks like. One also could argue about what constitutes "substantial portions." Additionally, like most plagiarism definitions, this one ignores critical distinctions between different types of plagiarism.

Three Different Reasons for Plagiarism

Intentional Theft

There are several reasons why students might plagiarize intentionally. They might feel pressure to get good grades, but are not confident about their writing skills. Research also shows that students believe that many of their peers engage in plagiarism (Scanlon & Neumann, 2002). In order to compete, students may succumb to peer pressure and behave the way they believe their peers do. The stereotypical plagiarism case is the stressed-out student working late into the night towards an impending morning deadline, and hastily pasting together a document, fully aware that the information belongs to someone else. Likewise, students who buy an entire paper from the online paper-mills, or borrow a paper from friends and submit it as a product of their own work, are also guilty of this most egregious form of academic dishonesty.

Surveys indicate that somewhere between 25-30 percent of college undergraduates admit to some form of intentional plagiarism (e.g., McCabe & Trevino, 1996). Despite growing concerns that the Internet is a fertile breeding ground for increasing plagiarism, Scanlon and Neumann (2002) reported that students were equally likely to plagiarize from conventional sources (e.g., books, magazines, journal articles), as from the Internet.

A Source Memory Error

In contrast with intentionally motivated plagiarism, there is a volume of research suggesting that people can plagiarize *unintentionally*. This type of plagiarism can arise in the context of writing a paper when a student has completed the requisite background research and is attempting to write the paper. It is important to note that these students may have a decent understanding of plagiarism, and might even be actively trying not to plagiarize, but they do not have perfect memory for the sources of the information they are using. During the writing process, they might fluently generate a sentence, phrase, or idea that they perceive as their own, when in fact it is not. In this case, because students fail to carefully assess where the information originated (i.e., is that my phrase or did it come from one of my sources?), they inadvertently present someone else's thoughts as their own.

Misapprehension

When students are accused of plagiarism, many claim that they did not know they were doing something wrong. Although the cynical view is that these students are claiming ignorance in hopes of escaping without penalty, there is evidence suggesting that they may be telling the truth. Roig (1997) collected data from undergraduates indicating that they were largely unaware of how to properly paraphrase other people's work. In one study, Roig presented undergraduates with several different paraphrased versions of a paragraph and asked them to compare each paraphrasing to the original passage to determine if the authors received proper credit. All too often, the undergraduates claimed that passages that had undergone only superficial wording changes or lacked an appropriate citation were properly paraphrased.

The Plagiarism Conundrum

Clearly, plagiarism and other related forms of academic dishonesty are too common (e.g., McCabe, 1999). Although plagiarism can arise for very different reasons, the same problem exists regardless of the causal mechanism: a student has misappropriated someone else's ideas and a professor must determine the appropriate way to handle the matter. Most academic institutions do not distinguish between these different types of plagiarism; the same penalties apply to a student who purposely downloads an entire paper and the misguided student who commits an unintentional act of plagiarism.

Reducing Plagiarism

The techniques described below, used individually or in combination, should reduce the probability that students will engage in any of the three different types of plagiarism.

Make Plagiarism Guidelines Explicit

Students must understand what plagiarism is. It is unwise to assume that your students understand plagiarism, what it looks like, and how it occurs (Roig, 1997). As tempting as it might be to place a non-specific directive on the syllabus to avoid plagiarism and other forms of academic dishonesty, this is not an effective technique (Landau, Druen, & Arcuri, 2002). To avoid plagiarism students must first understand what it is. Therefore, it is important to spend part of a class defining, discussing and describing plagiarism in the overall context of the course. I typically try to have this discussion early in the semester to set the tone for the rest of the course. It is also a good idea to reinforce plagiarism avoidance using a brief reminder with each assignment.

During the initial plagiarism discussion, I explain to my students that plagiarism is a vague but punishable form of academic dishonesty. Because there are no universally accepted conventions (i.e., borrowing two, three, or four words in succession constitutes plagiarism), they will have to develop a variety of methods for avoiding plagiarism. I encourage them to concentrate on developing their own voice when describing psychological concepts and findings. One of the things that I look for when reading their work is that it is consistent with their overall writing style. If they are simply regurgitating what they read, that part of the paper will stand out. Instead of taking someone else's writing and changing a few select words, I explain that what they need to do is to incorporate the terms and ideas into their own knowledge base. Then, they can use their own words to describe the literature. I also make sure to emphasize that the finished product must be a product of their own hard work.

Provide Examples of Plagiarism and Non-Plagiarism

In any learning experience, providing relevant examples is an effective technique for helping students to understand underlying concepts. This tenet is especially true when it comes to plagiarism. Research indicates that students are best equipped to detect and avoid plagiarism when they have seen what it looks like (Landau et al., 2002). By showing them examples, they can begin to understand plagiarism and subsequently devise their own idiosyncratic strategies to avoid making this potentially costly error. This also is an excellent opportunity to discuss how to properly analyze, describe and integrate difficult psychological concepts.

You can also move beyond merely providing a description of plagiarism by giving students exemplars of how to present other peoples' ideas in a non-plagiaristic way. For instance, have students work in small groups or individually in class reading a brief journal article and then presenting the ideas.

No Quotes Allowed

One of the ideas that I emphasize in my classes is helping students to become better writers, and therefore I make sure that they do a lot of writing. However, I do not allow them to use direct quotes from the literature. This has two positive effects. First, I no longer read page-long block quotations that give me no indication of the student's understanding of the material that they quoted. Second, to meet this requirement, students have to carefully read and comprehend the information, decide which details are important, and then carefully piece together their own thoughts to share with the reader. In short, preventing students from using quotations makes them sensitive to using their own words and helps to increase their understanding of the literature because they cannot simply regurgitate large passages of text.

Incorporate Many Written Assignments

Detecting plagiarism, which can feel like searching for a needle in a haystack, is much easier when you are familiar with a student's writing. One way to increase the likelihood of finding plagiarism is to require many writing assignments across the semester so you can become more familiar with each student's writing level. This way, if a student does plagiarize, then this material will stand out because you are used to how the student usually writes.

Structure the Writing Process

McKeachie (1999) suggests that professors treat writing as a process that develops through a series of stages, which makes it much more difficult for people to turn in papers prepared by someone else. The writing process can be divided into many developmental stages including idea/topic generation, collecting sources, making and revising outlines, preparing rough drafts, submitting the paper to peer review, etc. (cf., McBurney, 1999). If students have to complete all of these tasks as part of the course, they would have to make faux outlines and rough drafts to cover up their cheating. Additionally, if you use a peer review process, then students will undoubtedly receive criticisms that will require further revisions. In the end, students will probably realize the enormous amount of work required to cover up their plagiarism and might decide against buying or borrowing someone else's paper.

Remind Students to Monitor the Source of Their Information

Avoiding unintentional plagiarism is complicated, but requiring people to carefully scrutinize the source of their ideas can reduce the likelihood that people will borrow from others (Marsh, Landau, & Hicks, 1997). Before students submit any of their written work, it is a good idea to (again) caution them about plagiarism by asking them to re-read the paper and provide a final check that they properly attributed information to its source. Although this check cannot completely rid every paper of plagiarism, it is likely that it will reduce the overall amount of unintentional plagiarism.

Submit Sources With Each Paper

Whenever students submit a paper that includes a literature review, I require them to also include copies of their sources. Although students may not be thrilled about making extra photocopies or entrusting you with a library book, this is a good deterrent for people who might intentionally plagiarize. If they know that you will have their source material, then they might think twice about lifting entire passages.

Create Dynamic Assignments

Creating writing assignments that minimize the opportunities to plagiarize is another way to reduce plagiarism. This goal can be accomplished in a variety of ways. Have students read the same articles and then ask them to analyze and integrate the articles. If they know that you have these articles and have read them, then they will be less likely to intentionally plagiarize the authors. More importantly, you can use this exercise to teach students proper paraphrasing techniques.

Another approach is to make students write in different styles or adopt a different perspective. Landau and Leynes (in press) demonstrated that if you require people to incorporate unusual information into their final product, they are less likely to plagiarize. Based on this experimental finding, I had my students read a psychological article and write an informal e-mail to one of their friends outside of psychology describing the results of the article. Because they had to describe the findings so their friend could understand it, they changed the types of phrases and sentences they would normally include in their summaries.

Learn About Web-Based Plagiarism Detection Services

Currently, there are a number of Web-based services designed to help professors determine the overlap between student papers and other collected papers. With many of these services, a professor (or the institution) registers with the site for a fee. Students then submit their papers electronically and the professor then forwards the papers to the plagiarism Web site for comparison with a large database of existing papers. The professor then receives a descriptive report detailing the overlap between the student's paper and the information in the database. Although these Web-based services are imperfect (e.g., they do not contain every paper, they cannot search all published material), students do not need to know this. Therefore, even if you are not computer-savvy, you could at least make it clear that you know about these plagiarism Web sites, which might reduce some of the intentional cases of plagiarism.

What Are Your Options When You Find Plagiarism?

Finding plagiarism, much like confronting a student who is cheating on an exam, is unpleasant. Earlier in my career, when I found plagiarism, I was conflicted about how to handle the situation. On the one hand, I could penalize students privately, assign them a failing grade for that assignment, and sternly admonish them against future transgressions. On the other hand, I could inform the department chair and other academic administrators that the student violated the academic honesty policy. Informing the administration usually results in a far more serious penalty and much more time spent dealing with a formal, bureaucratic process. At my current institution, the first act of plagiarism earns a failing grade in the course and a second a one-year suspension. Given that the penalty at the administrative level of most schools is similarly harsh, it is no surprise that many professors are not enthusiastic about formally pursuing suspected plagiarism. The formal definitions of plagiarism lack clarity and in most cases, the student denies any wrongdoing and this shifts the burden of proof to the faculty member.

The problem with handling the issue privately is that there is no mechanism, other than word of mouth, for determining if the student has committed plagiarism before. If you decide to handle this matter privately, then you are simply passing this student on to the next professor to test their adeptness at detecting plagiarism. In my experience, it is best to weigh the evidence for each individual case. I try to examine the reason for the plagiarism (i.e., intentional or unintentional) and then decide how to proceed. However, the appropriate course of action is a personal decision that each teacher must make.

Since I use many of the techniques described above, I have created several obstructions that deter most students from plagiarizing. If the rare, stubborn student decides to plagiarize intentionally, I have increased my chances for detecting the misappropriation. Consequently, I will not feel much regret about failing the student because I did all that I could to stop the plagiarism before it happened.

Conclusion

It is important for professors to acknowledge that not all of plagiarism is the same. Plagiarism can be an intentional act, can happen unintentionally, or it can arise from a lack of knowledge. My suggestion is to use some combination of the techniques described above to reduce the chances that you will be confronted with this problem in the future.

References and Recommended Reading

American Psychological Association. (2001). *Publication manual of the American Psychological Association* (5th ed.). Washington DC: Author.

Landau, J. D., Druen, P. B., & Arcuri, J. A. (2002) Methods for helping students to avoid plagiarism. *Teaching of Psychology, 29,* 112-115.

Landau, J. D., Marsh, R. L., & Parsons, T. (2000). Dissociation of two kinds of source attributions. *American Journal of Psychology, 113,* 539-551.

Landau, J. D., & Leynes, P. A. (in press). Manipulations that disrupt the generative stage decrease conformity to examples: Evidence from two paradigms. *Memory.*

Marsh, R. L., Landau, J. D., & Hicks, J. L. (1997). The contribution of inadequate source monitoring to unconscious plagiarism during idea generation. *Journal of Experimental Psychology: Learning, Memory & Cognition, 23,* 886-897.

Marsh, R. L., Ward, T. B., & Landau, J. D. (1999). Implicit learning expressed in a generative cognitive task. *Memory & Cognition, 27,* 94-105.

McBurney, D. (1999). Cheating: Preventing and dealing with academic dishonesty. In B. Perlman, L. I. McCann, & S. H. McFadden (Eds.), *Lessons learned: Practical advice for the teaching of psychology* (pp. 213-217). Washington, DC: American Psychological Society.

McCabe, D. L. (1999). Academic dishonesty among high school students. *Adolescence, 34,* 681-687.

McCabe, D. L., & Trevino, L.K. (1996, January/February). What we know about cheating in college: Longitudinal trends and recent developments. *Change,* 29-33.

McKeachie, W. J. (1999). *Teaching tips: Strategies, research and theory for college and university teachers* (10th ed.). Boston: MA, HoughtonMifflin.

Roig, M. (1997). Can undergraduate students determine whether text has been plagiarized? *Psychological Record, 47,* 113-122.

Scanlon, P. M., & Neumann, D. R. (2002). Internet plagiarism among college students. *Journal of College Student Development, 43,* 374-385.

Fairness in the Classroom

BERNARD E. WHITLEY, JR.
DAVID V. PERKINS
DEBORAH WARE BALOGH
PATRICIA KEITH-SPIEGEL
ARNO F. WITTIG
Ball State University

WHEN STUDENTS SUBMIT essays showing a poor grasp of course material, Professor Bovine draws a little cartoon of a bull flying through the air on their blue book covers. A student complained that the drawing insulted and embarrassed her and that she was doing the best she could, not slinging bull. Bovine defends his behavior by stating that students should learn that attempting to hoodwink an expert is a bad idea and not at all appreciated by the recipient. He views his technique as a harmless yet effective way of teaching this valuable lesson.

Professor Reach teaches her upper-division undergraduate Forensic Psychology class at a highly advanced level: She uses a textbook often used during the second year at law schools and although her lectures are well crafted, they are complicated and fast-paced. Students complain that they do not understand what is going on. In a meeting with the department chair, Reach strongly defended her teaching approach as the appropriate way to give the excellent students the edge they need to compete in today's marketplace.

Dr. Two-Standard admits to some frustrated students that she has two grading curves: one for psychology majors and a lower one for nonmajors. She argues that majors should know more about psychology and be better able "to think like a psychologist" than students who are majoring in other fields.

These three cases illustrate situations that most students (and many instructors) would consider to be unfair. Because fairness is a cornerstone of ethical teaching (Keith-Spiegel, Wittig, Perkins, Balogh, & Whitley, 1993), we doubt many college and university instructors purposely act unfairly. However, because fairness is a perception based on interpretations of behavior rather than on intentions, many instructors may inadvertently engage in what students perceive to be unfair behavior. Our purpose is to provide an overview of behaviors that can lead students to attribute (un)fairness to their instructors. Our discussion is based on Rodabaugh's (1996) typology of perceived fairness: Interactional fairness concerns the nature of the interaction between instructor and student; procedural fairness the rules for grading and classroom administration; and outcome fairness the distribution of grades. Each section contains tips for teachers on how to be fair and ethical, and thus avoid as many classroom problems as possible.

Interactional Fairness

Although one might expect students to be most concerned with outcome or procedural fairness because it affects their grades, Rodabaugh (1996) found that students consider violations of interactional fairness to be the most severe. There are five aspects to interactional fairness according to Rodabaugh: impartiality, respect, concern for students, integrity, and propriety.

Impartiality

Students expect an instructor to treat everyone in the class equally. Few professors intentionally favor certain students over others, but it is probably impossible not to like some students more than others. Differences in liking may foster differences in interactions, such as allowing certain students to dominate discussions. Even subtle differences in how students are treated may lead to perceptions of partiality where none exists. For example, Keith-Spiegel, Tabachnick, and Allen (1993) found that 90 percent of students surveyed thought an instructor's "being more friendly to some students than to others" was inappropriate in at least a minor degree and 45 percent thought it was inappropriate under many or all circumstances. Instructors should carefully monitor their behavior to avoid giving the impression of partiality.

Respect

Respect involves treating students politely. Keith-Spiegel et al. (1993) found that 85 percent of student respondents thought that ridiculing a student or calling a student's comment "stupid" was inappropriate in many or all circumstances. Similarly, Rodabaugh (1996) found that students expect an instructor to listen to, carefully consider, and give thoughtful replies to their ideas when they challenge the instructor's views. An instructor who is perceived as impatient or demeaning, either directly through comments or indirectly through tone of voice, facial expressions, or posture, loses students' respect.

Patience is especially difficult when students actively misbehave in class. However, students also expect instructors to be polite in those situations. For example, 45 percent of students thought it inappropriate for an instructor to "humiliate a student for falling asleep in class" in most circumstances (Keith-Spiegel, Tabachnick, & Allen, 1993). Instructors who face disrespect should try to remain civil and calm, thereby modeling the appropriate behavior for students. It is always appropriate to meet privately with an offending student, during which one can be more direct in communicating expectations for classroom deportment.

Concern for Students

Students expect their instructors to care about them and their academic performance. One can demonstrate such concern by learning and using students' names, talking to them before and after class, carefully answering questions, and inviting students who appear to be having problems with the course to discuss those problems and potential solutions. Concern is also expressed by giving due consideration to student complaints, taking remedial action when the complaints are valid, and carefully explaining one's position when the complaints are not valid.

Showing concern for individual students is especially difficult when teaching large classes. Nonetheless, some measures you can take to make students feel welcome and appreciated are shown in Figure 1 (see Page 348).

Integrity

Integrity means being consistent and truthful, and explaining one's policies, procedures, and decisions and why they are necessary, so that their fairness can be judged and understood. For example, an attendance policy may be justifiable because attendance is correlated with increased learning and better

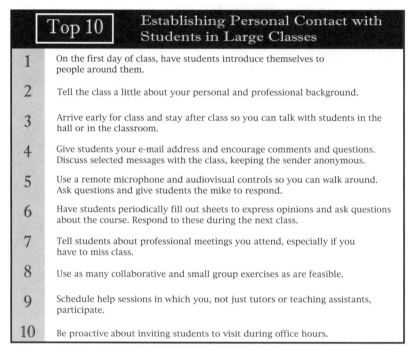

Top 10	Establishing Personal Contact with Students in Large Classes
1	On the first day of class, have students introduce themselves to people around them.
2	Tell the class a little about your personal and professional background.
3	Arrive early for class and stay after class so you can talk with students in the hall or in the classroom.
4	Give students your e-mail address and encourage comments and questions. Discuss selected messages with the class, keeping the sender anonymous.
5	Use a remote microphone and audiovisual controls so you can walk around. Ask questions and give students the mike to respond.
6	Have students periodically fill out sheets to express opinions and ask questions about the course. Respond to these during the next class.
7	Tell students about professional meetings you attend, especially if you have to miss class.
8	Use as many collaborative and small group exercises as are feasible.
9	Schedule help sessions in which you, not just tutors or teaching assistants, participate.
10	Be proactive about inviting students to visit during office hours.

Fig 1   Ten tips on increasing teacher-student communication and interaction before, during and after class.

grades. Explaining the educational goals of various types of assignments can also be effective. Greenberg (1990) found that a complete explanation of policies and practices to students who had initially perceived them as unfair led to acceptance of them. Instructors also should deliver promised rewards and penalties, and admit ignorance when appropriate.

Propriety

Propriety means acting in a socially acceptable manner and not offending students' sensibilities. Students expect instructors to follow the rules when interacting with them, even if the instructor believes there might be pedagogical value in breaking them. For example, 53 percent of students thought it inappropriate in most or all circumstances for an instructor to tell an off-color story or joke, and 80 percent thought the same about showing an emotionally upsetting film without warning students in advance. Students also expect instructors to respect their privacy: 88 percent thought that it was inappropriate to require students to reveal highly personal information in a class discussion. Finally, students expect instructors to maintain an appropriate social distance: 54 percent thought it inappropriate for an instructor to date a student and 70 percent believed it inappropriate for a professor to have a sexual relationship with a student (Keith-Spiegel, Tabachnick, & Allen, 1993).

Procedural Fairness

Students rate procedural fairness second in importance to interaction fairness and higher than outcome (grading) fairness (Rodabaugh, 1996). Four factors, based on a conceptual analysis, contribute to perceived procedural fairness in the classroom: course work load, tests, providing feedback, and making provision for student input.

Course Work Load

Although many factors (e.g., employment, extracurricular activities, low aptitude for the type of work done in the course) can lead students to perceive a reasonable work load as too heavy, some work loads can in fact be too heavy. If the knowledge base is rapidly expanding and instructors feel pressed to include everything they think must be covered in a course, many students may feel overloaded as well. When such pressure exists, instructors should review course content with an eye to pruning it back.

It is important to consider student ability when designing a course. A course for the general student population should be less technical than one designed for majors. It is also important to remember that many first year students are learning study skills along with the course content, and the difficulty of the course should be calibrated accordingly.

Tests

Three factors help a test appear fair to students. First, all the material on the test is relevant to the course's learning objectives and was covered in lectures, readings, or both. If one reuses test questions, one should double-check them to ensure their currency when revising lectures or changing textbooks. Second, the test is appropriate in difficulty for the course. As with work load, the proper level of test difficulty can vary as a function of the student population to which the course is directed. Students are especially offended by tests that seem designed to flunk people out of a course for the convenience of the faculty (e.g., to reduce the class size or the number of majors in a department).

Third, the test is well-designed, with clearly-phrased questions and, on multiple-choice tests, clearly phrased response options.

Providing Feedback

Providing prompt, constructive feedback on the results of tests and assignments is pedagogically sound and helps students perceive instructors as fair and concerned about their progress (Rodabaugh, 1996). Feedback should include not only telling students the questions they got right or wrong, but also explaining why wrong answers are incorrect, especially for items that are missed by a substantial proportion of students. This takes relatively little time even in large classes and provides large dividends in student good will.

Being Responsive to Students

Instructors should not only provide feedback to students, but also solicit and respond to feedback from students. For example, instructors should give serious consideration to student complaints that a test question was ambiguous or had more than one correct answer, and take remedial action when such complaints are valid. Instructors should ensure that students understand assignments, soliciting and answering questions about the requirements, procedures, deadlines, and so forth when distributing the assignment. Students should feel they have reasonable control over their outcomes in the class.

Outcome Fairness

Like it or not, grades are an important component of student perceptions of fairness. Students want grades to accurately reflect performance. If deprived of the grades they think they deserve, many will cheat to obtain what they see as their just due. Following are some guidelines for fair grading from the perspectives of both faculty (Ory & Ryan, 1993) and students (Rodabaugh, 1996).

Follow Institutional Practice

A department, college, or university may have specific policies concerning the proportion of each grade that may be given. When there is no formal policy, the actual distributions of grades in similar courses provide informal guidelines. Students compare grades with peers and will likely feel cheated if their grades for comparable performance are lower than those of students in similar courses taught by other instructors. Students who feel cheated may reciprocate by cheating.

Use Accurate Assessment Instruments

Assessment instruments — tests, term papers, homework, presentations, and other assignments — should yield accurate information about student performance. Instructors should continually review and update assessment instruments to ensure their accuracy. For example, questions in test banks supplied by textbook publishers are often written by someone other than the textbook authors. Questions may be poorly constructed when the writer does not fully understand the material or is under time pressure. Instructors should always check test bank questions against the textbook, and instructors who reuse test questions should check them when changing textbooks or moving to a new edition of the current book.

Exam and quiz questions that are poorly worded, ambiguous or were not covered in class or in assigned readings also reduce the accuracy of assessment. It is useful to have a student who has completed the course read questions for clarity.

Make Multiple Assessments

Some students do better on objective tests, others on term papers or essay tests. Consequently, accurate evaluation of student performance provides students a variety of ways to show their learning so that strengths can offset weaknesses. Similarly, multiple evaluations provide more accurate information about student performance than just one measure.

Tell Students How They Will Be Graded

The course syllabus should inform students what assessment instruments will be used and the weight each will have in determining course grades. Students should also know how grades will be determined, such as being based on preset cutoff scores or based on their relative ranking in the class (grading on the curve) and the reasons for using that grading method.

Grade Based on Individual Performance

Students want their grades to reflect their performance, not other people's. Grades based on preset cutoffs may be more satisfying to students than grades based on performance relative to the class mean. Students also expect to be graded individually for their contribution to group work. Individual performance on a collaborative project could include peer assessments or individual papers based on the assignment.

Don't Change Policies in Midcourse

Students expect grading policies to be firm. If alterations must be made, the changes and reasons for them should be fully explained. Ideally, the revised policy should benefit students, such as a new opportunity to gain points toward final grades. At a minimum, alterations in policies should at least balance costs and benefits.

The Syllabus

An excellent means of ensuring that students perceive an instructor to be fair, especially in terms of procedures and outcomes, is a complete syllabus. A syllabus should contain not only an outline of the course but also a complete description of ground rules for the course. In the context of grading, what number of points or percent of the final grade will come from each test, paper, or homework assignment? If contributions to class discussion are graded, exactly what does contribution mean and how will its quality be assessed? If extra credit is allowed, how much is it worth and how do students earn it? Due dates and penalties for late assignments should be clearly described. The syllabus should also contain procedural information, such as how much collaboration is allowed and the kinds of assistance students may receive. The syllabus is a contract between the instructor and the students enrolled in a course. Like any contract, the more complete and explicit the syllabus, the less room for varying interpretations and the less likelihood there is that students will perceive the instructor to be interpreting an individual situation in an unfair manner.

Conclusion

Ethical issues are often seen in terms of outright abuse of power or privilege. However, we have tried to show that where fairness is concerned, many behaviors that teachers may unthinkingly exhibit on a day-to-day basis, such as Professor Bovine's joking drawing on an exam booklet, may be perceived quite differently by students. Similarly, seemingly minor acts, such as delaying feedback on test results or making slight changes in course content and procedures during the semester or quarter, might have major impacts on student perceptions of teacher fairness. Perceptions of unfairness can, in turn, undermine the trust between student and teacher that is necessary for effective learning (Brookfield, 1990). Consequently, one must carefully monitor one's behavior and policies to ensure that they are not only in fact fair, but are perceived as fair by students.

References and Recommended Readings

Appleby, D. C. (1999). How to improve your teaching with the course syllabus. In B. Perlman, L. I. McCann, & S. H. McFadden (Eds.), *Lessons learned: Practical advice for the teaching of psychology* (pp. 19-24). Washington, DC: American Psychological Society.

Brookfield, S. D. (1990). *The skillful teacher: On technique, trust, and responsiveness in the classroom.* San Francisco: Jossey-Bass.

Goss, S. (1999). Dealing with problem students in the classroom. In B. Perlman, L. I. McCann, & S. H. McFadden (Eds.), *Lessons learned: Practical advice for the teaching of psychology* (pp. 209-212). Washington, DC: American Psychological Society.

Greenberg, J. (1990). Employee theft as a reaction to underpayment inequity: The hidden costs of pay cuts. *Journal of Applied Psychology, 75,* 561-568.

Keith-Spiegel, P., Tabachnick, B. G., & Allen, M. (1993). Ethics in academia: Students' views of professors' actions. *Ethics and Behavior, 3,* 149-162.

Keith-Spiegel, P., Wittig, A. F., Perkins, D. V., Balogh, D. W., & Whitley, B. E., Jr. (1993). *The ethics of teaching: A casebook.* Muncie, IN: Ball State University.

Ory, J. C., & Ryan, K. E. (1993). *Tips for improving testing and grading.* Newbury Park, CA: Sage.

Palladino, J. J., Hill, G. W. IV., & Norcross, J. C. (1999). Using extra credit. In B. Perlman, L. I. McCann, & S. H. McFadden (Eds.), *Lessons learned: Practical advice for the teaching of psychology* (pp. 57-60). Washington, DC: American Psychological Society.

Rodabaugh, R. C. (1996). Institutional commitment to fairness in college teaching. In L. Fisch (Ed.), *Ethical dimensions of college and university teaching* (pp. 37-45). San Francisco: Jossey-Bass.

Contributors

MARY J. ALLEN is Director of the California State University Institute for Teaching and Learning, the Executive Editor of *Exchanges*, and Professor of Psychology at California State University, Bakersfield. She is Past President of the Council of Teachers of Undergraduate Psychology.

PAMELA I. ANSBURG earned her doctorate in Cognitive Psychology from the University of Illinois at Chicago and has been teaching at Metropolitan State College of Denver since 1999. She began using web pages in undergraduate courses in 1999 and has developed web pages for several courses. Her web site can be found at http://clem.mscd.edu/~ansburg.

DEBORAH WARE BALOGH is Associate Provost and Dean of the Graduate School and Professor of Psychological Science at Ball State University. A Fellow of the Society for Personality Assessment, she is a former graduate program director and former Director of the Graduate Student Development Project, a BSU program designed to enhance the professional skills of graduate students, including those serving as teaching assistants.

DENISE R. BOYD holds a Bachelor of Arts in French, and Master of Education and Doctor of Education degrees in Educational Psychology from the University of Houston. She has been a Psychology instructor in the Houston Community College System since 1988. From 1995 until 1998, she chaired the Psychology, Sociology, and Anthropology Department at HCCS-Central College. With Samuel Wood and Ellen Green Wood, Boyd authored *Mastering the World of Psychology* (1st Edition) and *The World of Psychology* (5th Edition), published by Allyn & Bacon.

T. L. BRINK teaches Psychology at Crafton Hills College, California's San Bernardino Community College District.

WILLIAM BUSKIST is the Distinguished Professor of the Teaching of Psychology at Auburn University, where he has been teaching large sections of introductory level Psychology courses for the past 21 years. For the last 13 years he has taught a year-long course to first year graduate teaching assistants on the teaching of Psychology. His primary research interests center on excellence in undergraduate teaching.

E. J. CAPALDI is Professor of Psychology at Purdue University. His research interests are primarily in the areas of animal learning and cognition. Along with Robert W. Proctor, he has published a number of articles on issues in the philosophy of science as they pertain to Psychology. They are authors of the book, *Contextualism in Psychological Research? A Critical Review*, published in 1999 by Sage.

MICHAEL CARUSO earned his MA (and is ABD) in Developmental Psychology at the University of Akron in 1986. He is an Associate Professor and web master for the Psychology Department at the University of Toledo and has developed several course Web sites which can be accessed at http://homepages.utoledo.edu/mcaruso. He has given workshops on using the web in teaching, has authored study guide software and interactive web exercises to accompany Psychology textbooks, and has received grants for Web site and course software development.

WILLIAM CERBIN is Professor of Psychology and Assistant to the Provost at the University of Wisconsin La Crosse, La Crosse, WI. In 1992 he developed the first course portfolio. In 1998, as a Carnegie Scholar with the Carnegie Academy for the Scholarship of Teaching and Learning, he studied students' understanding in his own Educational Psychology classes and completed a multimedia portfolio of that work, available at: http://kml.carnegiefoundation.org/gallery/bcerbin.

TEDDI S. DEKA is an Associate Professor of Psychology at Missouri Western State College. She teaches courses in Introductory and Developmental Psychology. She received the 1999 National Institute of Psychology Award for Innovative Teaching and is a co-author of an instructor resource guide for an Introductory Psychology text. Her research interests include self-concept development and gender differences in cognitive abilities.

KAREN STIEGLITZ DEPALMA earned her Master of Arts in Special Education from Georgian Court College, and she has taught on the undergraduate level at GCC. She provides evaluation and therapy to young children in an early intervention program. Karen is interested in Child Psychology and siblings of children with disabilities.

TAMI J. EGGLESTON is an Associate Professor of Psychology at McKendree College in Lebanon, Illinois. She teaches Introduction to Psychology, Social Psychology, Biopsychology, Human Sexuality, Tests and Measurement, and SPSS.

REBECCA D. FOUSHÉE is Assistant Professor of Psychology at Fontbonne University in St. Louis, Missouri. She teaches a variety of courses, including Introductory Psychology, Developmental Psychology, Statistics, and Senior Research Seminar. Her research interests include prenatal and early postnatal development in both human and animal populations. She has also recently focused her work on examining the relationship between parenting style and academic success in adolescents.

PETER J. GIORDANO is Professor and Chair of Psychology and Director of the Teaching Center at Belmont University in Nashville, Tennessee, where he teaches General Psychology, Abnormal Psychology, Psychometrics, and Theories of Personality. He was the National Past-President of Psi Chi in 2002-2003 and is co-advisor of Belmont's Psi Chi chapter.

MELANIE C. GREEN is an Assistant Professor in the Department of Psychology at the University of Pennsylvania, where she teaches courses on Social Psychology, Political Psychology, and Research Methods. She received her PhD in 2000 from The Ohio State University in Social Psychology. Her research examines the impact of narratives on individuals' beliefs.

RAYMOND J. GREEN is an Assistant Professor of Psychology and Coordinator of the PhD Program in Educational Psychology at Texas A&M-Commerce. He received his PhD in the area of Social Psychology from Rutgers University in 1997. Being the father of two young children means that most of the movies he watches these days have cartoon characters as the leads.

DIANE F. HALPERN is Professor of Psychology and Director of the Berger Institute for Work, Family, and Children at Claremont McKenna College (Claremont University Consortium) in Los Angeles. She is the author of *Thought and Knowledge: An*

Introduction to Critical Thinking (4th ed.) and *Sex Differences in Cognitive Abilities.* She is the recipient of the APA's Distinguished Career Contributions to Education Award and the American Psychological Foundation's Distinguished Teaching Award. She is the 2004 President of the APA and Co-Chair (with Milton D. Hakel) of the APS Taskforce on Education.

ELIZABETH YOST HAMMER is Associate Professor of Psychology at Loyola University, New Orleans. She regularly teaches Social Psychology, Research Methods, and Introductory Psychology, and actively involves students in research. She was National President of Psi Chi in 2002-2003.

KELLY BOUAS HENRY is an Assistant Professor of Psychology at Missouri Western State College, where she teaches courses in Introductory, Social, and Organizational Psychology, in addition to Career Development and Senior Seminar courses. She coordinates the Personnel Psychology Program there, and has published several ancillary study guides to accompany Introductory Psychology texts. Kelly's research focuses on group structure and process.

BARBARA RAE HERBERT received her Master of Library Science from Rutgers University. She is the Behavioral Sciences Librarian at Georgian Court College.

SHARON A. HOLLANDER is Assistant Professor of Education at Georgian Court College in Lakewood, New Jersey. She is on the editorial board of the *Journal on Excellence in College Teaching.* Her current interests include TESOL, informal education for children with disabilities, interdisciplinary coursework, and children's literature.

PATRICIA KEITH-SPIEGEL is the Voran Honors Distinguished Professor of Social and Behavioral Sciences Emerita at Ball State University and currently working on a NSF grant from Children's Hospital, Boston/Harvard Medical School. She has written extensively on ethics and teaching since 1976.

ROSALYN M. KING is Professor of Psychology on the Loudoun Campus of Northern Virginia Community College. She also is Chair, Center for Teaching Excellence for the Northern Virginia Region and Director of the Center on the Loudoun Campus.

KATHERINE KIPP is Associate Professor of Psychology at the University of Georgia, where she teaches Developmental Psychology courses. She is a mentor to many graduate student teaching assistants, a member of UGA's Peer Consultation Team, and UGA's Teaching Academy.

SALLY KUHLENSCHMIDT has her PhD in Clinical Psychology from Purdue University, has been teaching at Western Kentucky University since 1986, and is Director of their Center for Teaching & Learning. She built her first Web page in 1996 and began teaching fully online in 1998 with a course about how to teach online. Her course materials (e.g., Behavior Modification, Psychological Tests and Measurement) can be accessed at: http://www.wku.edu/~sally.kuhlenschmidt.

JOSHUA D. LANDAU is an Assistant Professor at York College of Pennsylvania, where he has taught since 1997. He earned his PhD in Experimental Psychology from the University of Georgia. His research interests include mechanisms of inadvertent plagiarism and how imagination influences memory.

ASHLEY E. LOVELL graduated as a Psychology major at Belmont University and was President of Psi Chi and the Psychology Club at Belmont in 2002-2003. She has presented research projects at NCUR, SEPA, and APA. She is currently living in China and plans to pursue graduate study in Psychology in the future.

SANDRA GOSS LUCAS received her PhD in 1984 from Indiana University in Educational Psychology with a specialty in Teacher Behavior. She has taught at the middle school, high school, community college and university levels. She is Director of Introductory Psychology at the University of Illinois at Urbana-Champaign. She is on the program committee for the National Institute on the Teaching of Psychology and is an active participant in departmental and campus programs on effective college teaching.

LEE I. McCANN is a Professor of Psychology, Edward Rudoy Endowed Professor, and Rosebush Professor at the University of Wisconsin Oshkosh. He is a co-editor (with Baron Perlman and Susan H. McFadden) of *Lessons Learned: Practical Advice for the Teaching of Psychology* (1999, American Psychological Society), and the *Teaching Tips* column in the American Psychological Society *Observer,* and co-author (with Baron

Perlman) of *Recruiting Good College Faculty: Practical Advice for a Successful Search* (1996, Anker). His research interests include the social communication of dietary preference in rats, implicit learning in humans, Psychology teaching and curricula, and new faculty training and career development. McCann has presented workshops on faculty recruiting, teaching portfolio development, Psychology curricula, and several other topics at various national and regional conferences.

CATHY SARGENT MESTER is Senior Lecturer in Speech Communication at Pennsylvania State University-Erie, The Behrend College, specializing in Public Address Education. In her 32 years of college teaching, she has taught over 225 sections of general education courses for undergraduates as well as advanced public speaking courses, numerous workshops and seminars for educators and managers. She is the recipient of the college's Excellence in Academic Advising Award and the Benjamin A. Lane Award for Service and is listed in *Who's Who Among America's Teachers*.

PATRICIA A. MULLINS received her PhD in Psychology from the University of Chicago, committee on Cognition and Communication. She is a Senior Lecturer in the Grainger School of Business and a participating faculty member of the Industrial Relations Research Institute at the University of Wisconsin Madison. She teaches Statistics.

JOHN C. ORY is the Director of the Office of Instructional Resources and Professor in the Department of Human Resource Education at the University of Illinois at Urbana-Champaign. He received a Bachelor's degree in Psychology from Augustana College (Rock Island) and his Master's and PhD degrees in Educational Psychology from the University of Kansas. He has written articles and books in the area of student, faculty, and program assessment and he has conducted teacher/faculty workshops on testing and assessment at the secondary and post-secondary levels. He has also reviewed and developed testing and assessment programs for profit and non-profit organizations.

ELIZABETH WEISS OZORAK is Associate Professor of Psychology at Allegheny College. She also chairs the Values, Ethics and Social Action (VESA) program, an interdisciplinary academic program designed to foster civic engagement. She has taught a wide range of courses with service-learning including "Psychology of Language" and "Food & Hunger in Society" as well as the VESA core course "Ethics and Dynamics of Social Action" and various interdisciplinary freshman and sophomore seminars.

DAVID V. PERKINS is Professor of Psychological Science at Ball State University, Muncie, Indiana. He has been working on projects related to the ethics of teaching and ethics in the academy since 1992.

BARON PERLMAN is Editor of the APS *Observer's Teaching Tips* column. A University and Rosebush Professor at the University of Wisconsin Oshkosh in the Department of Psychology, he has taught Psychology for 30 years.

RETTA E. POE is a Professor of Psychology and Associate Dean of the College of Education and Behavioral Sciences at Western Kentucky University. She serves on the advisory council for the Center for Teaching and Learning at WKU, and she is a member of the editorial board for *Teaching of Psychology*. She earned her MA and PhD degrees in Counseling Psychology from the University of Missouri-Columbia.

ROBERT W. PROCTOR is Professor of Psychology at Purdue University. His research interests are primarily in the areas of basic and applied human performance. Along with E. J. Capaldi, he has published a number of articles on issues in the philosophy of science as they pertain to Psychology. They are authors of the book, *Contextualism in Psychological Research? A Critical Review*, published in 1999 by Sage.

DARREN R. RITZER served eight years in the United States Army while teaching part-time at George Mason University. He received a Teaching Excellence Award from GMU in 2003. He recently relocated to Winthrop University, where he is an Assistant Professor. His teaching interests include Introductory Psychology, Research Methods, Statistics, Industrial/ Organizational Psychology, and History and Systems.

SHEENA ROGERS is Associate Professor of Psychology and Head of the Department of Graduate Psychology at James Madison University. Her PhD is from the Royal College of Art, London. She did post-doctoral research in Experimental Psychology at the University of Oxford and previously taught Psychology at the University of Wisconsin Madison, St. John's College, Oxford, the University of Sussex, and the University of Nottingham. She is the editor (with William Epstein) of *Perception of Space and Motion* (Academic Press) and (with Judith Effken) of *Studies in Perception and Action VII* (Lawrence Erlbaum Associates), winner of the 1996 Wisconsin Power and Light Underkofler Excellence in Teaching Award, and of the 2003 CISAT Madison Scholar award at James Madison University.

BRYAN K. SAVILLE is an Assistant Professor in the Department of Psychology at Stephen F. Austin State University in Nacogdoches, Texas. He has taught classes in Introductory Psychology, Experimental Psychology, History and Systems of Psychology, and Group Dynamics. His research interests include the teaching of Psychology, Experimental Social Psychology, and Sport Psychology.

MERRY J. SLEIGH served as the Director of the Psychology Honors Program at George Mason University, where she received a Teaching Excellence Award in 2001. She recently relocated to Winthrop University, where she is a visiting Assistant Professor. Her teaching interests include Animal Behavior, Learning, Human Development, and Research Methods.

GABIE E. SMITH is an Assistant Professor at Elon University in Elon, North Carolina. She teaches Health Psychology, Research Methods, General Psychology, and Human Sexuality.

MICHAEL L. STOLOFF earned a PhD in Psychology from Johns Hopkins University in 1980 and taught at Towson State University and Northern Michigan University before arriving at James Madison University in 1981. He is currently a Professor of Psychology and Head of the Department of Psychology at JMU. Over the years his scholarship has included writing in the areas of Biopsychology, Forensic Psychology, computer use in Psychology, and innovations in college instruction and assessment.

ROBERT T. TAUBER is Professor Emeritus of Education at Pennsylvania State University-Erie, The Behrend College. Recently retired after 30 years of teaching at the high school and college level, Tauber is the author of six books on classroom management and communication. He has received the college's award for excellence in research as well as national distinction for his Psychology of Discipline distance education course, which won the 1996 Helen Adams Award for Excellence in Collegiate Independent Study.

BERNARD E. WHITLEY, JR. is Professor of Psychological Science at Ball State University, Muncie, Indiana. He has been working on projects related to the ethics of teaching and ethics in the academy since 1992.

STEFFEN POPE WILSON is an Associate Professor of Psychology and Associate Director of the Honors Program at Eastern Kentucky University, where she teaches courses in Developmental Psychology, Physiological Psychology, and a course on graduate school and career options for Psychology majors. She recently created a forum for discussions of teaching in her Department.

ARNO F. WITTIG is Professor of Psychological Science Emeritus at Ball State University, Muncie, Indiana.

TODD ZAKRAJSEK is the inaugural Director of Academic Excellence and also teaches regularly in the Psychology Department at Central Michigan University. Previously, he was the Director of the Center for Teaching and Learning at Southern Oregon University, where he taught in the Psychology Department as a tenured Associate Professor. Zakrajsek has written two introductory Psychology instructor's manuals for McGraw-Hill and a student study guide for Addison-Wesley. He received his PhD in Industrial/Organizational Psychology from Ohio University and currently teaches Learning and Memory, a first-year University experience course, and a graduate teaching seminar.

MARTHA S. ZLOKOVICH is an Associate Professor of Psychology at Southeast Missouri State University, where she teaches Developmental Psychology courses. She served eight years as the faculty advisor for Southeast's Psychology Club, and as the Psi Chi chapter advisor since 1992. She served a two-year term on Psi Chi national council as Midwestern Region Vice President and currently serves as National President of Psi Chi. Her research interests are college student study habits, beliefs, and retention, and adolescent and young adult sexuality and contraception.

Index

Guest speakers, 119-126; credible, 120-121; interesting, 121-123; reason to use, 119-120

Humor, 161-162

Internet. *See* Online teaching

Librarian, collaborate with faculty, 127-135; obstacles to faculty use of library, 128-129; student learning, 134-135

Non-traditional students. *See* Students, non-traditional

Online teaching, 81-89, 201-207; getting started, 84-86; objections to, 201-202; practical problems and frustrations, 204-206; technological hurdles, 203-204

Performance skills in classroom, 157-164; animation, physical, 159; animation, vocal, 158-159; classroom space, 159-160; enthusiasm, 157-158, 163; humor, 161; props, 160-161; role playing, 162-163; suspense and surprise, 162

Plagiarism, understanding and preventing, 335-343; definition, 336; options when discovered, 341-342; reasons for, 336-338; reducing, 338-341; web-based detection, 341

Popular media, use in teaching, 111-118; finding good material, 115-116; reasons to use, 111-113; requirements-grading, 116-117; use of, 113-115

Psi Chi Chapter, 323-332; faculty advisor, 324; leadership training, 324-327; scholarly activities, 331-332; service to department, 327-329; traditions, 329-331

Psychology club. *See* Psi Chi Chapter

Rapport, in teaching, 149-155; building 153-154; student perspective on, 152-153

Role playing, 162-163

Scholarship of teaching model, 21-29; use in classroom teaching, 23-28

Scientific methodology, 211-220; improving teaching of, 213-218

Service-learning, 137-146; definition, 137-138; importance of, 139-140; obstacles to use, 138-139; using in course, 140-145

AMERICAN PSYCHOLOGICAL SOCIETY

The American Psychological Society is the only association dedicated solely to advancing psychology as a science-based discipline. APS members include the field's most respected researchers and educators representing the full range of topics within psychological science. The Society is widely recognized as a leading voice for the science of psychology in Washington, and is focused on increasing public understanding and use of the knowledge generated by psychological research.

APS *OBSERVER*

The premier news publication for the field of psychological science, the APS *Observer* informs APS Members — as well as public policy makers, the media, libraries, and nonmember subscribers — of noteworthy events, activities, news, and opportunities affecting, and affected by, psychological science.

The *Observer* offers a host of information that is invaluable to the academic, research, and applied psychological community. Informative news articles and opinion pieces discuss issues such as important national trends, public policy, and research related matters of direct relevance to the discipline of psychology and its application. In addition, the *Observer* profiles Members making headlines, offers an inside look at Member efforts with provocative, exploratory series, and distributes detailed and practical "how to" information (including the *Teaching Tips* columns that make up this book) to psychological scientists in all stages of their careers.

For more information on APS membership, publications, conventions and other programs, contact APS at:

American Psychological Society
1010 Vermont Avenue, NW ♦ Suite 1100
Washington, DC 20005-4907
(202) 783-2077 ♦ Fax: (202) 783-2083
e-mail: aps@psychologicalscience.org
www.psychologicalscience.org